CATCHING SIGHT

CATCHING SIGHT

HOW A GUIDE DOG HELPED ME SEE MYSELF

DENI ELLIOTT

WITH **GRAHAM BUCK**

BEACON PRESS, BOSTON

Beacon Press
24 Farnsworth Street
Boston, Massachusetts
www.beacon.org

Beacon Press books
are published under the auspices of
the Unitarian Universalist Association of Congregations.

Text design and composition by Kim Arney

This book reflects recollections of experiences that happened several years ago. The names and identifying characteristics of some individuals have been changed to protect their privacy, some events have been compressed for better narrative flow, and most dialogue has been recreated.

Library of Congress Cataloging-in-Publication Data is available for this title.
Large print ISBN: 9780807024850

157214236

To the leaders, staff, volunteers, and donors who make guide dog relationships possible, allowing US guide dog schools to continue providing canine partners free of charge to visually impaired clients; breeders and geneticists who advance guide dogs' physical health and cognitive abilities with each generation; puppy raisers; dog trainers; the visually impaired people who choose to partner with guide dogs; and guide dogs everywhere. Each well-matched guide dog is literally the light at the end of a harness.

In gratitude to Dorothy Harrison Eustis, whose 1927 **Saturday Evening Post** article about dogs leading blind people pioneered US guide dog training.

CONTENTS

FOREWORD

When I selected Deni as a student in the Accelerated Training Option (ACTION) program at Guiding Eyes for the Blind in 2012, I was already coloring outside the lines with her. ACTION had been open only to Guiding Eyes alums, those who had proven to be extremely competent guide dog partners. With Deni, we were taking a student who'd never even had a dog from Guiding Eyes into the accelerated program. Some members of the committee had been reluctant to admit her into Guiding Eyes at all. But as the sole trainer of ACTION clients and their new dogs, I got my way.

Part of the Guiding Eyes application was recorded video from the home evaluator of Deni under blindfold, guided on harness by her privately trained

German shepherd. In an interview with the home evaluator, Deni talked openly about her problems with the dog. But when the dog was wearing his harness and she was under blindfold, the video showed her following his lead competently, figuring out how to deal with a confusing move that he made, and praising him for his good work. I could see how well she would work with a smart, creative, appropriate guide dog. Other than her unusual admission, Deni didn't at first seem particularly different from the hundreds of clients I had introduced to new guide dogs over the years.

The dogs and the clients—those are the essentials. I always remember that without the dogs and graduates, there would be no Guiding Eyes for the Blind.

The dogs, nurtured and raised from birth, have no way of knowing just how important they will become in the life of a future guide dog handler. Yet each one, through dedicated training and careful matching with their person, offers the highest level of service by becoming a vital link to a blind individual's mobility and identity.

These dogs work without question, relying on their handlers for communication and support.

The graduates—courageous, fearless individuals—have paved the way for guide dog partnerships since the beginning. They have all faced challenges head-on, refusing to let obstacles stand in the way of their independence or ability to move through the world with confidence.

With every step, each team not only forges a clearer path for themselves but also opens doors to a broader view of the human experience.

After more than twenty years working at Guiding Eyes, I knew that every client had their own story. Some had been totally blind from birth, while others had lost vision suddenly later in life. Still others, like Deni, had experienced a decline in their vision over time. Some were angry, some were very sad, and others were determined to excel at what they wanted to do, regardless of their lack of vision. I had learned over the years to be empathic and to meet clients on their own terms. I learned that I could teach a student only where they are, not where I wanted them to be.

When Deni arrived on our campus in Yorktown Heights, New York, she was watchful and reserved. As she was my only student for the ten days that we worked together, it didn't take me long to understand that she kept her distance from others to hide her vulnerability. Other Guiding Eyes instructors may have found her cold or unfriendly, but I saw that her stoicism was protecting a compassionate and giving person inside.

I have always been drawn to courageous and resourceful people. My favorite

Shakespeare quote is "Sweet are the uses of adversity." I took it as a compliment when a college friend once told me, "Graham, you can turn a bad situation into a circus." I do like challenges, and I like working with clients who are willing to challenge themselves.

Deni and I spent many hours together in the Guiding Eyes van as I drove us to our various training destinations. I tried to keep the sites varied and interesting. We worked on a bridge across the Hudson in Poughkeepsie, all over the Upper West Side of Manhattan, and in Peekskill on a very windy day, which may have been the first time a client accused me of torture. Deni said I was intentionally working her in the cold so that I could see how she functioned under stress. The dog, Alberta, and I had thought it was a perfectly nice day for early March; it hadn't occurred to me that someone from Florida might experience the weather differently.

Through our long workdays together, Deni and I found that we admired in one another strengths that we lacked in ourselves. Poise and determination are essential elements of Deni; mine are creativity and calmness. We also found that we shared some of the same ideals and a love of making positive change in the world. We told each other stories about how our leadership positions in our careers had given us power to provide opportunities for people marginalized by race, ethnicity, gender, and gender identity, as well as by disability.

Deni never hesitated to tell me what she thought. I was raised by a mother who was also a no-nonsense, let's-get-this-done person, so Deni's personality felt familiar to me. I also liked that Deni didn't try to mow people over with her beliefs. She was what I call a Martha Stewart type of activist. She was quick to tell me that she appreciated my positive outlook and the years of experience that had brought me to this moment in time with her. Deni assumed that every new person she met would be unique and important. She praised what they had to offer. She believed that every person wants to be as good as they can be at everything they try, and that they don't mind reflecting on their own choices. That assumption alone brings out the best in others.

Throughout the training, when I told Deni what I had planned for the next lesson, she'd almost always say, "Well, how about if we do this instead?" Because I prided myself on facilitating rather than forcing a newly created guide dog team, I searched for good reasons to explain my choices. Reaching for reasons helped me reexamine why I did things a certain way. Deni recognized my willingness to think creatively rather than say, "That's the way we always have done things." I learned to have fun collaborating with her to figure out what made sense next in the training for all three of us.

Years later, when Deni suggested that we write a book about her and Alberta, I was resistant. I had my own experiences to share and my own story to tell. Deni worked to convince me that I could tell my story by sharing my side of our training experience. We stayed in touch, talking sometimes about the book idea but mostly about her guide dog and our lives.

Then came COVID-19. It was time, said Deni, to write our book. Guiding Eyes had pretty much closed down, suspending home trainings as well as classes on campus. Dogs weren't being bred, litters weren't being born, and puppies didn't get trained, which ultimately caused a more than two-year backlog of clients in need of dogs.

Around the same time, I left Guiding Eyes to start my own dog training business, Buck's Best Dogs. Starting the new venture amid the pandemic restrictions, I realized that I finally had the time to work with Deni on our book.

Collaborating with Deni on the book was both hard and easy. Deni expected me to write or dictate copious notes weekly. At first, she set no limitations. She wanted to hear everything I could tell her about my background, my experience at Guiding Eyes, and my work with Alberta. One day I might feel like talking about technicalities of dog training. Other days I wrote reflectively about myself and my colleagues. I didn't worry about getting everything right. Deni always had follow-up questions.

Deni insisted that our communication for the book move forward when I most wanted to back out. She wrapped my memories and beliefs around her experience at Guiding Eyes. She showed me how telling my story was essential to the telling of hers.

My own writing got more focused as I absorbed Deni's suggestions to be specific and explicit. I learned how to make my work empathic but efficient.

She introduced me to what she called my "disfluency," while laughing about her own use of unnecessary filler words that editors had pointed out to her. I remember Deni saying, "If you learn anything in this process it will be to just stop saying 'just' when you write a sentence about something happening now."

My collaboration on **Catching Sight** raised me up, professionally and personally. Doesn't everyone need a Martha Stewart in their life? Now if only Deni could bake.

—Graham Buck
December 1, 2024

AUTHOR'S NOTE

This book was not intended to be a memoir.

In 2020, when I began framing the book, my plan was to introduce people to the seemingly astonishing capabilities of dogs professionally trained to guide people with visual impairments. I wanted people that pass guide dog teams in public to understand the extraordinary display of communication, interspecies interaction, and shared leadership happening in front of them. I wanted people with pet dogs to get more out of their canine-human relationships by applying some of the wisdom developed over more than one hundred years of guide dog breeding and training. I wanted to share what I learned firsthand about what guide dogs can do. That I happened to be visually impaired seemed irrelevant to me when I started this project. Here's the scene that initially inspired me:

> "That dog can read numbers," one hotel guest said in awe to another as they walked past my guide dog and me in the hallway. I smiled, feeling like a magician, able to make an already incredible reality appear even more astonishing. As they approached me, Guiding Eyes Alberta walked in harness a few steps ahead of me on my left. Her harness connected to a rigid twenty-inch-long handle that I held in my left hand, allowing me to follow her movement with ease. Alberta slowed as she neared the room that she knew to be ours. Unprompted, she pivoted left to face the door and stopped. I turned with her and felt her wagging tail brush my left leg. She was proud of herself. I told her I was proud of her too.

I let go of the harness handle and placed my left hand softly on her snout. She was using her nose to point to the doorknob. The insertion slot for the key card was just above the knob. I touched the slot with my left hand and inserted the key card with my right. The door unlocked. Alberta and I walked into the room and I closed the door. End of show.

I couldn't see the difference between the top or bottom of the key card. My dog couldn't read room numbers. We each had our tricks. When I had checked in the day before, I'd asked the hotel clerk to clip the top right corner of my key card so that I would know how to orient it for insertion. Then I told Alberta, "Follow," as the bellman escorted us from the lobby.

In the elevator, I asked our escort to show me, by touch, the button for my floor. I memorized its position and noted that it had a raised number 8 on it. I also noticed that the Lobby button was labeled with a raised L and was different from the floor labeled 1. Good to know. In some hotels, the first floor is also the lobby floor. Not here. Now I felt prepared to meet the one navigating responsibility that was mine and not Alberta's: exit the elevator on the right level.

We followed the bellman to our hotel room. I opened the door to make sure that the key was marked correctly before handing him a tip and sliding my suitcase into the room. From then on, I trusted Alberta to use her canine scenting abilities to guide me from the elevator to our room. Neither of us needed to know the room number.

In March 2013, I met Alberta, a small yellow Labrador retriever at Guiding

Eyes for the Blind, and Graham Buck, a tall guide dog instructor ten years younger and one hundred times better than I was at understanding how dogs process complicated concepts. Every day I learned something new about dogs who understood they were serving as the navigators for the humans holding the rigid handles of harnesses strapped to their backs and bellies. I wrote thoughts and observations on my laptop throughout my ten-day training period. I knew by the end of that experience that I wanted to share what I learned about what guide dogs can do. It didn't occur to me that I was changing how I saw myself. In the process of my writing, I realized that my time at Guiding Eyes was pivotal in my transformation from being a visually impaired individual who pretended to be normally sighted to a person comfortable coping publicly with a disability.

Dozens of drafts and two title changes later, **Catching Sight** is the story of how

I grew to be ready for my partnership with Alberta, mostly through handling my visual impairment on my own, including attempts to make do with dogs who performed guide dog tasks without having the big picture of their work. It is the story of the dedicated work of Graham Buck, then assistant training director at Guiding Eyes for the Blind, who helped Alberta and me move with such synergy that friends called us Denberta. Graham shared his story in the process of helping me tell mine. It is the story of the many staff members and volunteers who helped shape Alberta into the kind of dog able to take responsibility for my safety as well as her own as we navigated busy city streets and isolated wilderness trails.

As is fitting after my long career as an ethics professor, an author, and an ethics consultant, I think of **Catching Sight** as an ethics book. This is a book about taking personal responsibility and about how people should treat other people and dogs as well. It developed into a memoir that explores my disability denial and how my acceptance made me a more authentic person. It is a book about how treating a dog with respect and positive reinforcement can result in the dog choosing to take on important responsibilities. It is a book that takes an inside look at the work of Guide Dog Mobility Instructors (GDMI) and how they choreograph the intricate dance of interdependency between canine and human that defines a successful guide dog partnership.

The story is told primarily from my perspective. Graham dips into the book as narrator in scenes I was not privy to until long after I completed my training with Alberta. We both do our best to express Alberta's perspective. Her story is that of being a spunky little yellow Labrador happy to spend her life sharing with her human partner her vastly superior combination of all that a dog can see, hear, and smell.

—Deni Elliott
August 2025

CHAPTER 1

CHASING SIGHT

The ophthalmologist put down his retinoscope and picked up his fountain pen. The pen scratched paper as he wrote his notes. He said nothing. I kept silent and distracted myself by analyzing the sound of his heavy-handed writing. Was it an expression of authority? Frustration? Maybe he needed a new pen. I hated waiting. I worked to identify the birds I could hear chirping outside.

When I'd arrived at the doctor's office that March morning, the sky was blue, the air crisp in Missoula, Montana. Bright sun warmed piles of snow, and water from the melt trickled down the street behind me. Spring was on the way. I was ready for new beginnings. I was sure I had finally found a doctor who could prescribe glasses to make my vision as sharp as my imagination. I'd pulled the mountain air deep into my lungs before walking into his office. I felt ready.

The pen scratching stopped. The doctor's chair squeaked as he turned from his desk to face me.

"You are legally blind," he said. He spoke evenly and slowly, as if I might have trouble understanding his message. "There are no glasses or contact lenses or surgery or treatment that will make your vision normal. You are going to have to learn to live without much vision."

I said nothing. My initial response to conflict or unexpected bad news is always silence. "I know that you have worked hard to hide your low vision," he said. "But that is not going to work anymore. Intellect," he said, "will not trump biology."

The doctor handed me a prescription for yellow-tinted glasses that **might** cut out some glare. He said the prescription **might** help cohere the broken letters that I struggled to read. A scanner and computer screen with stark contrast and high magnification **might** make it easier for me to read documents, which **might** make my teaching and research easier.

He paused and sighed. I know he was watching for my reaction. He sounded weary of reciting what-might-help when he knew that all I heard was nothing-will-fix.

The doctor knew I worked at the University of Montana as a full professor in the philosophy department and director of the campus-wide ethics center. I had been hired eight years out of my graduate work with tenure and an endowed research chair—perks only a few scholars get, and usually far later in their careers. The doctor and I had professional colleagues in common. I hoped that he wouldn't violate his professional ethics by telling anyone about my limitations.

The doctor stood to indicate that the appointment was over. Still mute, I stood too. He said his office would call the appropriate state agency and that a social worker would be assigned to my case. At that, I felt myself flinch. I'd come in wanting better glasses. I was leaving as a "case."

The doctor hesitated, perhaps unnerved by my lack of response. He decided to state the bad news one more time: the world three feet past my nose would continue to dissolve into blurred bits of color and movement. My close vision would always include the splotches that obscured the text I was trying to read. My peripheral vision would probably continue to narrow. I said, "Thank you," and when I heard him open the exam room door, I walked out into the lighted blur beyond.

No doctor had ever told me I was blind. I shook from the same shock that I felt when I walked into doors and walls that I hadn't noticed were there.

I stepped outside into the morning glare. The sun stabbed at my eyes. In the parking lot, remnants of winter ice stood sharp and jagged as the Rocky Mountains that surrounded the valley before me. Suddenly, the world felt dangerous.

I was barely out the door when I recognized the shape and color of our dark blue Subaru Outback. My husband, Paul, pulled up in front of the door. He must have been watching for me. He had gone to the grocery store during the appointment, calling this an efficient use of time. I called it escape and avoidance. I don't know that I would have wanted him to be at the doctor's appointment with me, but it wasn't worth the fight if I had. Paul detested interaction with any stranger who might be intrusive, and doctors were at the top of his list. Despite his friendly and outgoing public persona, my husband was pathologically private.

Paul was the only person I knew who bought shoes without trying them on and bought cars without a test drive. He didn't like strangers watching him make personal decisions. He felt trapped by the intimacy of sales transactions.

"How did it go?" Paul asked as he wove the car through city streets and onto the road that would lead to our mountain home. "Interesting," I said.

I didn't know what to say. If the doctor was right—if I really was going to be legally blind for the rest of my life—the impact on Paul would be profound. I had always tried to appear fully sighted around him. Paul seemed annoyed when I failed at that: when I tripped over his shoes left in the middle of the hallway, when I ran into a trash can by a building entrance, when I lost him in a crowd and stopped in my tracks to wait, as my mother had taught me to do when I could no longer find the family member or friend I had been trailing.

As a scholar, Paul specialized in visual communication. Yet, despite my attempts to describe to him how the world looked to me, he'd never responded in a way that showed he understood. I was puzzled by his lack of interest, given his profession, but I guess he preferred not to think about it much when it touched him so personally. Paul usually remembered to clutch my hand as we walked in crowded or unfamiliar areas. He understood that I walked slightly behind him so that I could feel when he stepped up or down to clear a curb, or when we reached an escalator or stairs. I suspected he was sensitive to my needs in public because he knew that I would draw attention to us if I tripped or ran into an obstacle. Unless Paul chose to put himself on display, he preferred to slip through the world unnoticed.

Despite our differences, our work and lifestyles harmonized. He taught in California. I taught in Montana. We were both comfortable with a long-distance relationship. Good academic jobs for two full professors at the same university were nearly impossible to find. Although we didn't live together full time, we shared a professional and personal connection.

My previous relationships had usually ended because my fervent love of my work in higher education and as an ethics consultant wasn't compatible with my partner's interests. Then there was the one who, after I described my visual limitations to him, said, "I couldn't stand to have a blind wife." I sighed and replied, "Then it all works out. I couldn't stand to have an asshole for a husband."

With Paul, I finally felt loved by someone who was my workmate, my playmate, and my soulmate. We both liked to travel, eat great food, and drink fine wine. Our academic specialties meshed well enough that we received invitations from around the world to conduct workshops together—to teach others what we did so well. We were a smart, interactive, and attractive professional couple who fed on each other's intellect and magnetism. People were drawn to us.

After seven years of contributing to each other's work, Paul invited me to Paris for our first date. For as long as we'd known each other, he had told me stories about his beautiful, charming daughter and her artistically talented mom. Paul and his previous wife had gone their own ways years before Paul invited me to Paris. I didn't care why or when they'd broken up; what I cared about was that they could manage their differences and support one another in maintaining a loving relationship with their daughter, Allison. When Paul met me at Charles de Gaulle Airport and escorted me into the subway to get to our hotel on the Seine, he picked up a rose he spied discarded in a trash can, placed the flower in my hands, and kissed me. "Be mine," he said.

Now, as he drove us home from the doctor's, I didn't tell Paul that my limited vision might be permanent. I'd barely considered that possibility myself. No matter how fast my vision loss progressed, I viewed it as a temporary limitation. As my vision worsened, I needed to work harder to successfully hide the problem or I needed to shorten eye-intensive work sessions, but I held on to the belief that eventually my eyes would improve. As Paul liked to hold my hand, I could appear normally sighted when we walked together. Alone, it was not so easy.

I had thought about learning how to use a long white cane to navigate airports when I traveled on my own. People unexpectedly appeared in my narrow visual field. Suitcases they rolled in front of them, behind them, or next to them popped into the fragmented area where I could see when the tripping hazard was only a step away. I thought that a white cane might keep people out of my way. When I tested out the idea with Paul, he made his feelings clear: "Do what you want when you are alone," he said, "but keep that thing away from me."

I chided myself for being surprised by the doctor's pronouncement. Achieving normal vision was a dream that I should have given up in childhood. In the many years I had been chasing sight, no doctor had produced glasses powerful enough to make my vision 20/20 or give me normal peripheral vision. As I'd continued to search for the doctor with the right treatment, my vision had only gotten worse.

Once home, Paul retreated to his computer in our shared office. Our desks faced windows that stretched six feet tall, framing the Sapphire Mountains towering across the valley. Spring break was almost over. In a few days, Paul would return to California to complete the semester, joining me back in Montana for the summer.

I made myself a cup of tea, sat on the couch in the sunken living room, and stroked Oriel, my golden retriever puppy. I looked east at the mountains. Even with details blurred, I knew the view was magnificent. Nothing could change my appreciation of this house and the thirty acres that spiraled out from it. I had owned the house and property for several years before Paul and I became life partners. Here, I was grounded.

I held Oriel's face against mine, felt her soft fur on my cheek. **Canine aromatherapy**, I thought, breathing in her soothing puppy smell, still noticeable although she was almost a year old.

My decreased vision had already affected Oriel's life. I had reserved this puppy long before her birth, planning for her to compete with me in my favorite dog sport, agility. An agility ring is an inviting puppy playground, with jumps and tunnels and poles to weave through. As dogs in training get comfortable with the easier equipment, the more challenging A-frame and seesaw are added. In competition, dogs and handlers memorize the pattern the judge has laid out for the dog-handler teams to follow through the ring while being judged on their ability to handle each obstacle confidently, quickly, and accurately.

A month before my ophthalmologist appointment, I'd discovered that I had lost too much vision to handle the sport. When Oriel and I went to our weekly agility class, I tripped over the knee-level tunnels and jumps. I walked into the A-frame and the elevated dog walk. After a few weeks of class, the instructor told me that Oriel was now hesitating when I asked her to run through the tunnel or sail over a jump. Rather than trusting me to give her directions, the dog was watching me, concerned that I might trip or fall. We stopped going to the class. I didn't want my problems to make Oriel fearful or overly cautious.

As Oriel and I sat on the couch, I told myself that nothing about me had changed at the doctor's office. My lack of vision was no different now than when Paul had dropped me off. This latest visual decline was not sudden or recent. I had been refusing to think about it. I still had a successful career, despite seeing the world differently from normally sighted people. It helped that I had become proficient over the years in comprehending text in print or on a computer screen while looking around my optically projected shadows or fragmented words. I considered my ability to function with my limited vision as well as those with clear sight a point of personal pride and amusement.

I did understand the irony of teaching ethics while keeping my low vision a secret. As someone who lectured and published extensively on deception, I continually asked myself if I had a moral duty to tell people about my vision problems. All the relevant variables that create "a duty to tell" figured into my thought process. Intentionally telling a lie is always a morally questionable act. It is the wrong thing to do unless the liar can explain what special circumstance provided ethical justification. However, silence amounts to deception only some of the time. Sometimes we are legally required to tell the complete truth, like when we're on the witness stand or filling out income tax forms. Sometimes we make promises that make it unethical not to tell, like when promising to be sexually exclusive with a partner or to care for a friend's pet when she is out of town. Silence counts as cheating if we sneakily break a rule that we know everyone is reasonably expected to follow. Sometimes we have a duty to tell some people certain information, so I am being deceptive if I simply smile at a student who says, "I'm doing okay, right?" when I know she is failing the class.

I never claimed to have perfect vision. My silence violated no code of ethics. If I had a duty to tell only some of the people some of the time that I had low vision, which ones? When? Why? Each time I'd run the analysis, I'd decided that it was ethically permissible to remain silent. If people around me assumed that I was normally sighted, that was their problem, not mine.

Intellect does **trump biology**, I told myself. I nimbly walked straight down my well-worn analytic path, avoiding the murky ditches of feelings and relationship complications that I preferred not to explore. However, I was also beginning to recognize that my familiar path felt unstable and crumbly underfoot.

Ultimately, I had to admit to myself that everything **had** changed in that doctor's office. Until the doctor's pronouncement, I had held on to the dream that one day I would have normal vision. I had been waiting patiently to find out what the world looked like without peering through the ocular equivalent of a dirty screen door. I wanted to write notes on a piece of paper without shadows obscuring what I had written down. I wanted to give up my lifelong charade. It was uncharacteristic for me to feel trapped in an either/or situation. But that's the way it had always been with my vision. I could imagine only two possibilities: my eyesight could improve or I could continue to pretend than I had normal vision. I was afraid to consider other alternatives.

I mulled over this new social identity the ophthalmologist had bestowed during my appointment. **Legally blind.** This was not an exclusive club. I had drifted into membership with more than a million Americans whose distance vision could not be corrected better than 20/200 or who could not see more than 20 percent of the normal 170-degree visual field that included looking up, down, and side to side in addition to central vision.

The land of the legally blind is primarily populated with people like me, who have some vision. When sighted people close their eyes or put on a blindfold, they mimic the experience of only fifteen out of one hundred people who are in the legally blind camp. Eighty-five percent of us have at least the ability to tell dark from light. Yet most normally sighted people seem to think that someone is either totally unable to tell dark from light or sees the world exactly as they do.

I could pass as sighted in familiar settings, relying on color, light, movement, and blurry shapes to guide me. I didn't venture out of my campus office between classes, when students were rushing around in unpredictable directions. I arrived at my classroom door before the students from the previous class had been dismissed. I chose my moment to walk down to my favorite coffee stand or counter in the cafeteria and place an order when classes had been in session at least fifteen minutes.

When my drink was ready and the barista said that it was "over there," I didn't let on that I had no idea where she was pointing. "Can you please hand it to me?" I asked with a big smile as I pushed money for the tip across the counter.

Sometimes, outside, I could see a blossom six feet away with sparkling clarity, even as the rest of the bush was wrapped in translucent fuzz. But when stress or exhaustion saturated me to my visual dew point, a soft fog blurred my perceptions of color and shape too.

When I brought a bouquet of flowers into the house, I could distinguish daisy from snapdragon. But when I glanced back after crossing the kitchen to fetch a vase, the arrangement fractured into a kaleidoscope, making it difficult to determine the size of the vase needed, except for visual memory or the memory of how the bouquet had felt in my hands. Visual memory is an important asset for those of us with limited vision, but it can deceive. My visual memory might make a countertop look clear when in fact a wine glass or a plate was sitting in what would be, for a sighted person, plain view. Clutter was my enemy. A kaleidoscope was my best description of how things usually looked beyond my three-foot visual boundary: sometimes sharp, sometimes blurry, always fragmented.

Reading text and using computers are far easier for me than seeing at a distance. I credit my mom and sister with teaching me how to make sense of the fragmented letters that I saw. They first taught me to read with my fingers.

When I was two, my mom taught me to sort classic two-inch wooden blocks by using my finger to identify the embossed letter on each one and distinguish one block from the other. My sister Debbie, at seven, knew the full alphabet by sight, but she liked to close her eyes and guess along with me. As I traced the contours of a letter, my sister or mother spoke the phonetic sound that it represented. With practice, my brain connected each letter with its sound.

The next step was to connect those shapes and sounds with images I could sort of see. Debbie handed me three blocks: the **D**, then the **E**, then the **N**. On her command, I held up each one. "**D**-**E**-**N**," she said, "**Den**," which was her nickname for me. "ME!" I said happily. Debbie carefully drew the letters in thick black Magic Marker on a big piece of paper. It was harder to read with my eyes than with my fingers because parts of the printed letters blurred or were hidden under an ocular blob. Once I realized that she'd printed my name, I understood that I could use my knowledge of a word to help me identify the letters within it. If I knew I was looking at my name, for example, I could easily add to the fragments to recognize the individual letters.

Our reading lessons moved into field study. As we sat in the back seat of the family car, Debbie encouraged me to look out the window. "Find the stop sign," she'd say, sometimes turning my head in the right direction. "Say the letters out loud." I was delighted to learn that the world was filled with letters that made words, and that words were best understood in context. Then, back at home, Debbie would ask me to recall the words we'd seen. Together, we worked at spelling them, admiring the thick letters glistening on the page.

By the time I started first grade, I knew numbers were harder to understand than letters. I couldn't figure out a context for numbers the way that I could with letters, words, and sentences. I tested at the fifth-grade level in reading comprehension. I couldn't complete my first-grade arithmetic homework without my sister making sure that the numbers I'd added or subtracted were, in fact, the numbers printed on the page. I understood the concept of addition and subtraction but couldn't help that the number **6** sometimes looked to me like an **8** or **5** or **3**. When I got problems wrong, the error was almost always in what I'd read the number to be.

As I grew older, my father taught me how to identify pieces of money, even if I couldn't easily read the numbers on them. A dime and a penny might be similar in size, but dimes have ridges on the side and pennies don't. Quarters have ridges and nickels don't. He handed me paper money folded in different ways so that I'd learn to quickly distinguish dollar bills, fives, tens, and twenties when pulling them out of a wallet or pocket.

These relatively simple work-arounds, learned early in life, would serve as the foundation for more complicated ones as I navigated my career. Technology was not always the answer. Early in my academic career, I was introduced to Excel as an aid in performing calculations. Despite my eagerness to learn the program, I soon realized that regardless of Excel's computing power, I still needed help to type the correct numbers in the correct cells. The colors and columns were so confusing that I gave up trying to crack the code. Instead, I hired a graduate assistant, who regularly and patiently reviewed numbers with me whether we were reconciling a grant budget or thinking about data to be used in analysis. Once I learned that standard accounting practice requires two people to review financial records, I felt no need to justify my process.

Calculating student grades was easy. I reviewed individual assignment grades privately with each student. They were sure to tell me if they'd calculated a higher grade. This being an ethics class, I told them I expected them to tell me also if the grade they had calculated was lower. At the end of the semester, I met with each student in my office to talk through their class experience. During that meeting, we tabulated their final grade together. I asked the student to read the numbers to me from individual assignments to make sure we were starting at the same place. We'd then compare our calculations.

As I sat in my mountain house with Oriel, continuing to process the doctor's pronouncement, I decided that my task was simply to continue to overcome the obstacles that had always been there. The social worker would be coming sometime soon; maybe she'd have some new ideas to share with me. Besides, the doctor had said only that my vision would not get better. He hadn't said that it would get worse.

"Enough of this," I said to myself, and walked Oriel out to the meadow in front of the house to play ball. The sun on the snow had made the meadow soggy and fragrant with the smells of early spring.

By the time I toweled off the wet, tired dog, all felt right in my world. It was months later before I realized the doctor had no need to tell me that my vision would continue to worsen. That happened without his prediction.

CHAPTER 2

HAPPY ACCIDENTS

The letter that my eye doctor had sent to the state's agency included diagnosis and prognosis, and it described my functional limitations: some trouble reading print and computer text, more trouble finding landmarks when walking and identifying obstacles in my path.

By the time the social worker called to schedule her meeting with me, Paul had gone back to California. He and I never did get around to talking about my new legally blind status. I didn't bring it up. Paul had a lot on his mind as he prepped for his classes and did his research. I could guess how that conversation would have gone. He would have asked me what this new label meant for our life together and how it might impact him. I wouldn't have had an answer.

All I knew was that my vision had been getting noticeably worse for more than five years. If I hadn't been avoiding eye doctors for longer than that, I might have been labeled legally blind sooner. I gave up regular ophthalmologist appointments once I became an adult. I'd had enough of that as a child. Growing up, I'd gone to the ophthalmologist four times a year. When I learned how to make graphs, I imagined the results of these quarterly examinations as a downward progression, with plateaus between drop-offs. Sometimes there were steep drops. All the visits resulted in stronger eyeglass prescriptions that helped for a little while, but the overall trajectory never changed.

As an adult, I'd kept alert for anything that might help my vision in a significant or permanent way. If I heard of a possible treatment, or a doctor who seemed particularly creative, I made an appointment, always hopeful that I had finally found the right doctor in the right place at the right time. In retrospect, I can see how deluded I was about my eyesight, but I also couldn't deny that everything usually turned out just fine for me.

I thought of my life as a series of what Aristotle, the ancient Greek philosopher, called "happy accidents." It had been a happy accident that I'd had parents who'd forced me to stretch beyond my limitations, even if that focus on achieving made it difficult for me to seek help. It had been a happy accident that I'd had teachers and professors who'd convinced me that I could succeed. Choosing to be an ethics professor also felt like a happy accident. I'd learned in college that I thrilled to theoretical analysis and concept building—to creating guidelines for determining the conditions in which certain acts are or are not ethical. Growing up during the civil rights movement and anti–Vietnam War protests, I wondered about the ethical obligations of government and social institutions like medicine, law, journalism, and education. I didn't need eyesight to do the work I loved.

Trying on the idea that there might be no cure for my limited vision helped me to think about the future differently. I was weary of pretending to see what I couldn't. I was running out of work-arounds to compensate for the vision I didn't have. I blocked out three hours early every morning to complete the most visually dependent tasks of my job—grading papers, reading academic articles, writing for publication. Those were the hours when I could read text fastest and most accurately. I might be able to tack on another hour or two in the late afternoon if I could work under natural light. As I had never explored accommodations for visual impairment, I was curious and hopeful about what new technology the social worker might offer. Maybe there would be tools that I could use in the privacy of my home office. Then I would know what, if anything, I needed to tell Paul.

On the day of our meeting, the social worker arrived at my door, introduced herself, and entered my house, her arms full of equipment and paperwork. When she spied the kitchen table, she dumped everything she was carrying onto it and excused herself to go back to her car for more. She added that to the pile, looked around, crossed the kitchen, and started down the few steps into the living room. "We'll talk in here," she said.

Whose life is this anyway? I wondered silently as I followed her into my living room and then sat while she listed the litany of services that the state could provide me due to my newly diagnosed disability. I didn't interrupt, but I mentally crossed off each service as she described it. I didn't need someone to teach me knife skills or how to measure ingredients for cooking. My mom had done that and more before I even started school. I knew how ripe cantaloupes and perfectly baked bread sounded when tapped. I knew how fully cooked meat felt when bouncing back against a finger push. But when she started to talk about computer skills, I listened more closely. I asked about how to use voice control on my Apple computer. She said we would come back to that.

I wanted to feel grateful instead of annoyed that she had decided what I needed without knowing me or my life. The state's interest, she told me directly, was to keep me employed.

She stood and we walked into the kitchen. We took inventory of what she had dropped on the table. There was a battered oversized computer keyboard with bold black letters on bright yellow keys. "That looks like kindergarten surplus," I thought. There were some computer disks containing software that she said would read emails out loud to me, speak words as I typed them, and transcribe my dictations into typed sentences. I perked up at that until she added that, unfortunately, the software was designed for PCs rather than Apple computers.

One piece of equipment made the entire meeting worthwhile: a flatbed scanner that could magnify documents by a factor of thirty and display them on a twenty-seven-inch screen. After we plugged it in, she showed me how to adjust the size and contrast of the text so that any student papers, books, or academic articles that I laid on the scanner bed would appear on the screen at the magnification level and contrast that worked best for me. This setup could live quietly on the desk in my home office. This had promise.

She moved on to how the state would help me navigate the physical world. She had arranged for me to meet with an orientation and mobility specialist, who would teach me how to use a long white cane for navigating when I walked. "Not likely," I thought, imagining how that might look to my colleagues. Yet I still thought that a white cane might be good to have while traveling. I wouldn't use it around Paul or on campus, but it might come in handy if I was in an airport that was new to me or trying to get through a crowd.

I mentioned to the social worker the name of an optician I'd found who specialized in low-vision devices. I appreciated what she had brought, I told her, but only the scanner and screen seemed like they would be helpful for me, and the optician might be able to introduce me to more options.

The social worker said that I was free to meet with whomever I wanted—at my own cost, of course—but the resulting recommendations would make no difference to what the state could offer for accommodations. Directly coping with my vision loss was new territory to me, and I hadn't thought about building an argument to defend my belief that I should be able to choose accommodations that fit my needs. I got it that it was in the state's interest for me to stay employed, but having equipment that supported my research and writing would help me stay employed in what I did best. This wasn't a job; it was my whole career.

Finally, it dawned on me that, to her, as a client, I had no credibility regardless of my education or experience. This was the first time that, as an adult, I knowingly encountered a professional who thought they knew my needs better than I did. I suspected it wouldn't be the last. I didn't appreciate this dose of paternalism.

Her intervention made me feel even more desperate to cling to my identity as a successful professional woman who was not really disabled. I would continue to keep my visual limitations as private as possible. I had a still valid driver's license that I had kept secret from doctors and now social workers. I was grateful that no decision-maker I encountered had ever asked me directly if I drove or bothered to check with the Department of Motor Vehicles.

I felt like a living example in one of my lectures on deception. Is there a morally relevant difference between information that is legitimately private and information that someone chooses to keep secret? I was back to my lifelong professional quandary: What information did I have a duty to disclose, and to whom? As I had managed to legally get a driver's license when I was seventeen and had legally transferred it when I moved out of state, I decided that I had no duty to share the fact that, occasionally, I still drove a car.

I had lived alone most of my adult life, and I rationalized that I had decades of experience in determining if the conditions—weather, light, time of day, route, and destination—were safe for me to drive in. When I could not get a ride from a neighbor heading to or near the university, I drove to work and back, stopping at the dumpster, the post office, and the grocery store along the way. I timed everything to account for the daylight and traffic. I talked my way out of any event that would require me to be out after dark. As I had internet access to the library, I needed to be at the university only two or three days a week and only during daylight hours. I used my new scanner and screen as I completed work for my classes and research from my home office. I drove infrequently and with planning and caution.

When the light was right and it was time to drive to school, I made my way down four miles of mostly private gravel road to the state road in the valley. The dusty road contrasted nicely with the greens of the trees and grasses on either side. The only traffic to worry about was an occasional deer or chipmunk. When I reached the state highway, I turned right, despite the university being in the opposite direction. If I turned left, I would have to cross a busy two-lane road that had no traffic light at the intersection. I knew from experience that someone could literally drive a Mack truck into the large black splotch in my right eye's periphery. So, I turned right and drove an additional mile to the next traffic light, where I drove into a parking lot, circled it, then waited for the traffic light to block oncoming traffic before turning left. I then drove ten miles north to the university well under the speed limit, staying in the right lane, making a right turn to my usual spot on the far edge of one of the university's parking lots.

I struggled with the contradiction of being an ethicist and now knowing that

I was legally blind. While my license had been legal, I was sure that it no longer was. I knew that my justifications for driving were as murky as my vision. Even if my neighbor with Alzheimer's continued to drive to the dumpster and to the post office, I knew that offered no justification for my actions. She was wrong; her family was wrong not to take her car keys away. I was wrong in driving at all. I had to admit that I was not being my best, ethical self.

"We are all ethically challenged," I told my students on the first day of class as I did in every ethics class every semester. I use a confessional tone: "No person always makes the best ethical choice. No person is always the best they can be. Even when we try our hardest to make the right choice, we often fail because our analysis is faulty.

"Have any of you ever, even once in your life, knowingly chosen to do something that you knew was wrong or that you knew might hurt someone?" I waited for the question to sink in, then added, "Oh come on, I'm not going to ask you to reveal the circumstances." I smiled as I heard the students chuckle. I knew that one by one hands went up. We had all had that experience.

"Yep, that's right," I said. "We're all human. We make mistakes. Being ethical starts with admitting that we make mistakes but doesn't end there. What makes a person ethical is having the ability to acknowledge intentional mistakes, unintentional mistakes, and the willingness to keep trying to be a better person. It is hard to accept, but always true, that each of us can be a better person than we are right now, today. Moral development is a lifelong journey."

I told them that my job as their ethics professor was to help them learn to analyze their own choices using sound criteria. I could not model moral perfection. Instead, I would be an example of a person who analyzes their choices and actions day after day, always seeking new information and deeper understanding.

"I am often wrong," I said, "and I accept that I am always incomplete in my reasoning. I never have all the information I need to make the absolute best decision. Knowing that keeps me open-minded. I am ready to change my mind when confronted by new evidence or a new level of understanding." My words gave me comfort. I promised myself I would drive only when I absolutely had to get somewhere and there was no other choice.

As I drove along my memorized route to the university, I sometimes thought of an ancient map with its mythical creatures drawn to portray unknown territories. There be beasties beyond US Route 93, bigger than my vision could handle. I could drive safely only if I didn't stray from my familiar path. The transition from being a legal "high partial" driver, who could see light, color, traffic signs, and shapes of moving vehicles and pedestrians, to a no-longer-legal-to-drive visually impaired individual was a struggle.

When I'd turned fifteen, old enough for a learner's permit, I approached my parents with the argument familiar to every teenager: an additional driver in the family would reduce the parents' need to chauffeur. I was ready to explain to them how I would compensate for my low vision.

I reminded them that with the good lighting in the ophthalmologist's office, the visual acuity in my left eye sometimes reached the magical 20/70 designation required for a driver's license. While the ophthalmologist said I had low vision, he agreed that I might qualify as having high partial vision and may qualify for a driver's license, probably with restrictions. I was already good at shifting my gaze or compensating in other ways for some of the major splotches in my mid- and long-distance vision.

I told my parents that driving would be safer for me than walking. In a car, I wouldn't trip over uneven places on the sidewalk. Driving, I wouldn't get hit in the face by tree branches that I didn't see coming. I wouldn't walk into poles too thin for me to notice.

All that I needed for a learner's permit was a parent's signature, proof of their car insurance, and their willingness to spend weekends shepherding me to empty parking lots so that I could safely get a feel for how to handle a car.

I remained calm, compelling, and rational, exuding maturity. I knew that my parents were reluctant to say no when I tried to get beyond my visual limitations. I wasn't surprised when they agreed to my getting a learner's permit. There were, after all, layers of examiners between a driver's license and me. As I could not drive without a parent in the car, they could determine if or when I could progress beyond maneuvering the car in a large empty parking lot.

And yet. From an older and wiser perspective, it seems to me that supporting a visually impaired teenager's request for a driver's license was reckless at best. They were probably caught in their own bind of convincing me that I could do anything regardless of my low vision. They also wanted to hope that someday I'd have normal vision. I don't deny my show of teenage rebellion. I knew I was holding my parents hostage. After fifteen years of being told I could do anything if I tried, I was calling their bluff by daring them to deny me.

Learner's permit in hand, I waited impatiently on weekends for my mother or father to take me to an empty school parking lot so that I could practice. I followed their instructions: turn right, go slow, speed up, stop. Drive in a big figure 8. Now do it in reverse. Park the car inside the spot portioned off by bright yellow lines. Now, drive out of the parking spot and then back in.

When I pressed to begin driving on actual streets in our quiet community, my driving lessons included memory tests. My parents knew I didn't have enough vision to monitor other vehicles and pedestrians while I was also scanning for stop signs or traffic lights or the names of cross streets. The splotches in my visual field prevented me from quickly scanning my environment as other teenaged drivers would. I could look around the splotches, but that took time. They quizzed me at dinner: "Describe the route to your mother's office," my dad would say. I took him on a verbal tour of the one-and-a-half-mile trip, describing every intersection and whether it had a stop sign, yield sign, or traffic light. I learned to do the same for the two-mile drive to the grocery store and the three-mile drive to my high school.

They agreed to let me try driving on the streets. In full daylight, I could see moving shapes that I recognized as cars and trucks. I showed the parent in the passenger seat that I could safely judge the distance between our car and the moving and parked vehicles around us. I stayed in my lane, even as roads curved. Relying on movement, shape, and color, I could differentiate pedestrians trying to cross the street from the trees or bushes that also stood nearby. My sixteenth birthday had long passed before my parents agreed that I appreciated the enormous responsibility that came with driving a car. They had watched me demonstrate my caution and focus. They were unwilling to promise anything beyond taking me to the driver's license bureau. "Good luck," they said as I studied for the written test.

My mom drove me to my scheduled appointment at the DMV. She brought along a book to read while she waited with the other parents in this rite of passage. She barely had time to finish a chapter before I walked into the waiting room. I had failed the vision test, so I hadn't even gotten to progress to the written exam or road test. I tried a second time a few months later. Again, I failed the vision test. Aside from sympathetic smiles, I got no advice or consolation from my parents. I was on my own.

As my parents had taught me, I worked to think creatively about how to work around my obstacle. I enlisted my sister to repeatedly drive me along the route that my friends said that they had driven for their road tests. This was the late 1960s. Debbie was a rebellious twenty-one-year-old who had a long history of helping me work around my visual limitations.

As she drove the streets most likely to be used for my driving test, she described the environment for me. "Den," she said, "at this intersection, you need to look for the traffic light on the right corner. At the next intersection, the light is hanging overhead in the middle of the street. I'll pull over here so we can review. Tell me which intersections have stop signs and which have lights and where you'll find those lights." I passed these memory tests and was ready for more.

Debbie also gave me advice on how to use cues from other drivers. "Don't panic if you can't find the light at an intersection," she counseled. "Let the other cars tell you what's going on. Look to see if cars at the side streets are stopped or not. If they are stopped, keep going. If you can't find the traffic light, follow the car in front of you as close as you can. If the car in front of you is moving, the light is green. Or yellow."

I waited for my next stronger eyeglass prescription to schedule my third attempt, so that my vision with glasses would be at its best. And I booked the test for mid-morning, when Debbie and I had determined that the route would be least busy. I memorized the correct answers for all possible questions on the written exam but expected the multiple-choice test to be the easy part.

I decided this time to make the eye examiner my ally rather than adversary. "I can see the letters," I said. It was true that I could see some parts of most of the letters. "But sometimes I have trouble saying what they are. It's kind of a reading problem." Again, that seemed true to me. Not being able to tell the difference between a capital **F** and a capital **P** certainly qualified as a kind of reading problem.

The tester agreed that I had gotten enough of the letters correct and had been able to find her wiggling fingers outside my central vision often enough for her to pass me on for the written exam. I aced that and proceeded to my road test. I mentally reviewed the location of every stop sign and traffic light. I quickly scanned just the right spot at each intersection, looking for red or green and then focused on the cars and pedestrians around me. The in-car assessor told me that I needed to drive faster, but that I'd passed the test.

The examiner made me agree that I would see my eye doctor about new glasses soon. With no hesitation, I assured him that I would. That was true. I never missed my quarterly ophthalmologist appointment. "I can't believe it!" I congratulated myself as I danced toward the waiting room. I found my mother there pacing, an hour into her wait. She met my smile with a bemused expression. "I'm proud of you," she said. Her too-tight hug suggested something more complicated.

My parents decided that I could drive to the local Safeway if I parked at the edge of the parking lot and walked to the store from there. I campaigned successfully to drive my mom to work and then myself to school, picking her up at the end of her workday. After six months, they trusted me to drive to the strip mall two miles away, where I got my first job as a short-order cook in a diner. I was now seventeen years old, a senior in high school. For the first time, I felt independent. I felt in control of my life. I could drive; I could make my own money. I was free.

In the decades that followed, I realized how well my parents' determination had served me. I focused on my strengths and ignored my weaknesses. As I worked my way through college and graduate school, I jumped through academic hoops in record time. I wasn't smarter than my colleagues—I knew that I needed to put in twice the effort of my peers who saw clearly. Before Paul, no person, no relationship, nothing had been more important to me than professional success. I shed relationships when I felt them getting in the way of what I might achieve.

With Paul still teaching in California that spring, I could continue to avoid telling him I was legally blind. I did let him know that I'd gotten some new equipment that helped me read student papers more quickly.

I did not tell him that I was learning to use a white cane. The cane teacher judged me competent after I crossed successfully at the intersection of a busy six-lane highway. I felt more vulnerable than successful—at each lesson, I faced the possibility that I might end up squashed like a bug. I now knew how to properly use the cane, but I was far from enthusiastic.

Home alone with the cane, I tried to befriend my new helper, unsnapping it from its accordion fold to its full length, listening to the different sounds it made when tapped on a rug, tiles, or a wooden floor. I avoided looking at it, but it was hard to miss. Its luminous white length and tapered six-inch red tip broadcast my eye problem to anyone around me with any vision. It was designed to be undeniable and unambiguous. I hated it.

Nevertheless, I remembered to take it with me when I traveled. It was tucked in my backpack if I needed it when walking in a crowded airport or crossing a busy street. The cane helped part crowds. It found stairs or obstacles before I fell over them. But the tip sometimes got stuck in uneven pavement or in sidewalk cracks. When the tip jammed, the cane jabbed me in the stomach or thigh. Other times, as I walked, I felt the tip of the cane flail in open air, with no solid surface to land on. Then I would screech to a halt so I didn't trip off a curb or tumble down a flight of stairs.

The cane, however, didn't stop me from ramming my elbow into car mirrors or walking into tree branches. The battle scars from outings with the cane were often no fewer than when I walked without it.

As I couldn't reliably spot landmarks, the cane teacher said I should count city blocks and keep a mental map of the campus and neighborhood. That was helpful, but my memory map was not always up-to-date. I tripped over objects in the landscape that weren't in my memory map—sometimes in the form of the ironically named safety cone.

It was April, only a month after the doctor's pronouncement, and I was already searching for a work-around for the cane. A guide dog? How different life might be, I thought, if I moved with a beautiful dog at my side rather than behind the sweep of a white cane.

Dogs have been depicted in art leading blind people since the first century CE, according to the International Guide Dog Federation. A painting from this period shows a large dog with pricked ears and a long flowing tail leading a person while wearing a leash and collar; the person is carrying a long staff for further assistance in finding their way. By the sixteenth century, guide dog teams appeared regularly in street scenes in Asian and European art. It's not surprising that people would have long ago figured out how to use dogs to compensate for low human vision.

However, sight is rarely a dog's best sensory ability. Dogs' visual acuity is roughly 20/75—compared with normally sighted humans, they are nearsighted. In some states, dog vision wouldn't be good enough to qualify for drivers' licenses. However, because dog eyes are positioned more toward the sides of their head, they have a wider visual field than humans. And their superior senses of smell and hearing give them a huge sensory gulp of the environment that is ultimately much broader than what any human can achieve. They get the environment in ways beyond human imagination.

As I analyzed the situation, I knew that if I had a guide dog, I would be broadcasting my visual impairment. However, I was already doing that when I used the white cane. With the cane, I walked hunched over and tense, and I imagined people murmuring with pity as they saw me. If, instead, I were to walk tall and confident with a dog at my side, maybe people wouldn't pay attention to whether the dog was on a leash or on a guide dog harness. I had often walked my dogs on leash in the city or around campus. Most people noticed the dog—saying "Hi, pup!" and "Aren't you beautiful?"—and paid no attention to me.

I imagined how it would feel to have a dog in a guide harness giving me subtle cues so that I knew when to stop at curbs. A guide dog could help me avoid people and trash cans and safety cones on sidewalks. I'd always treasured the pet dogs who had been part of my life. When I signed my first apartment lease, I adopted a golden retriever before I bought a sofa. I could always be found at the local dog training club a couple nights a week, teaching my current dog to find and return objects with my scent or to weave through the slalom poles that are part of agility competition. My dogs and I often spent weekends at dog obedience competitions, either competing ourselves or cheering on friends from the club. I never had more than one dog at a time but my deep attachment to dogs was lifelong. It had begun when I thought that our family dog, a black Newfoundland named Marty, was my big brother.

CHAPTER 3

MARTY

"Marty is Deni's guardian angel," my mom told my dad when they brought me home from the hospital. It was mid-December in 1953—the day I'd been expected to be born, a month after the day of my birth. As I slept in my crib, the black Newfoundland stuck his nose between the wooden bars and rested his chin on the mattress, watching me. As I slept, he curled up to nap on the rug next to the crib. He stood when he sensed I was beginning to wake and rushed off to find my mother. He ensured that she almost always made it to my side before I started to cry.

"Marty is so good to you," my mom said as she laid me on a blanket on the rug, the dog stretched out close by. By the time I was five months old, I clutched Marty's ear or fur to soothe myself to sleep.

"He takes care of you," my mom said, as Marty lay across any doorway that she indicated, creating a canine baby gate. When I began to stand and walk, I entwined my fingers in Marty's fur to keep my balance. Marty led me around toys and furniture that I didn't yet realize other people could see.

When the obstetrician lifted me from the slice he'd made across my mother's belly, I was floppy and blue—not surprising for a baby born a month early in 1953. The good news was that the hospital had an incubator available that forced highly concentrated oxygen into my underdeveloped lungs. The incubator saved my life. The highly concentrated oxygen limited my sight.

When my parents brought me home, the doctor cautioned, "She's fragile. Maybe she's retarded. We can't tell yet if she's blind or deaf. We'll have to wait for what happens next."

My parents soon realized that my vision was limited, but they also noticed that I was precocious in other ways: I talked earlier than my peers, and I took my first steps at nine months without bothering to crawl first. I craved books. Before I was a year old, I could identify my favorite books by color and size. I handed my mom or dad the one I wanted to hear. They poured the stories into me, feeding my hunger to listen, to imagine, to know. They thought I could manage as well as a normally sighted child if they provided me with enough information and experience. They committed to teaching me independence—"Figure it out." "You can do it." "Use what you have."—and enlisted my big sister, Debbie, to do the same. All three of them cheered me on, holding their helpful hands behind their backs. "Look what you can do," they said with glee and determination.

I learned to fake my way through social niceties. I smiled and nodded appreciatively in the direction of a person's voice when I understood that they were pointing at something I should admire, even if I couldn't see enough to make a detailed comment or see where they were pointing. And I learned to pick up important details through context. When my mom, my sister, or my dad asked me, "How do I look?" I responded with increasing accuracy, "I like your sweater," "Great tie," or "Is that a new hat?" My job was to notice something, anything, and make an appropriate comment. My family helped me push my limitations into the background, making my visual loss unimportant to me and hidden from others.

It didn't occur to me that they were teaching me to pretend I could see. By the time I went to school, I effectively hid my visual loss most of the time. Other kids thought I was shy or unfriendly. My parents told the teachers and principal that I couldn't see well and needed a front row seat in the classroom. They explained I might get lost in the playground or the hall if I wasn't focused on following other children or holding an adult's hand. Oh, and I might need help reading numbers. The best they thought they could do for me was help me learn how to compensate for my low vision while appearing normally sighted.

I started first grade at the Catholic school when I was five years old, taking the bus with Debbie. My mom went back to work nursing part-time so she could be home by the time the bus dropped us off after school. We got a snack, then went straight to homework. My big sister helped me read the worksheets that I brought home. Debbie checked my work, but it was Marty who curled protectively around me as I did my assignments. I told Marty everything I'd learned that day.

One afternoon, my sister and I returned home from school to find the babysitter waiting for us. "Your parents had an errand to do," she said.

"Where's Marty?" I asked. "They took the dog with them," she said.

It was odd that my father had taken off work without telling my sister and me ahead of time. It was odd that they had taken Marty somewhere without waiting for us to get home from school so that we could go with them. It was odd that the babysitter was washing dishes in the kitchen instead of talking with us about our day at school and the homework we had to do. Debbie and I sat quietly on the couch close together, waiting for our parents to return.

They came home without Marty. "Marty was very old," my mother said gently. That wasn't a surprise to me. Everyone in the family seemed old to me. "Marty's gone to Heaven," she said. "He's there resting and happy. A long, long time from now, when you get old, you'll go to Heaven and get to play with Marty again." I tried to imagine what it might be like for Marty and me to play together when we were old. This felt like a lot for me to understand. "You won't see him again in this lifetime," my dad added. I could hear the sadness in his voice.

Debbie and I did our homework together, feeling Marty's absence. We whispered about what had happened. Debbie didn't know where Heaven was; neither did I. I remembered my teacher, Sister Marcie, saying that Heaven was God's special place. So, she must know. I told Debbie that I would ask Sister to help me get Marty to come back home.

The next day, I waited patiently at my desk for a chance to ask the nun how to get Marty home from Heaven. Sister was busy with a classroom full of children and chaos and didn't notice when I raised my hand. The more I thought about how my father had said that I would not see Marty again, the more I felt trapped in the hole in my heart. I put my head down on my desk and sobbed. Then Sister noticed me. She quickly led me down the hall to the office of the principal, whom we children called Sister Superior.

I sat on the principal's lap, crying and holding the big cross that hung from a thin strip of leather around her neck. As her cross was twice as big as my classroom teacher's religious sign, I reasoned that the principal must have more influence with God. Sister Superior could probably drive the convent car right to Heaven's gate to fetch Marty. I ran out of tears.

"Can you tell me what's wrong?" the nun asked gently, rubbing my back. I nodded, trying to talk through my hiccups. "My big brother died," I said. "Oh, you poor dear," she said and held me close as the next wave of tears engulfed me.

The secretary brought the principal my mother's work phone number. The principal reached for the phone, keeping one arm wrapped around me. The nun's voice was compassionate when my mother answered. "How are you holding up, dear?" she asked my mother. She seemed perplexed by my mother's response. Her next questions were more explicit. "If your son died, why did you let this child come to school today? And what are you doing at work?" I felt Sister Superior stiffen, and her tone changed. "A dog?" I heard her ask, incredulous. "A dog?!" She looked at my grieving, puzzled face as I tried to figure out her confusion. "You should still come get her."

I sat in the outer office, folding and unfolding the worksheet that my teacher had given me for that night's homework, wondering how I could do my assignments without Marty. My mom appeared at the principal's office. "Come on," she said, "let's go home."

As we walked to the car, she said, "You know that Marty was a dog and not your big brother, right?" I could tell she wanted me to agree with her. "Yes, ma'am," I said softly.

My mother's question didn't make sense to me. The feelings I had for Marty were exactly the same as the feelings I had for Debbie. If my sister died, I knew I'd miss her just as much as I missed Marty.

Decades later, as I was learning to use a desktop magnifier that made printed material appear more easily for me and how to use a white cane to avoid tripping over obstacles, I remembered how safe I'd felt with Marty. One afternoon, a month after the doctor's appointment that had changed my life, I sat in the living room and stroked the head of my golden retriever thoughtfully. "Hey, Oriel," I said. "What would you think about becoming my guide dog?"

Oriel napped at my feet while I talked myself into the idea. The fact that Oriel had become alarmed in agility class when

I fell or tripped was a good sign. If she was that attentive to me, then she could learn to lead me around obstacles that I couldn't see. "Let's see if we can find you a trainer for that," I said.

I called guide dog schools around the country, only to learn that none of them would help me train my own dog. "Training guide dogs starts at birth or even before that, if you take genetics into account," one admissions counselor said.

"How we handle dogs from early canine development through advanced training is based on decades of experience at our school," said another.

Each school had its own special breeding and training program. I learned that fewer than 50 percent of the dogs born and trained at these schools would ultimately have the right temperament, physical stamina, and initiative to graduate to guide a visually impaired partner. The dogs' training programs lasted from birth until sometime between their second and third birthdays. With those averages, I understood why the schools wouldn't take a chance on a dog whose breeding they hadn't controlled and whose puppyhood they hadn't supervised.

When I described my eye condition, the admissions counselors said that I would probably qualify for admission. They offered to send me the forms for my doctor and mobility trainer to complete. I politely said, "No, thanks." I already had a wonderful dog. And I had already decided that a school-bred and -trained guide dog would come with other problems.

I wondered how blind people could trust a two-year-old guide dog that I assumed had been randomly assigned to them. I suspected that guide dogs carried emotional scars, as their young lives were full of separations. As I understood the process, guide dog puppies stayed with their mom and littermates until they were eight weeks old. Then they were each packed off separately to spend at least a year living with a foster family. After growing attached to that family, they then returned to school for advanced training. The young dog had to transfer their affection and trust to their instructors so that they could be trained to guide. If the dog made it through training, they were matched with a blind partner. But guide dog partnerships work only if the dog and person bond with one another. If the initial match didn't work, the dog might be handed over to another potential "forever" partner or released to live as someone's extremely well-bred and -trained pet.

Human children who experience continual separations from their caregivers often grow to be emotionally impaired adults who have difficulty forming connections with other people. I wondered if anyone had ever studied guide dogs to see if they suffered from a canine equivalent of attachment disorder.

Since US guide dog schools are funded through donations rather than through health insurance or federal or state governments, I suspected that the schools prioritized pleasing their donors over meeting the needs of clients. I couldn't imagine spending weeks on a guide dog campus, with staff treating me like a charity case. I expected that they would watch my every move, continually reevaluating if I was worthy of one of their dogs.

I didn't want a damaged dog, and I didn't want to be treated like damaged goods. Being a "case" for the state was bad enough. I did not want further interference from specialists who thought they knew what was best for me.

I told myself I didn't have time to go to guide dog school, even if I were inclined to give up the three or more weeks that the schools required new clients to be in residence. I was director of the university's ethics center and a full-time professor in the philosophy department. It was the middle of spring semester. I had workshops and lectures at other campuses scheduled into the following year. I was too busy for guide dog school.

I returned to thinking about what Oriel would need to learn to be a guide dog. She would walk in a guide dog harness, on my left, out a few steps in front of me. My connection and communication with her would be through the rigid harness handle rather than a leash. When she was walking with me in harness, she would have to assess the path ahead to make sure there was enough space for both of us to walk through. She would need to stop at the edges of curbs and stairs so that I could reach down with my foot to feel the drop. She would learn to place her front foot on any upward steps that we encountered to alert me to that change in elevation. She would need to be quiet and calm while traveling with me on planes, trains, and subways, and she would need to lie calmly at my feet when I taught classes or gave a lecture on a stage. She would need to be happy spending long hours chewing on a bone or snoozing on a dog bed in my home office or in my campus office while I worked.

The next question I explored was, aside from the dog's ability to help steer me around obstacles I could not see, what made a dog a guide dog? I knew that guide dogs were allowed to be with their partners where no pets were allowed. I learned that guide dog partnerships had a long history of respect.

The Seeing Eye, America's first guide dog school, began graduating dog-handler teams in 1929, following the success in Europe of matching dogs trained to guide soldiers blinded in combat during World War I in Germany. Lawmakers and citizens could see for themselves that these specially bred and trained dogs behaved appropriately around people, animals, and other distractions while keeping blind handlers safe crossing streets in New York City. As early as the 1940s, federal policies allowed guide dogs to travel with their visually impaired people in airline cabins. Guide dogs were allowed on college campuses and in workplaces. During World War II, guide dogs were given their own meat rations. Through their success, The Seeing Eye planted the seeds for the dozen guide dog schools that spanned the nation by the start of the twenty-first century.

I reached out to Travis, a dog trainer I knew who had expertise in helping dogs use their abilities to assist people. He trained "hearing" dogs to alert their partners to sounds as different as a knock at the door and a baby's cry. With the help of local assistants, he trained puppies to do tasks for people with mobility issues: tug cords to open cabinets, push elevator call buttons and handicapped-access buttons, retrieve items that their owners dropped, and behave appropriately in public as they walked on the left side of someone using a wheelchair. When the dogs were two years old, Travis considered their adult personalities apparent. Appropriate dogs could then be matched with their human partners. The mobility service dog tasks were different from what I needed, but I trusted Travis to know if a dog was appropriate for assistance work. Travis had had experience with guide dogs who helped people with visual impairment.

Travis confirmed that dogs could be trained to guide without graduating from a guide dog school. The Americans with Disabilities Act (ADA), signed into law in 1990, guaranteed people with disabilities the civil right to access public services and privately owned businesses, including restaurants and stores that were open to the public. Barriers like curbs and steps that obstructed access were declared discriminatory and illegal unless ramps and elevators were provided. The ADA and rules that were written to implement that act expanded the notion of service dog beyond those who guided visually impaired people. The act described a service animal as "any guide dog, signal dog, or other animal individually trained to do work or perform tasks for the benefit of an individual with a disability." No certification or registration for the dog was required. In this way, the US differed from almost every other country in the world. Some countries limited public access to only guide dogs. Other countries granted certification to the schools who trained dogs for public access and granted public access only for dogs trained by those schools. Almost every other country had a process for ensuring that people who had public access with their dogs were registered with the government. In the US, all that was essential was whether Oriel had the ability to do the work I needed her to do.

Travis took Oriel out for an afternoon, watched her interact with other people and dogs, and gave her the temperament test he used with dogs he was considering for mobility service training. "She's very attentive," Travis said, "and she wants to please. She is a very calm dog." Travis was willing to help me train her to guide.

I hatched my plan without discussing it with Paul. He was still in California, finishing up his semester's teaching. He would not be back on the hill in Montana until the end of June. By then I'd know if my experiment with Oriel was working. If so, I hoped that I could show him how Oriel traveling at my side would make life easier for him too.

Oriel continued to live at home with me while she spent her days training with Travis, his assistants, and the puppies in his mobility service program. An assistant picked her up in the morning to take her to training and then returned her and her homework to me at the end of the day. Oriel went on field trips to shopping malls and nursing homes and the local airport.

She rode buses and met farm animals. She learned to ignore other people and dogs she passed on the sidewalk. She learned to pay attention to her trainer and stay focused on the task she was asked to complete. At the end of the day, the assistant demonstrated the day's lesson so that we could practice together in the evening.

A local leather shop made a guide dog harness for Oriel in the same design used by guide dog schools: soft leather straps looped over her shoulders and buckled under her belly. A rigid U-shaped eighteen-inch handle clipped to her shoulder straps for me to hold.

In early June, Travis said that Oriel was ready to work on harness. We stood where the gravel driveway met the walkway to my house. I buckled Oriel into the harness and stood tall at her side. I smiled as I felt Oriel push into the chest strap, which I interpreted as her saying, "Ready."

I said, "Forward." Oriel stepped out, and I followed a second later, walking next to her hips, her wagging tail brushing my leg. I held the harness in my left hand, my arm extended slightly so that I could feel as Oriel moved right or left or stopped. We walked to the end of the driveway, where Oriel stopped, waiting for me to tell her which way I wanted to walk on the private road that branched in three directions: left, right, or forward.

Following the dog in harness felt different from trailing a cane. While the cane swept an arc on the sidewalk a few feet in front of me, Oriel walked only inches from my left side. When Oriel turned corners, we moved as a unit, my hand on the harness handle, the dog leading. The two of us thinking and making choices was easier than my trying to interpret the changes in environment that I felt when the cane bumped into something. The cane located obstacles; Oriel avoided them. As Oriel and I navigated down the sidewalk together, I felt confident. I had found my answer for dealing with low vision.

I joked with my colleagues and students about having a "guide dog with training wheels." I wasn't willing to admit that Oriel was a guide dog in the same way as one professionally trained at a guide dog school although I didn't know what made them different. I wasn't willing to admit that my loss of vision was substantial enough to need a dog that well trained for the job. I didn't talk about the details of my vision or my need for the dog, saying only that Oriel kept me from tripping over things when I walked. They said, "Hi, Oriel," along with "Hi, Deni," as we passed. Oriel wagged her tail in recognition while continuing to guide me. People on campus who didn't know me now referred to me as that lady with the dog.

One neighbor on the hill was returning to the university to complete her undergraduate degree later in life, and another neighbor worked 9–5 in an office only a half mile from campus. Either could be counted on to get me to the university when I really needed to be there.

Oriel easily learned the location of my classroom and my office, and she led me without hesitation from one to the other. When people asked, "Are you training that dog?" I smiled and responded ambiguously, "Every day is a training day."

In late June, Paul arrived, and we settled into our rhythm of living together and working in our shared Montana home office. He noticed the large screen and flatbed scanner that I now used to read printed materials. He noticed my oversized high-contrast keyboard, but said little aside from a sarcastic, "Nice!" The cane and guide dog harness were tucked in a closet. "We've got to talk," I said one evening. Allison, Paul's eleven-year-old daughter, would be arriving soon to spend the rest of the summer with us. I needed him to know before then how our life was changing.

I told Paul I was now classified as legally blind. He noted that nothing had really changed aside from that label. He understood that my new desk equipment was helpful, but it seemed to him, he said, that I functioned at least as well as I had prior to the doctor's pronouncement. I said, "My vision has been getting progressively worse for a while. It wasn't until the doctor's appointment and meeting with the social worker who had ideas about how I might better cope with diminished vision that I started really paying attention to the problems I was having." I spoke with unusual confidence, not trying to convince Paul to see the world from my point of view. For a change, it felt irrelevant to me that Paul trusted his perceptions over my experience.

Although Paul objected to being seen with me if I had my white cane, he didn't object to my working with Oriel as a guide dog even if he was with me. When the three of us walked around town together, Paul told me that people stared at us. He said it was rude. He returned their stares with equally pointed glares back at them.

Paul liked that I was less dependent on him when I had Oriel with me in harness. He could see that I was more confident following Oriel than I'd been when I'd clung to him. He didn't have to put up with me squeezing his hand too hard when I felt stressed. He didn't have to worry about me getting lost. Oriel didn't lose track of him in crowds. I noticed that Paul sometimes walked far enough ahead of Oriel and me that people couldn't tell that we were together.

When Allison arrived for her summer vacation with us, she was happy that Oriel shared so much of our lives. She liked the attention our foursome got from strangers and had exceptional preteen talent for coming up with snappy comebacks to intrusive questions. She was delighted to discover that neither her father nor I would tell her to stop being rude when she was keeping people from distracting Oriel. When asked the dog's name, Allison might say, "We call her Squat Bucket." When asked where we put the dog on airplanes, she sounded almost credible as she said, "We used to put her in the overhead compartment, but people complained about the dog hair on their suitcases. So now she just rides at our feet." Oriel had yet to take her first flight, but it was true that she would ride at my feet. "How do you come up with these responses?" I asked Allison one evening as she, Oriel, and I went for a walk through the wilderness behind the house. She said, "I only say what I think would be funny if true."

When we went on road trips, Oriel liked to stretch out. Allison wanted her fair share of the back seat. They finally compromised with Oriel resting her head on Allison's lap. Oriel pouted outside Allison's bedroom door when she and her friends gathered for sleepovers and didn't invite the dog to join them. Allison and I developed a relationship that was independent of her father, and we talked together about Oriel and the difference the dog made in my comfort when walking. I felt grateful to have Allison in my life. Allison's mom supported her daughter in her decision to call me Mom 2.

After Allison returned home in early August, Paul and I prepared for Oriel's first flight. We were going to a journalism education conference in Phoenix, with a connecting flight in Salt Lake City. Airline terminals and airplanes would be a new experience for Oriel. Air travel with a guide dog would be new for me.

At this time, the summer of 2000, most of the people using dogs to mitigate disability were those with guide dogs. I tucked Oriel's health certificate in my wallet in case I was asked to prove that her inoculations were up-to-date. I packed dog food and poop bags in my carry-on, along with a few toys. I brought a small blanket to serve as her bed on the airplane floor and in the hotel room. Travis gave me an ID from his service dog organization confirming that Oriel had been trained to helped mitigate my disability and that she had passed a public access test that showed she could conduct herself appropriately in stressful public settings. A call to Delta Air Lines confirmed I had all I needed to travel with a dog who had been specially trained to help me get around obstacles I could not see.

We arrived at the Missoula airport with plenty of time for Oriel to go potty outside before we checked in, per the sensible routine that Travis recommended. I couldn't explain to the dog how long we would be on the airplane or when she might be able to go out again, but she would learn with experience that it might be a very long time between opportunities. She did not get breakfast the morning we traveled and had only a small bowl of water.

Check-in at the Delta counter was easy. The agent took my suitcase, which sported a bright yellow luggage strap to help me find it at the other end of the trip. She handed me my boarding pass and gave me careful directions for how to get to my gate. I happily noted that when people knew I had visual limitations, they provided detailed information I didn't get when I pretended to be fully sighted.

We boarded the plane. I removed Oriel's harness and stored it in the overhead bin. I slipped a dog vest over her head that had GUIDE DOG embossed on the back. The vest also held my business card in one pocket and a pee pad, wet wipes, and poop bags in the other. We were ready for any emergency.

I had requested the window seat in the bulkhead, as that provided the most space for my legs and for Oriel. I unhooked the two clips on her leash and looped her leash around a metal support under the seat, clipping both ends to her collar to keep her in place. If I got up to use the bathroom and she ignored my command to "Stay," she could not move as far as the aisle. Paul sat in the seat next to us and busied himself with reviewing one of his upcoming presentations. Oriel sat quietly for a while and watched other people board the plane. She got bored and curled up on her blanket. She slept through takeoff and the hour-long flight, awakening just as the plane was landing. "I can tell your dog is used to flying," said the man across the aisle as I put Oriel back in harness.

"That's a good start," I thought.

As we walked to the gate for our connecting flight to Phoenix, Oriel wagged her tail, seemingly enjoying the crowds, this new place full of people and food court smells. Paul said, "I wish people would stop staring at us." "I'm sure you do," I said, but refused to feel that I had responsibility to make his experience easier. I realized I was glad I couldn't see the stares. Limited vision had its benefits.

At the journalism education conference, Paul had presentations and meetings lined up with his colleagues in visual communication. I would be equally busy with the media ethics crowd. We co-ran a session on image ethics. As participants filtered into the seminar room for that session, some colleagues who had known me for years came up to the front to ask me about the dog. I began to appreciate that any of the participants might consider a visual communications professor, an ethicist, and a guide dog sharing the podium as an unusual combination. I started off our session by saying, "So, a vis comm scholar, a legally blind ethicist, and a guide dog walked into a bar . . ." Participants laughed as they thought about the possibilities.

"I'll give you the punch line during happy hour this afternoon," I said, knowing that I had already shared the important information. Whatever those who knew me thought about my vision, if they had thought about it at all, they now knew I was legally blind.

Friends asked me later if there was a punch line to the joke. There wasn't.

They asked me what happened with my vision. I started admitting that I had been dealing with low vision all my life. Regardless of who asked, I learned to smile unabashedly and say that I was visually impaired and that Oriel was my guide dog. Others wondered what I could bring to the discussion of image ethics without having clear vision. My skill in asking specific questions that led people to describe in detail what they found troubling showed that often the answer lies not in what you see but what you know.

I identified a grassy spot outside the hotel for me to take Oriel potty throughout the day. During the plenary sessions, Oriel gazed up, entranced by the crystal chandeliers on the ballroom ceiling. When I gave presentations in smaller rooms at the conference, she napped under the table next to the podium or the chair where I was sitting, just as she did when I taught my classes at the university. She didn't seem fazed by being a thousand miles from home. Traveling with a dog felt safer to me and far more fun than reaching for a cane or traveling without assistance. There was, however, one downside. When I used my cane, people shied away from me. Nobody wanted to pet my cane. When I was with Oriel, strangers walked up to us, reaching to pet her. I tried to keep them from distracting the dog while I fielded their questions: "How old is your dog?" "What's your dog's name?" "Are you training her?"

I was stunned by the expectation that I talk about my guide dog with anyone, anytime, anywhere. People intentionally tried to distract her by snapping their fingers or calling, "Puppy, puppy." I developed a standard response: "Please don't; she's working."

The worst situation occurred when we boarded a crowded elevator after a long day of conference sessions, heading to the hotel's rooftop lounge for happy hour. As the doors closed at the lobby level, a man behind me asked, "Why do you have that dog?" My shoulders sagged. The elevator fell silent. While I was deciding how to respond, Paul turned to him and asked loudly, "Do you ask people why they're using their wheelchairs?"

The analogy was apt, but it made everyone on the elevator (except Oriel) uncomfortable. No one made a sound until the man exited on the twenty-fourth floor. "I bet he never does that again," Paul said. Others in the elevator laughed. I was surprised but pleased that Paul was angry at the clueless stranger rather than at me.

Maybe he was adjusting to my diminished eyesight better than I thought.

Oriel and I also learned that weekend that the environment could hold unexpected perils. As we were crossing a street in the hot midday sun, Oriel suddenly yelped and jumped backward. She had burned her paw on a metal sheet that was covering part of the crosswalk. From then on, Oriel refused to walk on metal. She balked at riding escalators and walked around metal grates on the sidewalk. Oriel's generalization from one bad experience was extreme, but if avoiding metal was her worst trait, I could work around that.

Oriel and I reached other agreements on what it meant to work together. She kept track of everything below my knees, which were conveniently located at her head level. I used my residual vision to watch for obstacles above. Oriel moved more slowly than I would have walked on my own, picking up her pace only when she thought we were heading home. I learned to slow down and remind myself that a steady pace with a dog was far better than the halting, hesitant cadence I'd had when trailing a cane.

Oriel had one bad habit that I couldn't excuse or correct: she grabbed food she thought she could reach without me noticing. Once she took a piece of chicken off a low table in an airline gate area. Another time I heard a young child scream as Oriel and I walked by her at the airport. I swiveled in surprise. "Your dog stole my daughter's pretzel," the angry mother yelled. I reached down to the dog's mouth to find that Oriel was indeed chewing the stolen snack. "Oops, sorry," I said, and then hurried to our gate. I was too embarrassed and short on time to offer to replace the pretzel.

I shared my stories with Travis, who confirmed that he thought Oriel was doing the best that she could. "The only way to get a guide dog with perfect manners," Travis said, "is to go to guide dog school."

When Oriel turned four, I had a travel schedule most people found appalling. I had left the University of Montana for an endowed chair in ethics at the University of South Florida in St. Petersburg while simultaneously working as the new ethics officer for the Metropolitan Water District of Southern California on contract. I knew having responsibilities on both coasts would be demanding. I couldn't resist the opportunity to build a governmental ethics office from the ground up. Twice each month, I flew from Tampa to LA for meetings with the board of directors, staying with Paul while I was there. Oriel slept through the coast-to-coast flights, and I used the time to work on my laptop. I kept my house in Montana so that Paul, Allison, and I could spend our academic breaks there.

My twice-a-month commutes to LA were scheduled so that I could best meet responsibilities on both coasts: Monday mornings before 7 a.m., I boarded a nonstop flight in Tampa. With the change in time zones, I landed in LA by 9:30. A driver from Metropolitan met me at the terminal and got me to my office by 10 a.m. At the end of the day, a driver from the fleet of vehicles used by staff at the water district office took Oriel and me to Paul's house. On Tuesdays, I put in another full day at the LA office, had dinner with a friend from work, and boarded a red-eye flight to Tampa, arriving back in Florida at 6 a.m. on Wednesday. That gave me enough time to get home, shower, change clothes, and be in my university office by 10. My bosses on both coasts had signed off on my double life, and the University of South Florida allowed me to adjust my teaching schedule to fit the travel.

I don't get jet-lagged. Some dogs, like some people, do. After a few months of flying back and forth between Tampa and LA, Oriel started to burn out. On our Tuesday mornings in California, Oriel would eat breakfast and then return to her bed. "Let's go, Ory," I'd say as the driver pulled up to take us to my office. Slowly, she'd get up, shake off sleep, and walk into her harness.

She was also reluctant to get into harness when we returned to Florida. Our first mornings back, I had to cajole Oriel to "get dressed" so we could walk the few blocks to my university office. Up till now, I had checked to make sure she wanted to guide me by her reaction to me holding out the harness. I said I knew Oriel was voluntarily consenting to guide when she walked into the harness when asked and pressed her chest against the strap, waiting to be buckled in. Now, she didn't want to get dressed. I called Travis.

"Oriel doesn't have enough stamina to keep up with your lifestyle," he said. "Initially, you bought her to be an agility competition dog. Sprinting around an agility ring for a few minutes takes a different kind of energy than running a marathon. Your lifestyle is a marathon. You are asking more than Oriel can give."

Travis had spent three months helping me train Oriel for guide work. Now, just two years later, the dog was showing me that she didn't want to be a full-time guide dog. I grappled with the realization that finding and training another dog would take a while.

Travis offered to start looking for Oriel's successor. He recommended that I go with a German shepherd this time. He knew a US German shepherd breeder who specialized in providing working dogs for law enforcement and search-and-rescue work. The dogs were unflappable and had high energy. A puppy from one of these litters would have what it took to keep up with my "marathon" life.

A call from Travis and a deposit from me secured a puppy yet to be conceived. The breeder told us that, if all went well, we could expect the puppy to be born in April 2006. From there, Travis and I developed a timeline. He would visit the breeder when the litter was seven and a half weeks old. Using the temperament tests used by guide dog schools, he would evaluate the puppies and choose the one who was best suited for guide work. He would bring the puppy to me in Montana in June.

Paul said German shepherds were his favorite dog breed and thought the plan sounded good. He predicted that people would give me more space when I was with a German shepherd than they did when I was working Oriel. Paul, Allison, Oriel, and I would spend the summer of 2006 teaching the puppy house manners and basic obedience commands. When I was ready to return to my teaching job in Florida in the fall, the puppy would go to live with Travis for a year of service dog training. In August 2007, Travis would return the sixteen-month-old dog to me in Montana, ready to work. Travis, the dog, and I would train together for a week to transition the dog to guiding me in harness. The cost of the puppy, along with transportation and the months of boarding and training with Travis, added up to thousands of dollars, but the money seemed reasonable for the outcome: a guide dog who had been chosen to work with me, who had bonded with me from puppyhood, and who was trained by a service dog professional I could trust.

With the plan for the new dog now in motion, I modified Oriel's schedule to help her better manage the guide work until she could retire. My biggest priority was being able to take her on my commutes to

California. I depended on her most when finding my way through airports, moving through the crowds on the streets, and working in my LA office. And so I began to give Oriel time to rest on either side of our bimonthly cross-country trip.

The Friday before my Monday flight to LA, I left Oriel at home and tapped off to my university office using my white cane. I let her continue to rest over the weekend. Come Monday, we were out the door at 5 a.m. to make our flight to LA, Oriel rested and eager to go. She tolerated the hectic two-day schedule in California, wagging her way into her harness when I announced that it was time to get dressed. After we returned to Florida on Wednesday mornings, I left her at home the rest of the week to recover from the trip. By Sunday, she was eager to walk into her harness and work again. I made peace with navigating by cane in town some of the time so that Oriel could work when I needed her most.

By this time, my colleagues on campus and at the Metropolitan Water District understood that I was visually impaired, even if I didn't discuss the specifics. I became comfortable with people seeing me with Oriel and got comfortable disclosing a little more about my experience.

Each semester, on the first day of class, I explained to my students that I couldn't see much. They could help me get to know their voices by sitting in the same seat in our circle of chairs. I warned them not to expect a response if they silently raised their hands—instead, they should get my attention by making some noise. I told them not to talk to Oriel unless we were on break and I had removed her harness.

I had to confront the inevitable question of what to do with Oriel when my new guide dog moved in. Paul didn't want to keep Oriel with him in California as his pet. If I kept Oriel with me after she retired from guide work, I would need to put her in a boarding kennel when the new dog and I were out of town. She would watch me harness up the other dog and walk out the door, leaving her at home every day. I thought that would be painful for her. I felt closer to Oriel than I did to most humans. She had been a far better guide to me than Paul, even when he'd been willing to help me out. Unlike Paul, Oriel never ran me into a tree or a bush along the sidewalk. She never forgot she was guiding me.

Oriel needed a fuller life than I could provide her after she retired from guide work. A friend in Montana, Maggie, who directed a shelter for unhoused people, offered to give Oriel a new home. When the time came, Oriel would move to Maggie's house and become the shelter's in-residence therapy dog, going to the shelter with Maggie in the morning and hanging out there with anyone who needed her. When she wanted a break, she could go to Maggie's office and its big fluffy dog bed. At the end of the workday, Oriel and Maggie would go home to kids, dogs, cats, chickens, and goats. Oriel would have a new, full life without me. I expected her move to feel as big a loss to me as the death of Marty, my Newfoundland, when I was a small child. But I believed that Oriel deserved a retirement built around her needs, not mine.

One evening, soon after all the plans were in place, a woman at a cocktail party commented on how carefully Oriel watched me as I stood chatting with others. I agreed that Oriel was a great guide dog and added that she was getting ready to start a new life. With pride, I shared Oriel's retirement plan. "How can you do that?" the woman asked, her voice rising in horror. "After all that she has done for you, how can you just give her away?"

Until that moment, I hadn't considered how bizarre my plan might sound to someone who had a pet dog to whom they were committed for life. I realized that not so long ago, I would have had the same reaction. But over the years that Oriel and I had worked together, I had come to understand that she had needs independent of mine. When she retired, Oriel would need more socialization than I could provide while working a new guide dog. That conclusion had been hard to reach, but simple to understand once I got there.

I smiled sadly at the woman. I told her that I understood why giving up Oriel sounded cruel, but that I was sure that my choice was right for her. "It will be awful for me to let her go," I said. "I am going to miss her every day. I think I owe her a full and better life for all she's done for me." As for the agony of letting Oriel go, I told myself I had more than a year before I needed to face it. I filed the feeling away until I needed to confront it.

A sunny June afternoon in 2006, Travis arrived in Montana with a carsick puppy. Eight-week-old Wylie Chimera weighed in at twelve pounds. His right ear stood up, while the left ear flopped down. As he was passed from Travis to me to Paul to Allison, he managed a small tail wag. When we placed him on the ground to meet Oriel, he ignored her and stretched flat in the stubbly meadow grass, seemingly glad to have solid earth beneath his sick tummy.

"Wylie hasn't spent a lot of time in a car," Travis explained. "You'll need to take him out for short trips until he gets used to the motion. I'd give him just a little rice and ground beef tonight. He'll feel better by morning."

After walking in the meadow and congratulating Wylie for peeing outside, we introduced him to his primary crate, located in the living room. From there, Wylie could watch whoever was in the kitchen and dining area, and he could also see the birds soar outside the living room windows. After a little dinner, Wylie napped in his crate while Allison and I collaborated on cooking our evening meal. Travis had explained to me that a crate provided puppies and working dogs a safe place to chill as well as making housebreaking and raising a dog easier.

After another trip outside, telling Wylie to "Hurry up" and applauding his success, we settled into our normal after dinner routine. Paul played tunes on the keyboard by the windows. Allison and I read, chatted, and tried to convince Oriel that she would learn to love this puppy. Oriel was not impressed by Wylie or his confidence in monopolizing her people's attention. Finally, we put Wylie in his crate and turned our attention to Oriel. When not under human supervision, Wylie lived in a crate with toys and bones. Identical crates in the bedroom and office meant that Wylie was always in sight or sound of his people, never underfoot, and had no chance to pee on the floor or rugs. Our vigilance paid off.

Within three days, Wylie had learned to nudge someone's leg when he wanted to go outside, and he sat quietly outside of the kitchen three times a day while his food was put into his bowl and taken into the doggy dining area in the laundry room. He worked hard to hoist himself up the stairs and happily tumbled down them as he worked to follow his golden retriever sister.

I was getting daily lessons in the differences between dog breeds. My previous experience with dogs had been with my childhood Newfoundland and the three golden retrievers I'd raised at different times through my adulthood. Oriel, like most goldens, welcomed every visitor as a new best friend. Not Wylie. If someone came to the door, Wylie sat at my side, observing the stranger, but not initiating contact. He wanted attention only from Paul, Allison, and me.

Oriel gobbled up any dog treat offered and all the people's food she could reach.

Wylie sniffed suspiciously at treats that I offered, deciding whether they were worth a taste. If he took the treat, he might swallow it—or he might spit it out. He dutifully ate the meals put into his bowl morning, noon, and night, but otherwise was uninterested in human or canine food. Food was not going to be a training tool for this dog.

Wylie's play style was aggressive, and his puppy teeth were sharp. I found Oriel sleeping on the beds to escape them, as Wylie couldn't jump that high. She wanted to play outside with me but only if I left Wylie in his crate. She didn't like to spar with Wylie for control over toys. She growled when he used her long, flowing tail as a tug toy.

Wylie did not respond to me like a golden retriever, but he clearly wanted my approval. Within a week, he could be trusted to jangle the bells that hung from the doorknob at the front door to ask to go outside, just as Oriel did. Wylie quickly learned to stand, sit, down, and stay on command for no reason other than because I would praise him for his good work. Travis stopped by regularly to play with Wylie, getting to know him and watching to see how he was progressing. Wylie came when called unless he was distracted by something more interesting. His off-leash recall got a boost one day when he chased a wild turkey into the woods instead of coming when I called him. The turkey led him into a wasps' nest and then flew off. The twelve-week-old puppy ran back, howling in pain from multiple stings. For the rest of the summer, he came when I called.

In August, after Allison had returned home to her mom in Indiana to get ready for the school year, Paul and I prepared to return to work for the fall semester. I got Wylie comfortable in the travel crate in the back seat of the car. Oriel jumped in to stretch out on the seat beside him. Paul turned off the water from the well and locked the door.

I patted the red front door, thanked the house for yet another wonderful summer, and breathed in the fragrance of sweetgrass, wild onion, and sage. I never left my Montana home without shedding a few tears. Whether walking the hill to the rhythm of bird calls and wind in the pine trees or hearing the house fill with laughter and music from friends who'd brought their favorite instruments to play under the high ceiling acoustics of my living room, this was a place where I felt happy and safe. As we left, I held my sadness while the car flowed down the gravel driveway to the dirt road, through the forest of pine, spruce, and larch. I sighed as the car curved to the right, the eastern edge of my land lapping at our wheels.

We headed west, first dropping off Wylie at Travis's western Montana home. Wylie would be at Travis's side for the academic year, sometimes in Seattle, sometimes in California, sometimes in Montana. I might or might not see Wylie before next summer, depending on how Travis's and my travel schedules overlapped. I wasn't worried about the puppy forgetting me. Paul, Allison, and I were imprinted on Wylie, as was my Montana house and land. Leaving the pup with Travis felt like a parallel to my long-distance marriage. Intense connection interspersed with time alone. If I could make it work with Paul, I could make it work with Wylie too.

An unusual teaching opportunity led to an unplanned collision of my professional and personal worlds. I accepted an invitation at the Bergin College of Canine Studies to teach a weeklong graduate-level course in the law and ethics of dog ownership and training. Bergin was a postsecondary school near Santa Rosa in Northern California focused on human-canine relationships.

The entire student population numbered less than one hundred. Some worked on two-year associate degrees; others were completing four-year baccalaureate degrees. I was hired as one of the faculty members for Bergin's first class of graduate students who were working on master's degrees. The campus population was also unusual in that at least a third of students and faculty had disabilities. Most of the graduate students I taught were preparing to train service dogs. For the first time, my visual impairment added to my credibility rather than making me worry that it might make me seem less capable. I started grappling with a new insight: all the years I'd worked to appear fully sighted might have been better spent learning to be honest about my limitations and open to help from those knowledgeable about the experience of those with disabilities.

My previous experience in teaching ethics included courses on law and ethics in journalism, governmental service, research, and medicine, as well as broader areas of teaching ethics and demonstrating how philosophical ethical theory can be applied to everyday life. When I had considered Oriel becoming a guide dog, I became intrigued by US federal and state laws regarding canine assistance for people with disabilities. They differed from those in other countries. Those differences became problematic as more people with more dogs asserted their right to public access. I now had a new field of ethics to teach and research: the role of dogs in helping people mitigate aspects of their disabilities.

Between 1968 and 2008, federal agencies, along with Congress, went from ignoring the civil rights of people with disabilities to inadvertently creating a service-dog honor system that invited fraud. The three federal agencies writing rules on the use of animals to assist people with disabilities—the

Department of Justice, Department of Transportation, and Department of Housing and Urban Development—did not coordinate to create a uniform system for determining whether, or how, to hold people accountable for their claims that an animal was providing benefits associated with a disability. The rules that allowed dogs to fly free and uncrated in the airline cabin were issued by the Department of Transportation. The rules that allowed service dogs to live with their partners in no-pet housing came from the Department of Housing and Urban Development. It was the Department of Justice that distinguished dogs providing service from those who were pets and determined that service dogs were legally allowed in restaurants and grocery stores while pet dogs were not. Each agency described helper dogs a little differently and created its own procedures for people wanting to gain special public access with their dogs.

Even within the rules from the Department of Justice that addressed dogs allowed through the ADA were interesting research questions to explore. For example, when was public access with a service dog "reasonable accommodation"? In some settings, particularly zoos, wilderness parks, or nature reserves, the presence of a dog, no matter how calm, might have a negative effect on the animals protected by the establishment. What about amusement parks? As allowing a dog on most rides with people could be dangerous, was it discrimination for a person with a disability with a service dog to be denied access to rides? How should service dogs be managed at Disney World?

I was also uneasy about dogs having public access without a veterinarian's okay. What if a service dog's vaccinations weren't up-to-date? Dogs can transmit ringworm, roundworm, hookworm, tapeworm, mites, Lyme disease, giardia, rabies, and other diseases to humans. What if the dog posed a danger to other people or dogs? Airline cabins and travel hubs, as well as other bustling public spaces, are stressful for dogs who are not bred and trained to handle crowds and noise. Dogs who are stressed are more likely to bite, posing an immediate risk to public safety.

The federal government's lackadaisical approach to service dog regulation stood in sharp contrast with other ADA requirements. The Department of Justice provided specific requirements for the dimensions of ramps and parking spaces designed to accommodate people with disabilities. ADA provided national standards for determining who qualified for accessible parking privileges. Regardless of the state, a person applying for a handicapped placard or license plate needed certification of disability from a licensed physician.

I had been invited to teach the summer class through Travis's recommendation, and I was eager to live up to his description of me as an engaging teacher who could help students apply ethics to real-life situations. The student experience at Bergin intrigued me as much as the opportunity to do new work in animal ethics.

Bergin College, named for its founder, Bonnie Bergin, offered course work that included service dog breeding, training, and placement of trained dogs with clients who had mobility disabilities or who were veterans with PTSD. Students learned through curriculum and daily application how to prepare the golden retriever puppies bred on campus for service dog careers. They worked with the genetics professor to decide which dogs to breed. As they strove to produce puppies with the calm and compliant temperament needed for service work, they learned which traits could be predictably passed down and which could not.

Students were present when the dogs gave birth. They handled the newborns daily, using their names and acclimating them to gentle human touch so that it would feel as familiar as their nursing mom and littermates. Students made notes about their observations, using standardized criteria to plot aspects of the puppies' personality development.

I quickly agreed with the students that more schools should give academic credit for cuddling puppies. Every few days, we'd convene our law and ethics seminar in the puppy room for an hour or so, snuggling the young goldens while discussing public access laws for people with disabilities and how states could extend federally established civil rights but not create laws stricter than those set by federal agencies.

When the puppies were eight weeks old, each was assigned to a student, who became their primary trainer and caregiver. The pups came to class with their assigned students and learned to lie quietly under the seminar table as students focused on the lesson. I learned to plan breaks around the puppies' bladder needs.

The service dog trainer supervised the students as they taught puppies to walk calmly next to wheelchairs, open doors, and pick up dropped objects. Puppies slated to become PTSD-support dogs learned to "check out the house" by flipping on light switches when they returned home and reassuring their human partner that there was no danger. These puppies also learned to sit in front of their person when strangers approached, creating a protective shield.

Students served on the selection committee for clients who had applied to the school to be matched with a service dog. Under Dr. Bergin's mentorship, they paired each dog with a client by considering the personalities of both and the lifestyle needs of the client. Then the students helped conduct the intensive two-week class in which clients learned how to work with their new service dog partners.

No service dog organization in the US could match Bergin College in the amount of personal attention and training that each puppy was given between birth and going home with a client. No organization could match the combination of hands-on experience and deeply theoretical education offered to each student at Bergin.

For my week of teaching, Oriel and I moved into the residence hall with a dozen students and the dogs they had each been assigned to train. I had never lived among people who were so professionally and personally invested in how dogs could mitigate people's disabilities. I had never been in a community where people with disabilities were treated no differently from those without, and where accommodations that leveled the playing field were automatically provided. No student using a wheelchair was isolated by stairs. Ramps and elevators and smooth paths made the entire campus accessible for rolling and walking.

I began thinking about how canine-human relationships were experienced by the dogs themselves and how that might enlarge ethical concerns. Now, in addition to considering whether the dog was truly assisting with someone's disability and considering public safety concerns for those who encountered service dogs, I began to think seriously about what humans owed the canines who served as their partners.

For the first time, I felt no need to apologize for Oriel's presence or to explain how she helped me. I didn't hesitate to tell someone when I couldn't see something important or to ask for directions to the library or kennel from my classroom. I realized that I could be a person with a disability without casting doubt on my professional expertise.

The dozen graduate students I got to know that week were all interested in training service dogs to work with people who had disabilities. Most of the Bergin graduate students had had experience training dogs as well as the life experience of someone in their late thirties or forties. This was in contrast to my usual graduate students who were completing degrees in their twenties. The Bergin students each had passion for their education. Most had a plan of how they would use their degrees. As impressive as they all were, one student, Pam, stood out from the rest. She won her peers' respect through her confidence, determination, and critical thinking abilities. Having worked as a journalist in a foreign war zone and still living abroad, Pam had taken a leave of absence to return to the US to earn this new master's degree in human-canine connection.

Pam had ambitions beyond what Bergin taught, but she was unsure how to plan her future. "There is so much that people don't know about dogs," she lamented. She wanted others to recognize that dogs have their own way of making sense of the world—one shaped by sensory abilities that humans can't even imagine. Dogs can tell via body language if other dogs are interested in playing or in attacking. They can tell if another dog is holding a toy to invite play or to guard anyone from taking it. Pam contended that dogs often try to share such information with human family members, only to be ignored. Even when pet owners are paying attention to their dogs' communication attempts, they often insist their dogs are experiencing the world just like them. If a pet owner is cold, they put a jacket on the dog too. People toss their pets potato chips while they watch football on TV, believing the dog wants and needs to be treated like a human. People might call themselves "pet parents," but dogs are never going to experience life as humans do.

I suggested to Pam that she consider one more master's degree, one in science writing at the University of South Florida. The focused program could hone her canine-related writing and provide some professional contacts as well. Given her abilities and experience, I thought Pam would be a great addition to the university's journalism department.

After Paul dropped Oriel and me off in Santa Rosa, he drove back to LA to get ready for the new academic year. When we talked on the phone that week, he was happy to hear that my teaching was going well. When I told him about how much I appreciated the students—Pam, in particular—he said he had made a similar connection with an outstanding young copyright attorney he'd met. I was glad for both of us. Paul and I shared a love of mentoring early career professionals who had high potential.

CHAPTER 4

ORIEL

After my week at Bergin, I flew from Santa Rosa to Tampa for the start of the academic year. As the autumn months passed, I noticed that Paul seemed distracted or unavailable when I visited him in California twice a month. He was gone a lot. He had meetings on campus or work that he needed to do at the library. And when I was in Florida, he no longer seemed able to maintain the phone calls we'd shared every evening. At first, he offered explanations—last-minute dinner plans with colleagues, a lecture that he needed to give at a night class. Then we stopped talking about why.

The less Paul and I talked, the more certain I was that he and I needed to spend Thanksgiving in Montana. When I learned that Travis would be in Montana as well and that Wylie could join Paul and me for the holiday week, I wouldn't take no for an answer.

Paul got to Montana a day before Oriel and I arrived; he bought groceries, turned on the well and heat, and stacked wood on the hearth. When he picked me up at the airport, we drove to Travis's to fetch Wylie. When we had last seen Wylie, he'd been less than five months old, a puppy nipping at Oriel's feet. Now, at eight months, Wylie towered over the golden retriever. Bigger and stronger, he outran her every time I threw a ball. He pushed Oriel aside to sit next to me, leaning his body into my leg. I learned to give Wylie crate time so that Oriel had time to relax and stay connected with me.

I looked forward to talking with Paul about the change I felt in our relationship. Whatever was going on, I was sure we could figure out a solution together. I was careful to prepare a mental list of nonthreatening statements about what I felt rather than how he had been acting. But that night, as we settled in at home, Paul seemed to have little interest in talking—about himself, or me, or us. Instead, he complained about being in Montana in November, which surprised me—it was our habit to meet in Montana when we had breaks in our academic schedules. "What's going on, Paul?" I asked. "You seem stressed."

"If I were in California, I'd be getting my work done and not be stressed!" he said and dismissed me and further conversation by opening his laptop and putting his focus there.

I unpacked, made dinner, fed the dogs, listened to the radio, and ignored Paul while he sat at the dining table and tapped on his computer. I knew we'd talk at some point.

After dinner, I sat alone with Oriel and Wylie in the living room, sipping wine and listening to the fire crackle. Paul read in the small library at the end of our downstairs office. Wind whipped around the house. I looked forward to the predicted snowfall. I was safe. I was home.

Paul announced he was going to bed. I let the dogs out for a final chance to go potty. Then Oriel, Wylie, and I trailed Paul upstairs to our bedroom. By the time I brushed my teeth, Paul seemed to be asleep at the far side of the bed. I snuggled under the comforters. Outside, the wind howled. Wylie settled in his crate at the end of the bed; Oriel stretched out on the rug next to me. I wondered again about Paul. **He's tired. He's stressed. Give him time to decompress**, I told myself. This wouldn't be the first time for either of us that work anxiety had gotten in the way of connection.

At 2 a.m., I heard Wylie rustling in his crate. He gave a small, sharp bark, telling me that he needed to go outside, NOW. I slipped on my robe and found my slippers on the floor by the stairs. At the front door, I exchanged my slippers for Ugg boots, slid a leash over the dog's head and walked out into what should have been a gentle snowfall. An exuberant west wind had created a whirling dervish. Wylie pooped so quickly and with such urgency that I knew he had diarrhea. Nothing to do but wait to see if he was okay in the morning. I stepped out of the boots at the door, put Wylie back in his crate, and slid under the comforters. Knowing Paul would be unhappy if I woke him with my frosty limbs, I wrapped a comforter tighter around me.

Two hours later, Wylie was up again. We repeated our earlier routine. This time, I tried to think of anything I might have in the house that could soothe Wylie's indigestion. I found some over-the-counter human medication for diarrhea in the bathroom on the main floor. I couldn't remember if it was safe to give to a dog.

Although the woodstove in the living room had faded to embers, the house still felt cozy. I put another log in the stove and noticed Paul's laptop on the dining room table. It was plugged in and turned on. Rather than going downstairs to turn on my own computer in the cold office, I decided I could more quickly and warmly use Paul's laptop here to search for **dogs, diarrhea, drugs**.

When I opened the laptop, I saw that Paul had left his personal email account open. I hovered the mouse over a new tab to do my search and watched multiple emails from the lawyer he'd mentioned tumble into his inbox. The subject line, "Hotel Confirmed," caught my eye. I clicked it open. Her email included a hotel confirmation and a brief note: "I can't wait to spend the whole night in your arms," it read. I caught my breath. Seriously?

I sat stunned, shaking. I took a deep breath and told myself, "Focus." I opened a new tab and entered my key terms in the search box. Reassured that dogs could safely take Imodium, I gave Wylie a pill, my hand trembling as I rubbed his throat to encourage him to swallow.

I returned to Paul's laptop. I methodically clicked through the email exchanges with his new friend. I knew what I was doing was unethical. I was intentionally disregarding Paul's privacy. I knew I had no justification. Yes, he had violated his commitment to me. However, I understood long before becoming an ethicist that two wrongs don't justify anything. I couldn't pretend that I was simply looking for proof of their affair. I'd gotten that by seeing the hotel confirmation. Finally, I stopped nibbling at the textual crumbs of their developing relationship. I was unable to read through my tears.

It was 5 a.m.—less than an hour since I'd first opened Paul's laptop. I sat on the hearth by the fire, closed in by the darkness at the windows. During the day, the windows gave natural light from every angle. This night, the dark felt oppressive.

Wylie curled at my feet, his tummy calmer now. All was quiet upstairs. I had at least an hour to sit with this new reality before Paul woke up. Not only was I legally blind—I'd been emotionally blind as well. How could I not have known? There were so many reasons I should have suspected that Paul was seeing someone else. If only I'd paid attention.

Paul had a history of extramarital affairs. His ex-wife had told me that she had ended their marriage because of his sequence of girlfriends. I knew I wasn't the only woman he'd dated in the years between his wife leaving him and our first date in Paris. I had convinced myself I was as different from the women in his past as he was from the men in mine.

At 6 a.m., I softly called Oriel to come downstairs. I let her out to pee and brewed coffee for Paul and me. We liked to have coffee in bed together when neither of us had to rush off to work. I fed Oriel and Wylie, then put Wylie in his living room crate. I didn't need dog distractions during the conversation I was about to have with Paul. I walked upstairs to the bedroom, set the steaming cups on my night table, and slid under the covers. That's when I realized that I'd come to this important conversation with no plan. In a truly unusual move for me, I had rehearsed nothing. I had no idea what I was about to say.

"Paul," I said, "we have a problem." I passed him a few pillows so that he could prop himself up and then handed him his coffee with half-and-half. Just the way he liked it. He took a sip.

"Wylie got me up during the night. He has diarrhea." I knew that I was rambling my way into the story, doing what journalists call burying the lede. That always annoyed my mother. "Give me the headline!" she'd demand with exasperation.

Paul sipped his coffee without comment. "I needed to figure out if I could give Wylie Imodium or Pepto Bismol. I opened your laptop to look it up. Your email was open." I paused.

"Oh," he said, sitting up more as he realized what I had seen. We both hesitated.

Finally, I asked, "How long has this been going on?"

"Uhmm, maybe a month," he said. I knew from the three months of email exchange he had saved that he was lying. I chose not to argue that point.

"So, now what?" I asked.

He shrugged. "I love you. I love her. That's the dilemma."

I wanted to believe our years together would ultimately have more weight than a fling, even if it had been going on for more than a month. He insisted that this was something that had just happened and agreed that perhaps he was infatuated instead of in love with her.

For the remainder of the holiday weekend, we talked sporadically about how to move forward.

After he returned to California and I returned to Florida, Paul told me that he and the lawyer were no longer involved. My twice-monthly trips to California told a different story. I found an unfamiliar book on the nightstand, a nightgown on a hook in the closet, shampoo in the shower that wasn't his or mine. There was always something for me to stumble across and pretend not to notice. When confronted, Paul admitted that he had seen the lawyer again and reassured me that she was once again in the past.

I wanted the girlfriend out of our lives. I tried to treat the situation as a problem I might research, or a scenario I might present to students to resolve. What were the choices, short-term and long-term? Who was the most vulnerable here? How could I make the ethical high ground compatible with self-care? What

was the ethical high ground in this case? I knew I couldn't control Paul or his girlfriend. My only power was to try to act in a way that demonstrated my best self. I tried to stay calm and be open to what Paul might share. I tried not to be accusatory or defensive or push him away. It was difficult. I didn't know how we could become the connected and committed couple I thought we always had been. I'd never been good at giving up. I also wanted to know the truth.

Finally, in May, the academic year ended. I flew to LA, where I met up with Paul, getting ready to drive together to Montana for the summer. I was as ready as I would ever be to cope with the emotional months ahead: figuring out how to heal my marriage, retiring Oriel, and beginning work with Wylie as my new guide dog. Allison, now eighteen, had decided to stay home for the summer. For once, I was glad she wouldn't be with us.

Paul and I stopped at our favorite vineyards on the way and planned parties to host: an ice cream social one Sunday afternoon for the neighbors and jam sessions with friends featuring a variety of instruments and playing styles. We didn't talk about the girlfriend. Paul had assured me again that she was out of his life.

She crept back into our conversation as we neared summer solstice. "She doesn't know me at all," Paul proclaimed, describing with derision the longest day party she had wanted him to attend with her. Our relationship felt less shaky as we prepared to celebrate solstice as we had in previous years: we walked to a hilltop a thousand feet above my home, drank wine, and enjoyed the 360-degree view of sunset.

The following Monday, I flew to LA for my usual day of meetings, planning to be back in Montana by nightfall. Paul dropped me off at the airport early in the morning; I kissed him goodbye and said I'd see him when he picked me up at the airport that evening. When I landed at LAX, I met the driver from Metropolitan at our usual spot. I got Oriel settled in the van and turned on my phone for the first time since leaving Missoula. I found a voice mail message from Paul.

"I'm sorry," he said. "I can't live without her." He was driving nonstop to California that day to be with his girlfriend. He didn't pick up the phone as I tried to call him throughout the day. I flew back to Montana that evening as planned. There was no reason for me to stay in LA if Paul wasn't answering my phone calls. I had no hope that my being at his house would make any difference.

The Missoula airport shuttle drove me out of town to my house on the hill. I walked into the house, feeling as though I was stepping into a reenactment of the moment, twelve hours earlier, when I'd left the house glad that our chat over coffee had felt more comfortable than awkward.

Maybe we have turned the corner, I'd thought as Paul drove me to the airport.

He later told me he was thinking, "What do I need to do before I can get on the road back to LA?"

That evening, in the quiet house, I felt wounded, but calm and curious about the future. I had a lot of practical "What nows?" to figure out. Paul had left me without transportation. The nearest grocery store was four miles away. I couldn't even take the trash out, as that involved driving a mile and a half to the dumpster in the valley.

I reached out to my sister and to my closest friend from college. They each said that Paul wasn't good for me and that I needed to move on. Both said of course they would come to Montana to help me out. My sister, Debbie, came first and stayed for a week, delighted to help me get angry at Paul. My college friend Loretta came the following week, encouraging me to connect with neighbors who might take me along when they went to the grocery store. They both knew me well enough to be there when I needed them and to give me space without hovering. Each morning, I left the house and walked miles with Oriel at my side, glad that we wouldn't be returning to an empty house.

I distracted myself with the gratitude I felt for my home, for the fence that encircled some of the acreage and for the gate I could close at the end of the driveway. I looked for the bright wave of color that signaled the changing clumps of wildflowers as I walked amid the trees and played in the meadow with Oriel.

I found a project. Using a wheelbarrow, I moved cords of seasoned pine and spruce from the woodpile by the driveway to the porch nearest my woodstove. The physical work felt productive and helped me appreciate what I could do. With my muscles sore at the end of the day, I felt strong—strong enough to stop trying to bend the world to do what I thought it should do. Strong enough to wait and see how the future might develop. I felt scared, confused, excited, and curious.

It wasn't until after I'd moved all that wood that I wondered if I would even be back at the house to light a fire in the winter. For the first time, not having an answer felt not like failure but like peace, quieting the "what if I tried this" scenarios that bubbled in my mind. I lost myself in the rustle of the tall grasses and let the pine-scented wind dry my tears.

Regardless of Paul and his girlfriend, I still had a job in Los Angeles. On my next trip to California, I moved my clothing from the house I had shared with Paul into a subleased bedroom suite in a friend's apartment. I had told Paul when I would be moving so when we crossed paths, I knew it was intentional on his part. I continued packing as he talked. Perhaps surprised that I was no longer offering any suggestions for how we might stay together, he tried to explain why he preferred to be with the girlfriend.

"I hold her hand because I want to," he said, "not because I have to." That wasn't what I needed to hear. I hadn't before considered that he might have stayed with me if I were normally sighted.

I flew back to Montana and prepared to face more loss. Oriel would move to her retirement home in August. When we returned to the hill, I watched Oriel wander the house and land—looking, I assumed, for Paul and Allison. I brooded over how much loss Oriel would feel when she moved to Maggie's.

In July, Oriel and I flew to Santa Rosa for two weeks of teaching at Bergin College. The new class of students would have a week of dog law and ethics with me. I would spend the following week working with the second-year students on their theses and culminating projects.

While we were there, I thought about the differences between human and canine experiences of relationship and loss. Students talked about which dogs were their favorites among all the golden retrievers at the school. They could scan a seemingly identical crowd of dogs and easily recognize the ones they had raised as puppies. Students said that the turnover they experienced in training different dogs over the two-year program was emotionally hard. The dogs, meanwhile, were clearly delighted to be in the company of any attentive human. They seemed happy to transfer their affection to whichever student was assigned to them. They didn't pull at their leashes when their previous raiser or trainer walked by.

"Let's talk about how differently dogs and people feel about one another," I suggested in the first-year students' law and ethics class. "When in doubt, who deserves the most consideration when we make choices for a working dog and for dogs retiring from work—the dog or their human partner?"

I reminded them, "Give your reasons when you express your thoughts on this." I was happy to hear their responses coalesce around the dog. "Yes," I said. "Exactly! Favor the most vulnerable. That's the way to think about this ethically."

I also reengaged with the previous summer's cohort, now preparing to complete their final assignments prior to graduation. I coached them in shaping their theses or in developing more practically oriented culminating projects.

Pam told me she had been accepted into the journalism program at University of South Florida and awarded the department's most prestigious graduate fellowship. She would be teaching and researching under the mentorship of one of my colleagues: a professor who wrote creative nonfiction books about animals. I was delighted that she would be joining the department in August and reassured her that I had not put my thumb on the scale for her acceptance or fellowship. She had earned it all on her own.

Having Pam in the program made me eager for the start of the new academic year. I was always excited to meet our new graduate students, knowing I would learn from them as they learned from me. I expected Pam to easily move into a leadership role with the other graduate students in the program.

Toward the end of my two weeks at Bergin, Pam shared a scheduling conflict. Her summer studies at Bergin required her to be in residence through the third Friday in August. She'd need to be in Florida exactly one week later for the first graduate assistant meeting. She could get herself, her golden retriever, Jana, and everything she owned to Florida by then, but would have no time to find housing. She needed an immediate, short-term rental that would allow her to have her dog.

"No problem," I said. "You are welcome to stay at my place. It's close to campus." I had plenty of room in my three-bedroom condo. Over the years, other graduate students had taken up temporary residence with me while they were in transition or commuting distances too far to drive after an evening seminar. I would be pleased to have a roommate for a while.

"You and Jana can stay up to a month with my new German shepherd guide dog and me," I said. "That will give you time to get to know St. Petersburg and figure out where you want to live." To avoid concerns about conflicts of interest, I called the department chair to let him know that Pam would be staying at my condo for the start of the semester. As we had done in the past with other temporary grad student boarders, the department chair took over any supervision that I would have done of Pam's academic work.

I returned from Bergin feeling less concerned with how Oriel would adjust to her new life. I realized that I had been projecting my own feelings of loss on her experience to come. Teaching at Bergin reminded me that canines' experiences are different from those of humans. When I thought about it from a dog's point of view, I felt sure the change would be far harder for me than for Oriel.

Travis's weekly reports brimmed with praise about how quickly Wylie was learning his guiding skills. He had a sweet, stable temperament and showed no fear or aggression. He got distracted by small animals, birds, and Frisbees, but it took no more than a stern voice to move his focus back to work. Travis said that my biggest challenge would be that Wylie had tons of energy and needed time to run every day. But the dog was ready to do guide work.

I arranged for Maggie to pick up Oriel a few hours before Travis was scheduled to bring Wylie home to me. Oriel happily hopped into the passenger's side of Maggie's car—the back seat was filled with her bed, toys, food, and dishes. I kissed the top of Oriel's head and slid my hands down her soft ears. She wagged her tail and looked out the car window, ready for the next adventure. I watched sadly as they drove down the hill, then squared my shoulders and prepared for Wylie's arrival. I set out his food dishes and bed. The toy basket was a mixture of new bones and squeaky toys and some older ones that Oriel had left behind.

When I heard a car driving up the hill, I returned to the driveway and waited for Travis to park. Travis knew that I referred to Oriel as "my minivan" because of her steady but pokey working speed. He stepped out of the car, asked Wylie to come, handed me the dog's leash, and said, "Here's your Porsche."

I held out the harness and asked Wylie to get dressed. He stepped into the guide dog harness, wagging his tail with slow, broad strokes. Wylie was taller and longer than Oriel. Unlike Oriel, who had pushed out her chest and shoulders to fill the harness, Wylie wore the harness loosely over his frame like a familiar, well-washed T-shirt. He padded forward panther-style, shoulders relaxed, head and tail parallel with his body as he curled and uncurled his legs in rhythmic stride.

Over the next week, Travis and I worked together with Wylie, and I adjusted to my new dog's working style. Wylie worked faster in harness than Oriel had, sometimes too fast for me to keep up with him and his signals. Oriel had trotted along, keeping pace with people around us. Wylie lacked patience. He threaded us past people who were in our way, not hesitating to nose the back of someone's leg to get them to move. "Hey, Wylie, I'm here too," I said. It felt like he thought he was in charge and that I was simply along for the ride.

Travis taught me how to slow Wylie down by giving "harness checks"—quick pops back on the handle—and saying, "Steady." Wylie and I walked miles with Travis each day, honing our partnership on the streets of Missoula and in all corners of the University of Montana campus. We stopped by the Missoula airport, getting Wylie used to the routine of going potty outside, entering the building, and finding the Delta ticket counter. He learned to indicate which suitcase was mine when we sent it on a ride around the luggage carousel. Wylie and I would take our first flight together when we traveled from Missoula back to Tampa for the academic year. At the end of the week, Travis left Wylie and me, saying I had a great dog.

Wylie and I established a routine of playing catch with the Frisbee multiple times a day. I learned to exercise Wylie in the full daylight hours, when deer were less likely to be in the meadow to distract him. After he'd burned off some energy,

Wylie often wanted to chase the sights, scents, and sounds of all the animals who called our hilltop home. He eyed hawks and eagles whose wings and songs I could hear overhead. He came back when I called him, reluctantly. As he slowly made his way back, I realized he was stopping to watch wildlife well out of my visual and aural range. "Wylie," I said with voice low and stern, "bring your dog back here now please." Although the structure of the command was unusual, it fit my own expectation that I treat my canine partner with respect. Asking a dog directly to take responsibility for themselves was a policy I had created years before. Even if the dog didn't understand the nuance, the phrasing reminded me that Wylie had his responsibilities, and I had mine. There was always a treat for him when he returned to me despite distractions. Sometimes he wanted the treat, but usually not. My rubbing his ears was enough.

On our last day in Montana, I closed the house, not knowing when I'd return. I patted the front door lovingly as I always did when leaving. Wylie and I got into the airport shuttle. We had a full day's travel ahead. I had food packed for Wylie and a bone for him to gnaw on during the flights and while waiting in airports.

Outside the airport door, Wylie peed in the grassy strip as asked. He led me to the Delta counter, where I checked my suitcase. He stood stoically while the TSA agent felt under his harness. He lay next to my seat in the gate area, watching everything going on around us. When called to pre-board, I was surprised to find that Wylie hesitated when I asked him to guide me down the jetway. I steered him into the bulkhead window seat, removed his harness, slipped his GUIDE DOG vest over his shoulders, and gave him his favorite treat. I praised the dog for his good work. Wylie watched other people board the plane. He sat and stayed, but shifted his weight paw to paw, side to side, front to back. He panted. He moaned. He started shedding in copious amounts, indicating very high stress. I stroked his ears and spoke gently to soothe him. I couldn't figure out what was making him so uncomfortable. I could tell that all he wanted to do was to get off the plane and run back down the jetway. His leash, wrapped tightly around my wrist, ensured that he didn't.

Once the plane took off, Wylie relaxed and lay at my feet. Whatever had made him anxious before takeoff was mirrored upon our touchdown and taxiing when we landed. Was it the sound and vibration of the engines? Wylie tensely waited for me to buckle him into his harness. Then he pushed passengers out of our way in his hurry to get off. As it turned out, this would be the best that Wylie would ever behave on an airplane.

CHAPTER 5

WYLIE

In Florida, I prepared lessons for the new semester, easily weaving new cases for my students to consider as I focused on helping students become more mindful, intentional ethical beings. I taught with clear learning goals for each class segment, using a seemingly infinite variety of resources I had created, adopted, or stumbled across while flipping through newspapers and listening to newscasts.

My new guide dog was much more of a challenge. Before we left the condo to walk the block to my office, I routinely checked Wylie's mouth, often removing a toy or tennis ball as we headed out the door. Wylie always guided me after I had buckled him into his harness, but he simultaneously tracked birds flying overhead and glared at squirrels jabbering in the trees.

The only time I felt that I had 100 percent of Wylie's attention was when we stopped at a street crossing surrounded by other people or when I paused on campus to have a conversation with a colleague. In those moments, Wylie glued himself to my left side, suspiciously watching the people around us. Hardly anyone reached to pet Wylie as they had with Oriel.

Pam and her golden retriever, Jana, arrived. They had a bedroom and bath on one side of the condo, with mine on the other. We crossed paths in the kitchen or when heading out the door. I could tell Pam and I would have an easy friendship. We shared a mutual interest in dogs. Neither of us talked much. We gave each other space.

As the weeks passed, Pam looked for an apartment of her own but couldn't find anything she could afford that was close to school and would allow a pet dog. As we were clearly compatible roommates, I suggested to Pam that she continue sharing my condo. We could help each other out. I would charge her only the amount of rent she could afford on her graduate assistant salary. In return, she could drive me to the airport and pick me up for my return when I commuted to LA. Living with Pam felt safe and uncomplicated. She communicated in a clear and direct style. She was a grown-up graduate student in her forties, sometimes happy with her decision to return to the US and sometimes not. She liked the university but didn't much like Florida, aside from the dog beach.

Several times a week, we took the dogs to the Gulf of Mexico dog beach, only a twenty-minute drive. As Pam and I both got up early, as did our dogs, we were often first on the beach, arriving at daybreak. We marveled at the seasonal changes in sea life. One morning, the beach was full of sea urchins. Another day, we found the tidal pools sparkling with starfish. Then there was the magical morning that three adolescent dolphins danced on their tails in the gulf at sunrise, whistling and clicking, while Pam, the dogs, and I stood in awe. I savored the companionship we shared without living with the responsibilities and risks of an intimate relationship.

My struggles with Wylie continued. When I taught my weekly three-hour graduate seminar, he was good at lying still under the table. However, he used his excellent internal clock to keep the class on a strict schedule. My usual routine was to teach for an hour, give the students a thirty-minute break, and then teach for the remaining hour and a half. Sometimes, break time snuck up on me when I was in the midst of making an important point or when students were engaged in discussion.

"Let's keep with this," I'd tell the students in those instances. "We'll take our break in five minutes or so." When Oriel had been my guide dog, she'd waited for the students to stand up for the break before getting up herself. Not Wylie. After a few weeks to learn the routine, at precisely the one-hour mark, Wylie sat up, blinking his eyes, lids heavy from sleep. He'd look around at the students, making eye contact with those who would look back. "Settle, please," I'd say to him. Instead, Wylie responded by putting his head back and yawning. Loudly. Invariably, the students laughed, and Wylie wagged his tail. The teachable moment was gone.

In my office at school, I left my door open, liking the informality of students and faculty dropping in to chat as they walked by. Wylie chewed on a bone or stood to drink from the water bowl in his corner of the office or lounged on his bed while I worked. The dog noticed people walking by, but he didn't respond to anything happening outside the office door. However, if someone stuck their head in the door to say hi, Wylie growled. I told him, "No," and posted a sign at my door: "Please knock before entering. Even if the door is open."

When I heard a knock, I made sure to verbally welcome people: "Hi." "Come on in." As long as I did that, Wylie was content. Still, I worried about his behavior. I knew that a guide dog should not growl at any person for any reason.

I was also finding that Wylie needed more exercise than I could provide. Throwing a tennis ball a dozen times in the park every evening had been enough off-leash exercise for Oriel. That was only the start of what Wylie required. Wylie wanted to run long and hard. Every day. Most evenings, I walked him to a nearby beach on Tampa Bay and removed his harness. There he raced back and forth along the half mile of coast until he was wet and tired. He ignored me if I called him. Only when he'd had enough exercise would he step back into the harness to guide me home.

Fenced-in dog parks were not an option for Wylie. He played well only with other dogs that matched his size and weight. Most dogs were smaller than this eighty-five-pound German shepherd. Before I knew how he felt about little dogs, I let him loose in a fenced-in dog park. Wylie found a small dog to chase. And chase. He ignored my increasingly frantic attempts to entice him back or to let me catch him. Finally, the smaller dog hid under a picnic table behind their owner's legs. The owner grabbed Wylie's collar so that I could leash him and get him out of the park.

I'd hoped that Wylie would get used to air travel, but he only became more traumatized by it. I brought a crunchy treat for him to have during takeoff and another for landing in case the air pressure change was bothering his ears. He refused the treats. On takeoffs and landings, he moaned, panted, and shed, ready to bolt off the plane at the first opportunity. After a half-dozen cross-country trips, Wylie began trembling and panting when we got near the airport.

I knew Pam could see the difficulties I was having with Wylie. She didn't offer advice. I didn't ask for any. Then she heard from other students that Wylie had growled at them when they'd come into my office.

One sunny, breezy Saturday morning in November, Pam and I strolled along the shore of the dog beach while our dogs ran and swam off leash. Wylie raced through the breaking waves, then turned and raced back to me. He stopped at my feet, panted, shook the water from his coat, and repeated the circuit. He ran as hard and fast as he could, darting around other people and dogs in his thirst for speed and release. After a half-dozen runs, Wylie had used up enough pent-up energy that he could walk by my side, panting from his exercise. Out of nowhere, Pam said, "You know that no guide dog school would have graduated this dog. Wylie is not a suitable guide dog under any circumstances. He is certainly not the guide dog you need."

"What?" I asked, startled. That was quite a speech, one that Pam had obviously been rehearsing. I knew I had trouble controlling Wylie, but Pam saw every day how hard I tried to make this guide dog relationship work. I knew that, in many ways, Wylie was not an appropriate guide for me, but I had run out of alternatives. I sighed. "I'm doing the best I can," I said.

"I see that," Pam said. "You are trying your best to turn this dog into what you need. But it's not going to happen. Deni, you've taught at Bergin for two summers now. You've seen how service dogs are expected to behave in public. You know that a successful working relationship requires that the dog and person be matched to one another's personalities.

"Wylie has too much prey drive to be a guide dog. He loves to chase things. Even when he's in harness, he's distracted by anything that moves. The fact that he growls ever, at all, under any condition, makes him unsuitable for working in public. It's like carrying a loaded gun." Pam was intense and clear. I could tell she had been waiting for a while to say these things.

"Even if we could take away his prey drive and aggression, you can tell Wylie doesn't like being a guide dog," Pam said. "He wants to walk next to you like we are doing here, not out in front in harness. We know he hates flying. You may not have noticed, but when he's with you at our faculty and graduate student meetings, he's always watching the men when they talk. He ignores the women. Whatever job is best for Wylie requires that he have a strong handler with a commanding male voice. That's not you. After watching you work with Oriel before she retired and then watching you try to work with Wylie, I can tell you this is a bad match. You need a dog who wants to help you and who wants to be your best friend." By this point, we had walked back to the car. We toweled off the dogs and drove home in silence. When we got back to the condo, I said, "I get it. Finally. A privately trained guide dog won't work for me."

Pam said, "You need to look at Guiding Eyes for the Blind."

Guiding Eyes was a well-known school in Yorktown Heights, New York, that began operations in the 1950s. I knew that Pam had direct experience with Guiding Eyes puppies. Pam had worked as the puppy training supervisor for a New England organization that trained service dogs for people with disabilities. The organization often received eight-week-old puppies who'd been released from the Guiding Eyes program because they lacked the confidence to override a visually impaired human partner's command. Yet the puppies, attentive and eager to interact with people, had the potential to become service dogs who mitigated other disabilities.

After dinner that evening, Pam picked up the conversation as we sat in the living room. "The Guiding Eyes puppies were the smartest and calmest puppies I ever trained," Pam said. "At eight weeks, they already knew to come when called. They sat on command. They were housebroken and could go up and down steps. The Guiding Eyes pups we got might not have been assertive enough to be guide dogs, but they were entirely appropriate for other service dog work. They were confident, eager to learn, and ready for any adventure, including trips to the shopping mall and the county fair. The pups Guiding Eyes kept must have been perfect for guide work."

Pam told me that I had misunderstood guide dog schools if I thought that they treated visually impaired clients like second-class citizens. "Guiding Eyes has high standards for their clients, just as they have high standards for their dogs. Neither the dog nor client makes it through the Guiding Eyes program without being able to navigate the streets and subways in New York City."

Clients at Guiding Eyes were more likely to be successful professionals than people unable to cope with their disabilities. From her own experience of working with puppies who had started off at Guiding Eyes, Pam knew that the school used only positive, not forceful, training methods. "Force makes dogs fearful or aggressive," she explained.

"So," I said, "one more big issue. What about attachment disorder? How can it be emotionally healthy for dogs to bond with their puppy raisers, then attach to their trainer, and then learn to love their visually impaired partner? I've wondered if that's part of Wylie's problem. He bonded with me, then lived and worked with Travis for more than a year and then was expected to bond with me again. It didn't work. Maybe he lost trust in me because of that."

Pam disagreed. "Wylie is unsuitable for the job he is being asked to do," she said. "Remember what you have learned at Bergin from watching dogs get switched between student trainers. Dogs get attached to their people, but it's different from how humans attach," Pam said. "Dogs never forget people who are important in their lives. If dogs get what they need, physically and emotionally, they attach to more people. And, they stay attached to the people they've learned to love and trust regardless of how long it's been since they were together. Look at Oriel."

I did. At that moment, Oriel was stretched out on the sofa between Pam and me, entirely at home with us, despite her year living on Maggie's farm. Now that Pam was my long-term roommate, I had someone who could take care of Oriel when I was out of town, and so I was able to welcome my old dog back home. Pam was eager for Oriel to spend her final years with us. The dog showed no trauma from having been uprooted again. Oriel was happily retired. She showed no interest in walking into the harness when I got ready to go to work. She was happy to stay home with Pam's dog, Jana, while Wylie and I headed off in harness.

I stroked Oriel's ear. Oriel responded by patting my arm with her paw. She was the only dog I'd ever had who liked to pet her people as well as be petted by them. "I'll think about it some more," I said.

Then, I lost the luxury of mulling over the problem of Wylie. He killed a cat.

It was February 2012. Pam and the dogs and I were in Berkeley; I was on a sabbatical leave for the semester. Pam had an invitation to work for Bergin. We were both eager to head out to the Bay Area for four months. Oriel, now twelve years old, had recently been diagnosed with an inoperable tumor. We hadn't expected her to still be alive for the road trip across the country, much less our stay in Berkeley. But she had made it to California with us and seemed to be thriving. Vets in Florida and California agreed that she wasn't in pain. Oriel was very happy with the special high-protein food that, thanks to her, all three dogs in our household were now being fed.

One afternoon, we took the dogs to an off-leash hiking area not far from our rental house. As usual, Wylie ranged and then came back to check in when he felt like it. The two goldens, Oriel and Jana, trotted alongside us, stopping occasionally to sniff a tree or branch.

Wylie was out of sight, around the bend in the path in front of us, when we heard an animal scream. A man yelled, "A

German shepherd just grabbed and killed a feral cat." Pam found Wylie guarding the cat's body. She leashed him. I leashed the other two dogs. We headed home in silence. The shock that Wylie could do such a thing shook me out of my complacency. It was past time for me to face the hard truth: I could not control Wylie. He could not be expected to work safely around other people or animals. He was not a guide dog.

I was humbled by how I had failed to meet this dog's needs. I also knew that the event that had shaken me awake could have been worse. Wylie might have responded to his stress about flying by becoming aggressive rather than timid. It was time for me to face up to my responsibilities. It was time for me to face up to my needs.

A week later, Oriel woke one morning unable to stand. After a quick call to the emergency vet nearby, Pam and I created a stretcher using a blanket. We carried her to the car, pausing to let Jana and Wylie sniff her, nose to toes. We drove to the vet's office and were met in the parking lot by an assistant with a cart to transport her. The vet confirmed that the mass in Oriel's liver had ruptured. She was bleeding internally. Ory was not in pain, but she was very weak from the bleeding into her belly. As the vet administered euthanasia drugs, Pam and I sat on the floor and held Oriel close as we said goodbye. I thanked her for the years that she had served as my guide, and for teaching me to greet each day with anticipation and joy. Oriel peacefully slipped away.

With Oriel gone and Wylie having proved beyond a doubt that he was unsuitable for guide work, I had reached the end of my twelve-year, expensive, ultimately unsuccessful experiment with private guide dog training. I could not handle my visual limitations on my own. I couldn't train my own guide dog. Pam was right. I needed to trust the experts.

As I completed the application for Guiding Eyes for the Blind, I grappled with explaining my previous guide dog experience, and why I now wanted a school-bred and school-trained guide dog. I was honest but not detailed. "I was lucky that my first privately trained dog worked as an adequate guide," I wrote. "My vision has deteriorated further and my current dog, who was also privately trained, has too much prey drive to be predictable. He is about to have a career change."

I sent my application packet, with doctors' reports and contact information for three references who were willing to attest to my ability to be responsible for a trained guide dog.

With Pam's help, I found a suitable home for Wylie. She had a friend who trained and placed dogs with veterans who had PTSD. The director of that program identified a young, active veteran as the right partner for Wylie. Wylie would be kept on leash when out in public. She promised that Wylie's new partner would take him for daily runs and earn the dog's respect as leader of their pack. Wylie would help the veteran stay out of a darker place than I'd ever been. When we left California, Pam and I first drove Wylie to South Carolina to begin his PTSD service dog training. She and Jana and I returned to Florida. I unfurled my white cane. I waited.

CHAPTER 6

ALBERTA

On April 25, 2011, Jane Russenberger, director of breeding and genetics at Guiding Eyes for the Blind, slipped her hand under Aloha's flank as the black Labrador curled in contraction and gave a final push. A golden puppy slid into Jane's outstretched hand, fitting easily in the cupped palm that had caught more than a thousand newborns. Jane's long fingers formed a fence to protect the puppy from falling.

Aloha reached around two nursing puppies to attend to the newest puppy in Jane's hand. Aloha licked her baby, swallowing strips of blood-streaked birth sac that clung to her head and back. The newborn struggled against Aloha's tongue and Jane's hand, wriggling in pursuit of her first meal.

"Just a minute," Jane said softly, although the pup's ears wouldn't open for weeks. "Let me take a look at you." The puppy looked like a sodden toddler's mitten, as they all did when they were a minute old. As Jane watched, Aloha's vigorous licking stimulated oxygenated blood to flow, and the puppy's nose and tummy and paw pads began to pink up. Jane placed the puppy on a blanket on a scale. This puppy weighed in at fifteen ounces, one less than her two slightly older sisters, Addison and Aggie.

"Name?" Jane asked. The volunteer helping with the delivery looked at the list on the paper at her side. "Girl?" she confirmed. "This is Alberta." The names for this "AA" litter born in April had been picked out weeks before. The Guiding Eyes convention is to start each new calendar year with the "A" litter, with each puppy's name beginning with the letter **A**.

The school had bred twenty-six litters so far in 2011. "AA" indicated that they were starting the alphabet all over again.

All the puppies that Aloha delivered that day had names that began with **A**. This convention would help staff keep track of all members of a litter throughout their lives. Some of the puppy names had been chosen by donors who had contributed six thousand dollars for the privilege; other names honored outstanding Guiding Eyes volunteers or staff. When more names were needed, the Canine Development staff members who cared for the puppies at Guiding Eyes from birth to eight weeks added in their tributes and favorites.

Jane fastened a tattered green cloth collar around Alberta's neck. The differently colored collars, washed and reused for sequential litters until they fell apart, made each puppy's development easier to track. Alberta's collar was green, Addison's was yellow, and Aggie's was purple.

Jane slid Alberta to the towel in the whelping pen, positioning the newborn an inch from her mom's swollen teats. Alberta struggled to raise her head. Following her nose, she blindly stroked her front legs to push forward and then tightened her jaws around the nipple that grazed her lips. She hoisted herself closer to her mother and sisters and contentedly sucked. Jane silently congratulated Alberta on her success. She had passed the first test.

"Good timing," she said, her hand on Aloha's flank, feeling the dog's core contract again. According to the ultrasound, there were five more puppies to be delivered. Aloha panted hard and then pushed. Jane knew this puppy was stillborn the instant the pale limp birth sac touched her fingers. Puppy number four felt like a lukewarm slimy bag of chicken bones.

"Sorry, Aloha, that happens sometimes," Jane said as the dog sniffed briefly at the dead puppy and then lay back down. "Puppy number four is a stillborn black male," Jane said to the volunteer taking notes in the composition book that would serve forever as the diary for the AA litter. "Normal interval," Jane added.

Jane placed the dead puppy into a rectangular petri dish she'd brought to the whelping room to hold any stillborn puppies. Later, Jane would examine the corpse for abnormalities, but she didn't expect to find any. Sometimes, some puppies simply didn't survive, even when the mom had had a smooth pregnancy and delivery, and even when puppies slid out like trains on a schedule, in what Jane called a normal interval.

The volunteer's composition book was as new as the litter, its pages pristine, its binding stiff. Over the next ten years or so, staff and volunteers would fill the notebook with different inks and handwritings as they recorded information about each puppy's development into adulthood. The documentation would continue until every dog had retired from their guide dog career, had been released from the program because they were unsuitable to become guide dogs, or died. Over time, the notebook would fall open to the pages that staff found most important in making future breeding decisions. These notebooks filled a bookcase in Jane's office. Taken together, they told the sixty-year story of Guiding Eyes, litter by litter, puppy by puppy.

By 2011, when Alberta was born, Jane was also using spreadsheets and computer-coded evaluation forms to create breeding indexes that demonstrated statistically significant results. Her genetics research influenced animal husbandry programs around the world. Yet when she was uncertain about a breeding, Jane still reached for the handwritten observations. Computer spreadsheets were good at showing larger trends, but they lacked paws-on-the-ground intimate details of how the puppies had developed.

Jane's lofty goal was for each Guiding Eyes breeding to be a complete success. Her definition of success was simple: graduation from Guiding Eyes with a visually impaired partner or selection as a breeder dog. Dogs kept by the school for breeding were qualified to become guide dogs but were the best even within that elite group. They were considered most likely to pass their superior health and temperament on to their offspring.

At even the best guide dog schools, the graduation success rate was no more than 50 percent. Some schools claimed higher success rates but might use a more generous definition of success, counting dogs who didn't qualify for guide work and were diverted into service training for people with mobility disabilities or PTSD. Some schools also included dogs who were released to law enforcement agencies for scent detection work or placed as pets for children with visual disabilities. But in Jane's book, dogs who didn't qualify to guide were not successes.

Within a few hours, Aloha had finished delivering. Seven healthy puppies nursed and slept: Addison, Aggie, Alberta, Alicia, Almond, Ariel, and Angus. Angus was the only black Lab and was also the sole surviving male in the litter. The six girls displayed a range of yellows as nuanced as Van Gogh's palette. Alberta was buttercream with toffee-colored ears and tail. Addison's coat had a golden weave. Aggie was honey blond. Alicia was platinum. Ariel wore the orange-tinged yellow of a dandelion at the end of a summer's day. Almond was toasty brown, coincidentally matching her name.

Jane chose breeding pairs based on their lack of genetic deficiencies and their abundance of genetic strengths. She paid no attention to the color of their coats. This litter displayed the color diversity in their heritage. Angus had a sprinkle of cream-colored fur on the top of his black head and at the base of his tail; Alberta's creamy coat was peppered with black strands.

Occasionally, a puppy was born with an exotic display of what happens when a toss of genetics results in duplicate recessive genes: a red-fox Labrador with a coat that gleamed like aged cherrywood, or a black-and-tan Labrador that strangers would later assume to be a Rottweiler mix. Even more rarely, a brindle Labrador emerged with a black coat and tan speckling on their feet and muzzle. Brindle Labs look like they have spent the afternoon playing in the mud. Visually impaired clients who were matched with these unusual and strikingly beautiful dogs were the envy of their classmates.

Such color variations reminded Jane that genetics produced unique combinations in each puppy. Statistically, she could successfully breed out some traits—such as susceptibility to ear infections, noise reactivity, or a dog's discomfort with the guide dog harness—and successfully breed in others. But even with all her careful calculations, she couldn't control all the variables at once.

Aloha, the mother of the AA litter, was a tall and graceful black Lab who danced lightly on small, tight feet. She'd first captured the attention of the Guiding Eyes breeding staff at four weeks old, when she distinguished herself in the playroom. Whereas her littermates responded to toys only when volunteers purposely worked to get their attention, Aloha eagerly explored new surfaces, obstacles, toys, and scents. When a toy squeaked or rattled, Aloha cocked her head, thinking about what had just happened. Then she pawed at the toy or grabbed it with her mouth, experimenting until she could get it to make noise again. She wagged her tail when she'd accomplished her goal and looked around for what else might be new.

Aloha also hopped up to grab the mobiles that dangled just above the puppies' heads, wagging her tail when she realized that her contact made bells ring and the fabric butterflies flutter. She found ropes for tugging and brought them back to her siblings, teasing them until she found a playmate to chase her and tug the toy. She stood out to Jane as a puppy who was particularly fearless and creative.

In contrast to the tall, lithe Aloha, Barlow, the yellow Labrador who had sired the AA litter, was built low to the ground, compact and solid as a tank. And he was unflappable. A sudden noise that startled other dogs and people might induce Barlow to look toward the distraction, survey the situation, and go back to sleep. Unlike Aloha, Barlow was not the dog who would jump in front to lead the parade. He was the dog who would have your back. Every time. He exuded that kind of confidence. He invited that kind of trust.

As different as Aloha and Barlow were from one another in looks and personality, they shared important genetic strengths. Like Aloha, Barlow had hips and elbows completely clear of the dysplasia common to retriever breeds. And despite these breeds' tendency to develop ear infections, Barlow, his siblings, and their parents and first cousins had never had a single one. Same with Aloha. An occasional ear infection may not sound like a serious defect for a guide dog, but the medication is difficult to get deep into the ears when the person administering it cannot see the ear canal or the dropper.

Despite Aloha and Barlow's peerless qualities, however, this AA litter was the one-and-only time that Jane would breed them to one another. Her breeder colleagues at other guide dog schools gasped when Jane told them her policy of only one litter per breeding pair. But her data had shown that repeat breeding of even the best dogs limited her ability to increase genetic diversity. Successive breeding of Aloha and Barlow could lead to a higher incidence of genetic disorders in later litters. Although Jane didn't particularly like this conclusion, she trusted the science.

Also, contrary to conventional wisdom, which called for spacing out pregnancies, Aloha would be bred each time she came into heat, until she'd produced four litters. Barlow would sire a total of ten litters in the same time frame, all with different mothers for the litters. Jane's research had shown that breeding younger dogs resulted in larger and healthier litters, and that the back-to-back breeding did no harm to the dogs who'd received the nod of approval from the school's veterinarian. By their fifth birthdays, Aloha and Barlow would be neutered, then continue to live out their lives as pampered pets with the same families that had fostered them while they were being used as breeders by Guiding Eyes.

Despite all her successes, Jane had also had her share of genetic disasters: litters in which no puppy had the temperament or physical strength required to become a guide dog. In such cases, unless she could identify the genetic defect with one of the breeding pair's other relatives, she retired both litters' parents. Repeated ear infections, stress-related diarrhea, thunderstorm sensitivity, or an inability to think their way out of unusual situations were also unacceptable traits for a Guiding Eyes dog. The failures were frustrating but inescapable.

Pairs like Aloha and Barlow made up for that. They helped maintain Jane's confidence that her careful genetic analysis resulted in continuing improvements for each new generation of Guiding Eyes dogs. When clients came to school to be trained with their new guide dogs, Jane met with each class and promised the students that the Guiding Eyes dogs they just met were terrific and that their next Guiding Eyes partner would be even smarter and healthier than the one they were training with right now.

When Aloha's puppies were a day old, staff members transformed their nursery into their first schoolroom. The lights came up, although their eyes were not yet open. The room filled with unusual scents and sounds. Puppies could experience new scents from birth, although their ears wouldn't be fully open for a few weeks. The puppies had their own audio playlist, one that grew more intense over time: lullabies until their ears began to open, then classical music with heavier percussion every day, and then rock and roll, rap, the **Star Wars** soundtrack, and finally discordant traffic sounds and thunder. Foam rolls under fleece bedding provided hills for the puppies to climb; strips of textured plastic gave them slippery surfaces to navigate. Eventually, a monitor would be placed in the half-open Dutch door, playing Disney cartoons and nature programs to add visual stimulation to their environment.

Every day, a development specialist lifted each puppy from the whelping box and onto their lap for a one-minute nose-to-tail massage. Throughout the massage, the staff member varied the nature of their touch and spoke the pup's name along with affirming phrases like, "Good dog," "Good job," and "What a good girl." The specialist made notes about each puppy's responses.

For Alberta, the fingertip massages that created small swirls in a slow clockwise motion from head to tail were soothing. She twitched at long strokes; those tickled her. Ariel and Almond squirmed at the clockwise touch but enjoyed slow, long strokes head to tail. Other puppies loved it all. By the time the puppies were two weeks old and their hearing and vision were keen, they associated their names and people with soothing connection.

Aloha nursed and cleaned her puppies diligently, but each day, she took more time out of the whelping box to snooze nearby on the cool tile floor by herself. Some mothers jump to respond when a puppy cries. Not Aloha. When a pup whimpered, she simply looked over to make sure no one was hurt, then she went back to snoozing on the floor. When she entered the whelping box, rather than lying down to make feeding easy for the puppies, she sat, letting her babies work their way over to her and reach up to find a nipple.

Jane approved. Research showed that puppies whose mom encouraged them to work harder to nurse become more resilient. Resilient puppies are more likely to become successful guide dogs.

By the time Aloha's puppies were three weeks old, the mom got more "me time."

When Aloha went outside to relieve herself, Jane introduced the puppies to a new morning routine: a mushy kibble breakfast. Breakfast came on a noisy cart, at first with a single stainless-steel weaning bowl big enough for all seven puppies to gather around. They stood on wobbly legs, stepping into the bowl or falling over as they nosed each other out of the way. When Aloha returned, they weren't hungry.

Aloha nursed them less and Jane fed them more. Three times a day, the puppies clambered at the Dutch door as they heard the cart being wheeled toward their nursery. They jumped, cried, barked, and attempted to climb over one another in anticipation. The resident kennel cat ran in ahead of the cart or rode on the cart into the puppy room, grabbing a bit of kibble for herself during the ride. When the food bowl was placed on the floor, the cat circled among the puppies, purring and teasing, quick to slap a puppy that became too aggressive.

Once they'd learned to crawl over the four-inch sides of the whelping box, the box was replaced with separate puppy crates lining the walls. This was their fourth week, and puppies graduated to individual bowls. At mealtime, each puppy was asked to sit and briefly wait outside their crate while their food bowl was placed inside. As with any fine-dining establishment, dinner was served simultaneously to diners, one waiter for each puppy. When they were released with the words "Free dog!" each puppy raced into their individual crate to eat. Since puppies automatically fall asleep after feeding at this age, they spent up to a half hour alone in their crates three times a day, eating and napping. Crate doors were left open. Soon, the puppies were choosing to spend time in the safety and solitude of their crates outside of mealtimes.

The puppies also began housebreaking themselves. No dog wants to soil the area where they sleep or play. Staff members placed a low-sided square box filled with wood shavings in the corner of the room. When the pups woke from their naps, they were lifted into the wood shavings and told, "Get busy." After a few introductions and praise for their success, the puppies visited the box on their own at other times of the day and night.

Each day, beginning with their fourth week, the pups were loaded into a cart and wheeled down the hall to the playroom. Jane's carefully planned curriculum of activities and stimuli changed daily. The puppies found people of different ages, colors, genders, ethnicities, and abilities waiting to play with them. Some were dressed in costumes with hanging fringe, while others carried jingling bells and keys, wore strong fragrances, or used walkers or wheelchairs. The people huffed and puffed and acted as unconventionally as they could without scaring the puppies. Every puppy that seemed uncertain was approached gently and slowly by the people who looked or acted in an unusual way.

Playroom attendants encouraged the puppies to examine three-foot-tall, inflated clowns and lifelike statues of dogs, cats, and farm animals. The people rolled and tapped toys that squawked and beeped. They called the puppies to follow them as they walked over a range of surfaces: spongy foams and soft, low blocks. Each activity was designed to teach the puppies something new. The cart ride down the hall got them used to being in a moving vehicle, eliminating any tendency for them to get carsick. The changing stimuli in the playroom taught them that the world is always new and different and waiting for them to explore. They learned that all people, no matter how they look or act, are safe and ready to help a puppy with any challenges.

Jane capitalized on the critical learning period that extends from three to twelve weeks of age. Experiences—or a lack of experiences—in this time frame make a lifelong impression. Puppies who are not exposed to a diversity of people are likely to react aggressively or fearfully later in life when they see people who look strange to them. Puppies not exposed to different surfaces, scents, sights, and sounds before they are twelve weeks old will be stressed or suspicious when they encounter new stimuli.

The teachers working with the AA litter built on the qualities of each puppy. Aggie, the puppy development team noticed, was the most cautious pup in the litter. When she happened upon a new toy or surface, she lurched to a stop, gave it a slow examination, and then only sometimes sought to engage. An analytical disposition can be a good guide dog trait, but Aggie also needed to develop confidence. And so staff and volunteers calmly approached her multiple times a day, petting and praising. Soon, she greeted strangers with anticipation rather than hesitancy, and she more eagerly engaged with new items and situations.

The puppies' one-on-one massage and socialization time expanded from a single minute in the presence of the mom and littermates to ten minutes alone with a staff member or volunteer. When alone with her teacher, Alberta wagged her tail when she sniffed a water bottle with small pebbles in it, one of the many props brought in for her session. When her teacher crinkled the water bottle in front of her, Alberta reached to pull the scrunchy plastic bottle to her tummy. She hugged it with her front paws, chewed on the cap, and kicked it with her back legs. When the teacher flipped Alberta on her stomach and rolled the water bottle on her back, Alberta squirmed away. Her back was ticklish. The pup reached to engage with the bottle in a different way, tugging the cap and swatting at the plastic bottle to make it roll and crackle.

The teacher turned the crank on a jack-in-the-box. Alberta watched it, wagging her tail in surprise when the puppet popped up. She sniffed the puppet, pawed at the flap, then sat in front of the box, waiting for her teacher to do it again.

During her individual lessons, Alberta met toys small and large, soft and prickly, and she figured out how to make each one a plaything. She learned to lie still while baby chicks hopped on and around her. She touched noses with a turtle.

When the ten minutes had passed or Alberta had signaled that she'd had enough stimulation by yawning or whining, the teacher switched to a one-minute massage and then returned her to the playroom.

For Aggie and Angus, even five minutes of individual stimulation was too much. They were the quickest to want to return to the playroom and find a quiet corner to nap.

"What's essential in this period," Jane told new volunteers and staff members at the Canine Development Center, "is pushing the puppies just far enough for them to get curious and maybe a little unsure but never overly stressed. Puppies build confidence by sorting things out on their own, in their own way and time, without being pressured or baited. Your job is to patiently wait, then praise and stroke them for being so brave. Some puppies are fast learners; some are slow. Some are fearless; some are cautious. We provide more opportunities for the brave puppies and safe places for the more sensitive ones to shelter and recover. We want puppies to trust that every human they encounter is watching out for them and will give them whatever they need.

"It's in this period between four and six weeks of age that they learn they have the power to make good things happen. A sit makes praise and food rewards appear. Jumping up or barking gets them nothing aside from a suggestion that they sit instead. We try to ignore bad behavior. We reward good behavior. We instill good habits now rather than create bad habits that will later need to be fixed."

In their fifth week, the puppies began to learn the "Close" command (as in, "Come close to me"). It built on what they already knew: "Sit" and connecting with people. Alberta was the first in the litter to learn this complicated maneuver. Her teacher sat on a chair, held out a dab of kibble mush on his finger, and called Alberta's name. Alberta approached and followed the teacher's finger until she had turned 180 degrees. Then when she responded to the request to sit, she found herself between her teacher's legs, facing out. "Close, good dog," the teacher said, letting Alberta lick the mush from his finger.

The "Close" command protects guide dogs throughout their lives. When visually impaired handlers sit in a chair, they cue the dog to "come close." The dog circles into position between the handler's feet, placing their hind end under the chair and their front paws between the handler's legs. In this position, the dog's entire body is safe from being stepped on or tripped over by passersby. Some dogs rest their head on their handler's knee and watch the world around them while sitting in close.

Within a few days, Alberta mastered the "Close" command, but staff had to stifle their laughter. Her teacher was very tall. Alberta's entire body fit within the arches of his feet, and her head didn't come much higher than his ankle. Alberta, who took herself and her accomplishments seriously, sat tall and proud. She was a dog with big ideas.

The puppies heard new commands each day. "Let's go" or "This way," the teachers said as they clapped their hands and called the puppies' names in group and individual training sessions. With a bit of kibble, the teachers induced the pups to follow them around the obstacles in the playroom.

Once the pups were consistently following the teacher when asked, they were introduced to leashes. The first lesson was nothing more than giving the pup a chance to feel the weight of the clip and see the leash dangling from their collar. Then the leash was promptly removed and offered to the puppy to sniff. Puppies who showed no stress might be encouraged at the next lesson to follow the teacher with the leash clipped to their collar and dragging behind them. At the following lesson, they might be asked to sit and then come when called, with the leash extended from puppy to teacher. At no time did the teacher pull the leash or use it to control the puppy.

Aggie initially responded to the attached leash by lying down, flattening her ears, and refusing to move. Almond looked back, then ran ahead in panic when the leash snaked after her. In both cases, the teacher removed the leashes and comforted the puppies. The teacher went back to the first lesson. She sat the puppy on her lap, attached the leash, and then immediately unclipped it. The puppy earned a treat for this small success. Next, the teacher gave praise and treats while the leash was still attached. Only when the puppy seemed relaxed with the leash attached did the teacher put the puppy on the floor. Rather than let the leash snake after a sensitive puppy, the teacher held the end of the leash and called the puppy's name, holding out soft kibble to entice the puppy in. The puppy could see the leash but did not feel impeded by it. Every puppy in the litter eventually became comfortable with the leash as a new way to stay connected with people.

Like her mom, Alberta was the first in her litter to notice challenging new toys in the playroom. One day she encountered a toddler staircase and slide, walked around it, and then struggled up the first step. Once on the step, she whimpered, thinking she was stuck up there. A staff member watched but didn't intervene.

Mid-whimper, it occurred to Alberta to try stepping back down to the floor. She put down a front paw, lost her balance, and tumbled onto the soft rubber matting below. She picked herself up, shook it off, and looked around the room for something else to try.

The next day, Alberta returned to the staircase, made it up two steps, and bunny-hopped down. On the third day, Alberta climbed up all three steps and then wagged her tail in happy surprise when she reached the large flat platform at the top and found a slide. Alberta slid and skidded down the slide and then raced to the staircase to do it all again. And again. Other puppies noticed her game and followed her lead.

Next, in their fifth week, the puppies were dressed in homemade, puppy-sized guide harnesses before going to the playroom for the day. The harnesses, constructed of wide, soft cloth straps, fastened with Velcro around their chests, bellies, and backs. Purse handles procured from the local thrift store were clipped to rings stitched on top of the soft harness. This was the puppy's first taste of what it would feel like to have a stiff guide dog harness handle lying on their back.

Jane was concerned about body and harness sensitivity with this litter because Aloha had exhibited that trait during her training. When she'd first been introduced to a proper guide dog harness, she had initially crouched. With encouragement and food rewards, she stood and walked normally, but she needed a harness that was modified to float an inch off her back rather than lying flat so that she wouldn't be distracted by the harness on her back. Once she was chosen as a breeder, comfort in the harness was no longer an issue. But it would be essential for her puppies, most of whom, Jane believed, would become guide dogs.

Jane was seeing more harness and body sensitivity among puppies born in 2011 than she had in previous years. Her analysis suggested that the sensitivity was a genetic trait, as it was more common in some family groups than others. When she'd started using data analysis in 2010 to make breeding decisions, she'd focused on physical problems that would eliminate dogs from the guide training program: dysplastic hips or elbows, mast-cell tumors, epilepsy, skin allergies. In 2011, Jane added body and harness sensitivity to the index as traits to breed out. She added confidence and curiosity as traits to breed in.

As they were adjusting to wearing puppy harnesses, the AA littermates were also finding new stimuli in the playroom. As the weeks passed, the room became a patchwork of different surfaces, including gravel, small rocks, and metal grates to simulate those found in urban sidewalks. A shallow tray of water helped the pups learn to walk through puddles. Balance pads and wedges gave them inclines to conquer. Interlocking foam grids and ladders allowed them to practice stepping over holes and taught them to pay attention to where they were placing their feet. The pups strengthened their problem-solving and coping skills as they worked through each new stimulus. Teachers stood by as a puppy resolved a problem, then praised the puppy for figuring it out.

Alberta, so good at taking risks, had issues with the harness and the irregular surfaces. Like her mother, Alberta crouched when she felt the purse handle on her back. She skirted around surfaces that tickled her feet. Pebbles were okay; bigger stones were not. Grass was fine, but she'd walk around a patch of Astroturf if she could. She also sidestepped the tray of water rather than splashing through it as her littermates did. There was no question that she had some harness and body sensitivity. The question was whether she could overcome it.

Staff members capitalized on what Alberta did like—human attention and food rewards. After her initial reaction to the harness, her teacher dressed her in something simpler: a strip of cloth around her shoulders and another strip around her belly. Then her teacher practiced with her the "Close" command that she liked so much. Once she seemed comfortable with the strips of cloth, the purse handle was added again. Alberta did not like that thing lying on her back. She turned her head and dropped her tail, twitching to try to make it go away.

"Close," said her teacher. Alberta turned her attention to the command and to the particularly good-smelling treats that her teacher had. They did the exercise again, three, four, then five times. Each time, Alberta responded with more confidence. By the time she was seven weeks old, Alberta was no longer irritated by the handle. Then the teacher started placing unusual surfaces between his feet. When asked to "Come close," she confidently circled and sat between her teacher's feet on a square of Astroturf or on a sample tile from Home Depot with a rough pebbly surface. Jane thought that they had gotten Alberta past the worst of her body sensitivity, but her puppy raiser would need to understand how vital encouragement was for this girl's success.

When the litter was eight weeks old, the puppies were ready for their first formal evaluations. Each puppy was tested in a room, alone, by a trainer they hadn't met. They were expected to follow the stranger when called by name and to remain relaxed while the person held them still and stroked them. They would see new objects, including a rocking horse and cat statue, and were expected to approach them with curiosity. When a person entered the room dressed in a clown suit, they were evaluated on their willingness to walk up to them without fear or suspicion. And they would have to walk calmly on a loose leash past a blowing fan and over slippery tile, Astroturf, carpet, and pavers. If a puppy startled or showed discomfort, they were given a minute to recover on their own before the evaluator provided reassurance.

All the members of the AA litter passed these tests, as do eight out of every ten Guiding Eyes puppies. Any pup who retreats from the test's challenges or waits for a person to reassure them is diverted to programs that assist people with mobility impairments. The main difference between a mobility service dog and a guide dog for the visually impaired is that guide dogs must be willing to trust their own judgment to veto a blind partner's planned route. Mobility service dogs must be comfortable handling unexpected situations in public spaces but aren't required to be able to overrule their human partner's commands. At the low end, some puppies showed stress when faced with the novel sights, sounds, or smells of the test. As they would not be up to working in public spaces, these pups would end up in homes as pets.

At the other extreme, some puppies exhibit too much drive or intensity. Guiding Eyes holds on to such puppies, waiting to see how they develop when placed in their foster families. With the right puppy raisers, and with careful handling in advanced training, high-energy puppies can mature into dogs suitable for guiding blind handlers in big cities, while mountain climbing, or in other challenging environments. They undergo more evaluations throughout their training. If they are not able to calm down enough to concentrate on guide work, they are routed to occupations in law enforcement.

After their eight-week evaluations, the AA litter was transferred from Jane and her crew at the Canine Development Center over to the puppy training staff, led by Kerry Lemerise. She and her team reviewed the videos and score sheets from the tests.

These staff members matched the pups with puppy raisers who would, for the next year, provide them with foster homes and teach them house manners. Before they could return to school to learn the special skills needed for guiding visually impaired partners, the pups first needed to grow up. They would learn basic obedience and how to be part of a family. Every person in a puppy raiser household was required to agree to follow the Guiding Eyes rules of not allowing the dogs on furniture and never offering people food or any treat from a human dining surface. They promised to give the puppy consistently positive feedback, look for opportunities to expose the puppy to novel situations, and take the puppy to weekly training sessions.

Prospective puppy raisers participated in six hours of seminars to introduce them to the variety of situations they could expect to encounter. In the seminars, Kerry also identified any volunteers who were not ready for the yearlong responsibility, helping them self-select out.

Kerry told potential puppy raisers, "This is not like having a pet puppy. Sometimes when you come to the weekly class, we'll ask you to swap the puppy with another raiser for a weekend. We want the pups to be exposed to different people and environments that all practice the same rules. Guiding Eyes staff members will evaluate the puppies on a regular basis. After an evaluation, we may decide that the puppy isn't progressing as we expect. We may try a different home or decide that the puppy isn't suitable for guide work and should be released. This is hard on everyone, but it's important that you not take it personally. We want you to be willing to try with another puppy."

Kerry warned the volunteers that a puppy can form bad habits surprisingly quickly. "Some puppies are single-trial learners," she cautioned. "If they can pull a piece of meat off a table one time, they may never forget that and will persistently look for another opportunity. Here's how to set your puppy up so that they don't counter-surf: Put something enticing on the counter or table. Have a better food treat in your hand. Give the pup the treat out of your hand for ignoring what you have put on the counter. Practice this until you can put food in easy reaching distance for the puppy, like on a coffee table, and then put it on the floor and teach the puppy to ignore what you put down. Puppies can have food only in their bowls or if handed a treat. It's up to you to help the puppy develop good habits early on. Bad habits may be impossible to break and will result in the puppy being released from training."

Every day would be filled with teachable moments. Kerry instructed the puppy raisers to start the day with thirty pieces of kibble in their pockets to use as food rewards. They should find opportunities to treat the puppy thirty times a day. This trains the raiser to reinforce the puppy's behavior every time they are pleased. "Reinforce behavior that you like," she said. If a raiser didn't go through the thirty treats each day, that meant the puppy wasn't getting enough exposure or rewards. "It's up to you," Kerry said, "to help the puppy believe that every challenge is fun and that their life is all about challenges." Truly satisfied guide dogs are like people so happy with their careers that work is indistinguishable from play.

Kerry categorized the volunteers into three groups. First were those who were good at encouraging puppies who slowed down or stopped when they became stressed. Second were those who could calm a puppy who zoomed around the room when overly stimulated. And third were those who could keep up with a smart, creative puppy who was ready to test every boundary the raiser might set. Such puppies would require absolute consistency so that they could not get around the rules. They would also need an enormous amount of stimulation and exposure so that they didn't get bored. Many of these puppies were overly sensitive to correction. The raisers would have to rely on encouragement to keep the puppy in line.

Alberta fit into the third group. She greeted every challenge as a new game created for her. She got bored with repetition and liked the bar set a little higher each time. Each success made her more confident. She expected the people around her to acknowledge that she was special. She pouted when told no.

Kerry identified Lisa McMains and her household as the best foster family for Alberta. Lisa lived in Massachusetts with her husband, George, and their daughter, thirteen-year-old Shaye, and son, eleven-year-old Owen. Alberta would be the family's second puppy from Guiding Eyes. "When we do something," Lisa said, "we do what we're expected to do and then do even more." Alberta the overachieving puppy would grow up in an overachieving family.

"Housebreaking Alberta was easy," Lisa later said. "Whenever George or I could not watch her, Alberta was in her crate. She was happy unless she had to potty. Then she'd whimper. We scooped her out of her crate and put her leash on while carrying her out the door. We'd set her down and give her the Guiding Eyes cue, 'Get busy.' As soon as she did, we praised her, gave her a food reward, and let her explore a little or play. Alberta was housebroken, going to the kitchen door to ask to go outside, within a week."

Lisa and George, along with Owen or Shaye, took Alberta to the weekly Guiding Eyes training sessions. Lisa decided that Alberta needed more exposure to other dogs. She discovered the New England Bully Breed Club and thought those dogs would provide new exposure for Alberta. When Lisa explained to the club organizers that Alberta was learning to be a guide dog, she was granted an exception to the "bully breed" requirement. "There were twelve pit bulls and Alberta," said Lisa.

During the summer, the McMains went to the ocean to scuba dive with friends. While George, Shaye, and Owen dived, Alberta played happily in the waves with Lisa, then napped on a rock or under the sun shelter while Lisa read a book nearby. When the rest of the family emerged from the ocean in wetsuits, holding scuba gear,

Alberta greeted them enthusiastically, despite their strange-looking garb. She learned to play carefully with the live lobsters they brought back.

At sixteen weeks, Alberta demonstrated to Guiding Eyes staff that she responded well enough to obedience commands to qualify for a "Guide Dog in Training" jacket. This opened more doors for her, as Massachusetts gives guide dogs in training the same public access as working guide dogs. She visited Boston's international airport. She was the only dog in attendance at a police officers' ball. She sat in the front row at a Cirque du Soleil performance, enthralled with the human acrobats. She rode the train, tucking herself under the seat when asked to sit "Close."

"When we were out among strangers, George and I were a tag team," Lisa recalled. "One would work the dog and the other would run interference. When people wanted to pet Alberta, we'd ask,

'Can you please walk by her? She needs to practice ignoring strangers.' On the other hand, if we saw a guy with a beard or a woman wearing jangling jewelry, we'd invite them to come pet the puppy. We wanted to expose Alberta to people who were different from what she was used to."

To celebrate Alberta's first birthday, Lisa presented her with a cupcake from the local dog-biscuit bakery. When Alberta realized that this treat was for her, she began to drool. Rather than immediately handing her the cupcake, Lisa asked Alberta to lie down.

Alberta dropped to the floor and looked at Lisa in anticipation.

Lisa put a candle in the cupcake and set it between Alberta's front paws. Lisa lit the candle, warning the dog, "Don't touch."

The family sang Alberta the Happy Birthday song. Alberta closed her eyes and turned her head to distract herself from the treat between her paws. Alberta opened her eyes when the singing stopped. Shaye and Owen blew out the candle and removed it from the cupcake. Only then did Lisa say, "Free dog!" Alberta eagerly responded by eating the cupcake.

Two months later, a trip to the grocery store showed Lisa that Alberta was ready to return to Guiding Eyes for advanced training. Lisa went inside to shop, leaving Owen outside with Alberta. She handed the young tween a sprinkling of kibble. It was always good for Alberta to practice staying focused on a family member rather than the passersby who clicked their tongues at her, calling, "Puppy, puppy," or stopping to pet her. Lisa wouldn't be in the store long.

"Either Alberta or Owen got bored," Lisa later said, "probably both. I looked up in the produce section to see Owen walking Alberta on leash in the store. They walked by me without a glance in my direction. Alberta heeled perfectly. She was attentive to Owen, not distracted by food or people or shopping carts. Although Guiding Eyes was not ready for her to come back yet, I knew then that our family had done everything we needed to do to get her prepared. She was only fourteen months old but ready to learn how to guide a blind person."

Guiding Eyes summoned Alberta back to campus in August 2012 at sixteen months of age. The McMains handed the kennel assistant a Kong dog toy stuffed with peanut butter and kibble to give to her once she was put in her kennel run. They gave Alberta a hug before she agreeably turned to walk away from them. The family wiped their tears, knowing that they would not see Alberta again until she was successfully matched and ready for graduation with her new partner.

"Turning over the dogs is hard on the raisers," said Kerry, "but not on the dogs. The dogs never forget their first families, but they don't grieve for them. They're on to the next adventure. Their lifelong experience taught them to trust every person they meet and always expect good things to happen."

Nine years and five Guiding Eyes puppies later, Alberta's picture was still the wallpaper on Lisa's phone. "No other dog had this effect on me," Lisa said. "I've never known anyone, human or canine, who took such joy in learning. Every challenge we offered her made her want more."

After returning their dog to Guiding Eyes, every puppy raiser waits nervously to find out if the dog they raised has passed the "in for training" evaluation, called the IFT. Passing is required for the young dog to move into advanced training.

Some dogs don't even make it to the test. Each returning dog first has a thorough medical exam to ensure that they are physically fit to be a guide dog. Their hips and elbows must be free of dysplasia. Guiding Eyes vets also examine the dogs' medical records from the previous year, looking for anything that would indicate food allergies, repeated ear infections, or digestive issues difficult for a blind owner to manage in a dog expected to travel everywhere.

Sometimes, dogs are released because of issues that developed in their puppy-raiser homes. "If smart, persistent dogs with good food motivation get into the habit of stealing food, they're not going to be able to live with a visually impaired person," Kerry said. "We can't place them in homes if they take food without permission or rummage in trash cans." However, persistence can be a strength in the right setting. Extremely persistent dogs are perfect for scent detection work and are immediately scooped up when offered to state law enforcement agencies.

During the IFT, an evaluator tests the dog's ability to remain focused on the human at their side while the pair negotiates stairs, slippery surfaces, heights, and objects that make loud noises, like fans and vacuum cleaners. The dog must quickly bond with the evaluator, a person new to them. Staff members, volunteers, and campus visitors, along with many puppy raisers, watch from the sidelines. Regardless of performance, they clap at the end of the test. Guiding Eyes staff are less surprised than puppy raisers when only about half of the dogs returned to school qualify for advanced training. Any dog who exhibits fear or reluctance is placed in a pet home. "If the dog's behavior says, 'Don't make me do this,' we won't," Kerry said. "We advance the dogs who we think will treat guide work as the best possible life. Otherwise, they won't make it through advanced training. The dogs that become detection dogs or mobility service dogs or pets are still going to change people's lives, just not in the same way. We try to help the dogs figure out what they want to do and then give them that life."

Alberta passed her IFT with an almost perfect score, scoring the maximum number of points on forty out of forty-two criteria. She'd lost a point for hesitating when she felt the harness handle drop onto her back, but she continued heeling with the evaluator, earning four out of five points on that exercise. Her only other single-point deduction was for scavenging. For a moment, the food that the evaluator dropped on the floor looked too good to ignore. The evaluator reminded her to focus on him. Again, she got four out of five for her good recovery.

Remarkably, no dog from the AA litter was released from the guide dog program. The AA dogs were all physically and psychologically fit for guide work. So far, they were Jane's fully successful, 100-percent litter.

Jane had already chosen two of Alberta's littermates, Addison and Alicia, as breeders, hoping to pass down the litter's genetic strengths for generations to come. That was high praise, as Jane rarely picked even one dog from a litter to breed.

Jane was impressed enough with Alberta's performance that she considered keeping her as a breeder as well. Alberta's unique combination of confidence and creativity could be an asset to future generations. But there was also her harness and body sensitivity to consider—a trait she appeared to have inherited from her mother, Aloha.

After a few days, Jane told Graham Buck, the assistant director of training, that Alberta should be spayed and started in advanced training. Alberta was smaller than most Guiding Eyes dogs. She crouched when the harness was dropped on her back. A comb run through her coat tickled her, causing her to squirm away. Alberta could be a good guide dog, despite her body and harness sensitivity, but she would not be a good breeder. Jane needed to breed that sensitivity out more than she needed to breed Alberta's motivation and creativity in.

The training department would provide Alberta with a modified harness that floated above her back. And they would take special care to help her with her sensitivity in other ways. The training director wasn't worried that Alberta was smaller than most of the dogs. Dogs didn't have to be big to do big jobs. The training department needed dogs with incredible drive who loved working anywhere and under any conditions. That described Alberta perfectly.

CHAPTER 7

CLICK

Graham Buck taught the Accelerated Client Training Option (ACTION), an intense ten-day individualized program that accepted only one or two students each session. The course was available to Guiding Eyes alums who had demonstrated excellent handling skills with their previously assigned guide dogs. They would be able to bond quickly with their new dogs and work safely with them in less than half the time of the regular residential class. For Graham, teaching the accelerated clients allowed him to keep his hand in instruction while also leaving time for his other duties. Although the ACTION students began on the same day as the rest of the month's class, they completed their training at Guiding Eyes in just ten days, compared to the twenty-one or twenty-eight days required for first-time students or returning students not interested in the accelerated class.

As new dogs progressed through advanced training, Graham kept an eye out for those who seemed to be ACTION-program material. His goal was to find a dog for each ACTION client at least two months before the clients were scheduled to arrive on campus. That gave him time to get to know the dog and do any custom training that the client's lifestyle would require.

When Guiding Eyes class supervisor Miranda Beckmann asked Graham to join her at the community run to look at the new dogs in advanced training, it was midafternoon, the first Tuesday in September. Graham had just returned from a three-and-a-half-hour drive to Cornell University. He was tired from the trip to Ithaca and back, but never too tired to look at promising young dogs.

His visit to Cornell had gone well. He had opened his presentation by following his host into the auditorium while wearing a blindfold. A young German shepherd guided Graham on harness. When they reached the podium, Graham asked the dog to lie down. Then he took off his blindfold and smiled at the audience of three hundred veterinary students.

"Here's what it's like to cover your eyes with a blindfold, pick up the guide dog harness handle, and say 'Forward' to an adolescent dog who has been in training for less than a month." Graham paused for his audience to put those elements together. "For me, the initial moment feels like when I throw myself off the face of a mountain onto a double-diamond ski run. Suddenly, I'm in motion, moving too quickly with too much external stimulation and too little sensory input. I don't know what's coming up. I brace for what I might hit. Every instinct I have screams 'STOP,' but I push through, knowing that the disorientation is momentary." The students listened silently.

"After a few long seconds, my white-knuckle hold on the harness handle softens. My shoulders relax. I'm not plunging off the side of a mountain; I'm walking with no vision, being led by a guide dog in training. There's another instructor following the dog and me to keep us out of serious trouble. We're okay.

"The dog's rhythmic pace and pull invite me to walk in sync with him. He stops at a street crossing. When I feel for the curb with my toes and find it just a few inches in front of my right foot, I know that the dog has stopped with his front toes touching right at the edge of the curb. Perfect. Now I can breathe. This young dog already understands what he's being trained to do. I ask for a left turn, and he tucks his hindquarters behind my left leg to pivot in place. That lets me turn left without tripping over the dog or the curb. The evaluator following behind us makes encouraging comments. 'This dog doesn't get distracted,' she says approvingly and lists what the dog has whisked me past so far: pedestrians, two leashed dogs, an overflowing trash can, and one cat.

"'This guy is okay,' I think.

"'Praise your dog,' the other instructor says.

"The dog I have with me today," Graham said to the audience, "has almost completed his advanced training. He'll meet the partner we matched him with at the start of next month's class."

Graham had worked at Guiding Eyes for more than twenty years, beginning as an apprentice trainer. Now he often served as the public face and voice of the school. The hosts on **Today** and **Good Morning America** knew him by name. A Guiding Eyes marketing director assigned him to speak anywhere there were potential donors. Graham took Guiding Eyes delegations to county fairs and other public exhibitions where people could watch the dogs lead their trainers while they were under blindfold. He explained how the dogs had been trained to help blind people maneuver through unpredictable environments as safely as any sighted person. The more people understood the time and effort required to breed and train the dogs, the more likely they were to contribute to the endowment—and the more educated they would be when they passed a guide dog team on the street.

Graham understood that the veterinary students at Cornell were more likely to use their money to pay off student loans than contribute to a guide dog school endowment, but he liked talking about the program with other animal professionals. The students asked detailed questions about how IBM's supercomputer, Watson, had helped Guiding Eyes crunch sixty years of data to aid in determining which puppies would succeed as guide dogs. The students were sold on the Guiding Eyes breeding program when someone in the audience excitedly told the others that the program's director, Jane Russenberger, was the same renowned researcher whose work they had studied in their class on cell biology and genetics.

"The dogs begin guiding an instructor under blindfold within weeks of having the guide dog harness on their backs," Graham explained. "As quickly as possible, we help the dog understand that leading a person with no usable vision is the point of all this training. We teach the dogs that the harness buckled in place signals that the dog is in charge. Truly giving the dog responsibility is important for the trainers as well as the dogs. It's natural for a sighted instructor to tense up when approaching a tricky maneuver or slow down as the dog approaches a busy street crossing. We don't know how much the dogs are depending on our unintentional cues until the dogs guide us under blindfold.

"When I'm blindfolded, testing the new dogs in advanced training, I walk the same six blocks with up to eight different dogs," Graham said. "Every dog feels different. Last week, I worked one dog who walked exactly in the center of the sidewalk. A few hugged the left side of the sidewalk, which got us rude comments from people coming the other way. In a right-sided culture, like the US, that is a tendency we need to fix.

"One dog had a rowboat gait, rocking side to side as she walked. One bounced and walked high on her toes, projecting a profile taller than she was. Compared to the Labs, the one German shepherd in the string felt smooth and long. When I started out with the last dog, a black Lab, I could feel he was trying not to put weight on his front-left foot. I stopped to reach down and run my fingers between his toes. Still blindfolded, I pulled out the pebble that had lodged there.

"This evaluation was just one of the many times that the dogs in training would lead staff members under blindfold. Apprentices always carry blindfolds when they're out with the senior instructors and dogs. Many times each day, the instructor will ask the apprentice to put on the blindfold and have a dog in training guide them through a maneuver the instructor wants to observe. The instructor follows as the dog leads the blindfolded apprentice instructors in and out of subway cars, up and down escalators, and through parking lots with cars approaching from unexpected angles.

"Putting apprentices under blindfold helps these novice trainers understand the clients' experience in learning how to handle guide dogs for the first time. It teaches guide dogs how to work with handlers who are new to walking with a dog in guiding harness. It continually reminds the dogs that they are the eyes for people who cannot see. It reminds instructors that we need to give clear, nonvisual directions. Instead of saying, 'Turn right at the next corner,' you learn to say, 'You will feel your dog slow down and stop when you reach the intersection. Then tell him to turn right.'"

Graham ended the talk as he often did: "When I work under blindfold, I follow two rules drilled into me by my first boss at Guiding Eyes: If you get confused, keep the blindfold on. Blind clients can't resort to vision when they feel overwhelmed.

"Next, never say, 'That was fun,' when you take off the blindfold. Being blind isn't fun. It's also not a fate worse than death. It's our clients' lives. When instructors treat the blindfold as nothing more than an interesting exercise, they create a barrier between themselves and their students. The client can't trust instructor or dog unless the instructor knows how it feels to walk sightless with this specific dog guiding and how to seriously confront issues, while blind, that this dog might raise."

Graham answered a few questions and acknowledged the applause. The group sat hushed as he thanked the crowd again, put on his blindfold, and picked up the handle of the regal German shepherd who lay harnessed at his feet. "Forward," Graham said. "Go find the car."

Once the dog found the car, Graham removed his blindfold, got in, and began the drive back to Guiding Eyes. During the drive, he thought of more stories he could have shared from his years working up the ranks from apprentice to assistant director of training. When he'd been training his first string of dogs, a young yellow Lab named Grady had walked him directly into a pile of full garbage bags on the curb. Graham was under blindfold but realized what they had waded into. He told Grady, "Back, back!" The dog ignored the command and began sniffing for tasty snacks instead. Graham knew that the garbage bags could contain dangers—broken glass, spoiled food, rat poison—but he couldn't find his footing and walk safely backward. The supervisor following them called, "Halt," and then gave Graham directions for the safest way out. After that, it had taken weeks for Graham to convince Grady to guide him around, rather than through, street garbage.

Graham also remembered when he'd trained Othello, about five years into his career. Othello was a black Lab who had walked a blindfolded Graham into a parking meter. The meter hit Graham in the middle of his chest. He bounced back and fell into the street. The supervisor who had been following Graham stopped traffic, helped him get to his feet, and apologized for not intervening sooner. Graham shrugged off the apology. He kept his blindfold on and comforted the dog. Trainers let dog and handler resolve their own problems if possible, shouting a warning only at the last second. Sometimes they were too late. That was a risk of this job.

Graham and the supervisor tried to figure out why the dog had walked him into the meter. "I must be giving the dog too much direction when I'm walking sighted with Othello," Graham said. "He hasn't yet learned how to make space for both of us when walking around obstacles."

Graham thought his job was as perfect as any could be. Looking back, he realized that anyone could have predicted his career choice. After all, he'd grown up among a pack of dogs.

In Graham's earliest memories, he had no recollection of his brothers or parents. He only remembered the Great Danes that seemed always present. In retrospect, that made sense. Graham was small; the dogs that his parents bred were very tall. From the beginning, he knew the dogs were at least as important as the humans in his family. He'd begun contributing to his family's dog breeding and showing business when he was four years old.

"Come with me," his mom said to him one day not long after his fourth birthday. She lifted Graham into a shallow wooden box in which Lily, the family's brindle Great Dane, lay. Graham sat down in the layers of newspapers in the box and watched Lily pant, grunt, and curl up in contractions. He gave his mom a worried look. His mom smiled at him, stroked the Dane's head, and said, "Lily's okay. Wait to see what happens next." Looking back, Graham realized that his mom had dropped him in the middle of it all so that she could keep track of a preschooler while helping the dog give birth.

His mom handed him a towel. The room bloomed with unfamiliar smells. A puppy emerged from under Lily's back leg. Graham's mom picked up the puppy, inspected it, and then handed it to Graham. She recorded the puppy's sex and weight and told Graham to gently towel it off. "That helps the puppy learn to breathe," his mom said.

Once the puppy was toweled off, Graham's mother instructed him to put the squirming newborn down at Lily's side. "Careful, slowly," she said.

He watched, fascinated, as the puppy began to nurse. When all four puppies were born and feeding, his mom said to him with pride, "They're in good shape now because you helped them." He understood that he had been part of bringing about this extraordinary outcome: four new, healthy puppies. He, his mom, and Lily were a team of three.

By the time he started school, Graham worked daily in the family business. He was the only kid in his class who was escorted to school by a half-dozen dogs. His dad, Jim Buck, was known as the first professional dog walker in Manhattan and had been profiled in the **New York Times** and the **New Yorker** magazine. A few years later, he was featured in a photo essay by Alfred Eisenstadt in **Life** magazine. He appeared on a popular TV game show, **To Tell the Truth.** While other people might have found his dad's career unusual, for Graham, being outnumbered by dogs was just daily life.

By the time Graham was in junior high school, he spent hours after school walking at least five miles each day with up to six leashed dogs, regardless of the weather or other ways he might have preferred to spend his time.

After high school, Graham enrolled in Unity College, a tiny school in Maine known for its teaching and research in environmental sciences. Graham wanted a career working with animals but didn't know exactly what was possible. He did know that he didn't see himself out in the wilderness counting birds or tagging bears.

The dedicated faculty members at Unity were experts at discovering the potential in each of their four hundred students. Each flourished in their own way. "Maybe," Graham told his adviser, "I could be a teacher and work with animals." As Graham neared graduation, a professor told him about an opening for a director of student interns at Lifeline for Wildlife, a wildlife rehabilitation center in Rockland County, New York. Graham trusted the professor to know what he needed next.

Graham was hired by Lifeline for Wildlife and lived on campus, supervising the dozen student interns who'd left their home colleges to spend a semester living and working at the rehabilitation center. Some were interested in the rescued birds; others loved the snakes and tortoises. Many mornings Graham and his students found a box left at the gate.

They always opened the box slowly and with caution, never knowing what might be inside: baby racoons, an injured skunk, or a bristling porcupine hissing at their intrusion.

Graham helped his students find new potential in themselves, just as his college professors had done for him, rotating them through the facility's wildlife to ensure they all got a range of experiences. When the day's work was done, Graham relaxed by training the four or five dogs that had been abandoned at Lifeline for Wildlife. Graham set about making each dog attractive for adoption. He marketed the dogs to the students, encouraging each to consider taking one home at the end of the semester.

After a year of working at Lifeline, Graham realized that his next career step should be something that involved helping people and dogs build relationships with one another. Then he learned that Guiding Eyes for the Blind, a well-established guide dog school just up the road in Yorktown Heights, was hiring apprentice instructors.

Graham was twenty-four years old on the cold February day that he interviewed at Guiding Eyes. Thirty years later, Graham still recalled details of the day, as one does with life-changing events. "I wore a patterned Norwegian sweater, jeans, insulated hiking boots, and a blue jacket with a red fleece lining," he said. "I wanted the interviewers to see that I was ready to work outdoors with the dogs. I didn't know how guide dogs were trained, but I knew without asking that the work would require me to walk miles every day, while communicating with a dog. I had been raised doing that."

Graham was hired and shown to his new home: an apartment above the kennel where dogs in advanced training lived. These dogs were too valuable to be left alone, and so the kennel assistants and apprentice instructors lived in the small cluster of apartments upstairs, always ready to respond to their needs. They checked on the dogs regularly. Graham felt at home. He was used to living with dogs and liked living where he worked.

"Then," he said, "my tour guide took me into the kennel. We walked through the door, and I stopped, in awe, taken in by the beauty of what I saw. There were one hundred dogs in there, two dogs in every kennel run. Every dog—golden retrievers, German shepherds, and Labrador retrievers—was a breathtakingly beautiful representative of the breed. Not one of them barked. Row after row of alert, calm dogs studied me intently with their tails wagging. The intelligence in their scrutiny was unnerving. It felt more human than canine. From their first breath, these dogs had learned to connect with people. From their first minute, they had learned to solve problems on their own. They were unlike any dogs that I had known."

Now, twenty years later, Graham agreed to Miranda's request to join her and the two class instructors, Gerri and Barbara, to observe the new class. They had six months to get the dogs ready to meet their new partners. One or two dogs were likely to prove unsuitable and be released from training. Usually, an additional one or two would be "passed back" to a later class because some dogs needed a longer training period. However, the trainers knew that they had to have at least a dozen dogs ready for the clients arriving the first Sunday in March. The class date loomed like a target.

Jane's breeding program produced dogs that were smart, confident, and healthy. The sixteen dogs in this new class included yellow and black Labradors of different sizes and shapes, with more than a twenty-pound difference among them, and one long-coated shepherd. Some were not yet two years old; the oldest was two and a half. Most were the sole representative from their litter.

Miranda, Gerri, and Barbara discussed how to divvy up the group into two eight-dog strings so that the two class instructors each had a good mix of personalities. No one wanted eight overly active, social dogs that all needed help staying focused on each new task. No one wanted eight introverted dogs that all needed encouragement and soothing through every lesson. As class supervisor, Miranda would evaluate the dogs along the way. She would determine which dogs needed additional training. She would work with the admissions committee to help match dogs to clients who had not yet been assigned a class date.

As Graham, Miranda, Gerri, and Barbara watched the dogs actively engage with each other, Miranda called out to a dog by name. The dog turned from play and immediately responded. Dogs who came when called were given a Charlee Bear treat and immediately told, "Free dog," so that they knew they were released to play some more. Charlee Bears are the treats that Guiding Eyes dogs come to expect for just about everything that they do right. They are small, low in calories, and easy for the dog to gulp quickly.

Soon, most of the dogs were coming when their name was called, eager for their reward. Some dogs ran to the nearest instructor no matter who had called their name. Others raced to the nearest instructor no matter which dog's name was called. The instructors identified those dogs as the most eager to respond. Guide dogs need to value human connection above everything else.

"I see a couple that I want to keep an eye on for the ACTION program," Graham said, without specifying which ones. He didn't want to influence the trainers. Within the next few months, he would see how good he was at recognizing raw talent.

The dogs' advanced training started the next day. First, they were taken through their usual morning routine: time in the community run to relieve themselves, then breakfast in the kennel runs. The bowls of kibble arrived on carts, accompanied by kennel cats. Then, more time in the community run. There, Alberta heard her name called. She ran to the instructor, Gerri.

Gerri handed her a treat, but instead of telling Alberta, "Free dog," and releasing her to go back to play with the other dogs, as was the usual pattern, she snapped a leash to Alberta's collar. "Let's go, Alberta," Gerri said with enthusiasm. The dog eagerly walked along at the trainer's side. They headed back to the kennel run, where Alberta found a stool and a two-foot stick. She sniffed the two new objects, then looked to Gerri for an explanation.

Click, Alberta heard in response. Gerri handed her a treat and then showed Alberta the clicker she held in her hand: a one-by-two-inch piece of plastic and metal. When Alberta glanced up at Gerri's face, the clicker again made its distinctive sound. She was handed another treat. The **click** has a singular and consistent meaning: "Notice what you just did. THAT was the right choice. A food reward is coming. If you do it again, you'll get another treat."

Gerri picked up the two-foot target stick, making circles in the air with the big red ball that was attached to the end. Alberta pawed at the ball and heard **click** in response. Still crunching her Charlee Bear treat, she touched the ball with her nose. **Click**—another treat.

Alberta followed each move of the target stick to touch the ball with paw or nose. Five times, ten times. **Click** and treat. Then Alberta touched the ball with her paw. No click. She looked back at the instructor but got no response. Gerri waved the stick and ball again. This time, Alberta touched the stick with her nose. **Click**—a treat followed. Alberta tested out other responses. She grabbed the ball with her mouth, she slapped the ball with her paw, she walked under and then around the stick that held the ball. No click or treat for any of those. Then she touched the ball with her nose. **Click** and a treat. Now that she had tried out all other possible responses, Alberta understood the rule.

Gerri decided that this was enough for the first lesson. She took Alberta back to the community run, made a few notes about their session, and started the same lesson with the next dog in her string. Over the next few days, Alberta would find the target stick sitting in the hallway on her way to the community run. When she consistently touched the ball with her nose wherever the target stick showed up, Gerri was convinced that Alberta understood the game.

Repetition is often what separates guide dog training from pet training. Pet dog owners may think that their dog understands a command, like "Sit," when the dog responds to the command a half-dozen times in the same spot. Guide dogs must repeat a behavior dozens of times in different environments, ignoring any distractions, before the instructor decides that the dog really understands what's being asked.

Soon target sticks mushroomed all around campus, inside and outside, anywhere a dog in advanced training might walk. The sticks were inserted into wooden blocks that held them upright, their distinctive red balls on top. The goal remained the same: nose the red ball, hear the **click**, get a treat.

Gerri, certain that Alberta now understood that her job was to nose the target, moved on to the next lesson. She placed the target stick in its holder on the top of a curb outside the kennel building.

To reach the red ball, Alberta needed to step up onto the curb. Gerri gave Alberta a verbal label that would serve as a cue throughout her working life: "To the curb." When guide dogs hear that phrase, they know to look for an elevation change, such as the start of a staircase or an intersection of sidewalk and street. Again and again, Gerri responded to Alberta's nosing the target stick by giving her the new cue, "To the curb," then **click** and a treat. Soon, Alberta stepped up on the curb to reach the ball every time she heard, "To the curb." After the hundredth repetition, the stick and ball disappeared from Alberta's life. Only the command—"To the curb"—remained.

Next, Alberta was introduced to her grown-up guide dog harness. At first, instead of a rigid handle, she had only a soft rope attached to the leather shoulder straps. Gerri told Alberta, "To the curb," then held the rope taut, creating an association between the phrase and the handle. Gerri added a new word: "**Forward**, to the curb." Alberta walked out with confidence. The dog stopped when her toes grazed the curb. Then Alberta began wearing the rigid U-shaped handle. The snaps were modified so that, when Gerri let go of the handle, it floated an inch above Alberta's back.

Some guide dog instructors say that, in advanced training, they teach dogs thirty-five commands. Taken together, those commands make up a curriculum bigger than the sum of their parts: They teach dogs how to make decisions with their human partner in mind as well as respond to individual commands. Alberta quickly figured out that when she was walking with Gerri on harness, she should detour around obstacles widely enough to accommodate the width of them together. Alberta learned to calculate which path provided the widest clearance. She then chose whether to walk to the right or the left of the obstacle. She learned to pause to alert Gerri that they were about to make a detour. She learned to stay on the sidewalk, if possible, while going around the safety cone or sandwich board or person standing in the way. Gerri praised Alberta for her good decision-making. "You are such a smart dog," she said with enthusiasm. Alberta wagged her tail and rose on her toes in response.

A month into training, one of the dogs in Gerri's string decided not to become a guide dog. Kyle, a sixty-pound black Lab, used the only language he had to say that he had had enough of this. After leading Gerri through the school parking lot to the curb for the tenth time, Kyle responded to Gerri's next "Forward, to the curb" by standing still and pulling his ears back in a classic canine gesture of discomfort. The instructors took turns comforting and encouraging him. That helped briefly; Kyle wanted to please them. Sometimes he'd walk a few paces before refusing to go any farther.

Training staff members searched their notes and tried to remember if there had been some external factor that had caused Kyle to balk. The parking lot and campus had been quiet during the training session. No car door had slammed; they could recall nothing that might have startled the dog. Maybe something had spooked him by the kennel door where the dogs were usually put into harness.

The next time, Gerri led Kyle by leash away from the building before putting him in harness. That didn't help. He continued to walk just a few steps and then refuse to move. After a week of this, the instructors accepted what Kyle was telling them. He did not want to do guide work. Instead, he was reunited with his puppy raiser and settled into the life of a very well-bred and well-trained pet.

Early in these weeks of training, the instructors called the dogs' attention to the apprentices when they put on blindfolds and picked up the harness handles. The dogs were reminded that they had the only eyes available for the person at the end of the harness. At first, the blindfold communicates to the dog that the person holding the harness cannot see. Over time, dogs will learn that some people cannot see, whether they are wearing a blindfold or not. The dogs learn that when they are in harness, they should assume that the person holding the harness is sightless. When they are matched with their new partner, they begin their work assuming that person is completely blind. If the person has some functional vision, the dog quickly learns what the person can see and how they can work as a team, using both of their abilities and strengths.

Eight weeks into training, it was time for Graham to formally evaluate the dogs for the first time as they led their instructors under blindfold. As the blindfolded instructor and dog wove their way through the streets of nearby White

Plains, Graham followed the teams closely enough to intervene, if necessary, while also hanging back enough for the dogs to understand that they were responsible for guiding their now sightless instructors.

Graham evaluated the dogs on how well they walked a straight line down the sidewalk and how well they alerted their partners to upcoming curbs and steps. The dogs were also judged on their ability to walk around obstacles that naturally occurred on their route, and on how well they ignored other dogs, squirrels, birds, cats, people, and food on the ground.

Alberta was the most confident of the dogs evaluated. When leading Gerri under blindfold, she stood tall and pranced down the sidewalk. She liked showing off her skills and seemed eager to keep working, even when the evaluation was over.

Gerri took the blindfold off. As she and Graham compared notes, Alberta got bored and started sniffing the ground, searching for dropped food. Alberta got the highest marks for her guiding skills that day, but she lost points for scavenging for food on the ground while Gerri and Graham talked. Even if they are not actively leading a person, guide dogs in harness aren't supposed to take advantage when the handler's attention is elsewhere. A moment of distraction when the handler is depending on the dog's vision can be life-threatening.

After the evaluation, Graham thought that the seven dogs remaining in Gerri's string were likely to make it through training. Barbara, the other instructor, had yet to lose any. So far, the dogs slated for the March class looked solid.

Graham told the training staff that he wanted every dog to work with a person under blindfold for at least a few minutes every day. Graham always had a blindfold in his pocket and a dog in the last stages of training in his office. When he had an errand to do on the Guiding Eyes grounds, he put on the blindfold and harnessed the dog. "Forward," he said as they left his office. "Right turn, then left, left." His verbal cues helped the dog anticipate which way they would turn when the hallway branched off. As he walked through the halls, it wasn't unusual for him to hear an instructor announce to a group of students surrounded by their newly matched guide dogs, "Graham Buck is coming toward us under blindfold with a dog in training. Keep doing what you're doing. It's good practice for the dog to maneuver around us."

As a dog training professional, Graham was always most impressed by guide dogs' ability to see the bigger picture of what they were being asked to do. However, in Graham's experience, members of the public were most intrigued by how the dogs learn to refuse to do as they are asked.

If a handler is attempting to cross the street in front of a moving car, for instance, a guide dog will ignore the handler's command to move forward. Alternatively, the dog might curl their body around the front of their partner's legs to block the person from walking. If the team is in the middle of the street and the dog sees an approaching car, the dog backs up to the safety of the curb behind them, putting backward pressure on the harness handle that the partner is holding, cueing the person to back up as well.

An untrained dog instinctively runs away from a vehicle heading right toward them. A guide dog in harness can't do that. Instead, they learn to face danger by standing still or backing up to protect their partner and themself.

Intelligent disobedience training starts on campus after the dogs have passed their first evaluation, with dogs learning to back up when approached by a person pushing a grocery cart toward them in a narrow chute. The lesson continues outside, with staff members slowly driving cars around the parking lot while the trainers teach the harnessed dogs to keep at least a six-foot buffer between themselves and the vehicles.

Alberta had already figured out that she had important responsibilities while in harness, even if she sometimes got distracted by nearby food. She didn't have to be told not to walk her person in front of the moving car in the parking lot. When Gerri told her, "Forward," as the slow-moving car was about to pass in front of them, Alberta instinctively stopped instead. Then she heard her favorite phrase, "Good job!" After the car passed them, Gerri again said, "Go forward," and rewarded Alberta for obeying. The exercise got trickier when the car began to turn right in front of them when Alberta least expected it. The dog learned to listen for approaching cars on her left side or on her right. At the curb, she watched the passing cars, ready to step back from the street if one turned into her path. Otherwise, she learned that it was safe to walk past cars that were idling, parked, or moving parallel to her, as long as she kept the six-foot buffer.

Soon, traffic training moved from the safety of campus into the adjoining neighborhood, where the dogs learned to watch for cars moving in or out of driveways. At first, exercises were staged with Guiding Eyes vehicles. Later, members of the public became unwitting co-instructors.

Instructors look for real-world opportunities to test their dogs' willingness to disobey. When a courteous driver slowed down to let the guide dog team cross the street, the instructor waved the driver on while telling the dog "Forward." Drivers were puzzled and sometimes angry, but the point of the lesson was for the dog to back up while the car sped on.

Traffic training was when Barbara had to release the first dog from her string.

Mandy, a tall yellow Lab, trembled the first time she saw a car back out of a driveway in front of her and her instructor. She turned to run from the moving car. Two repeats of that anxious behavior were enough for trainers to respect Mandy's choice.

Mandy joined the other released dogs in the kennel, who were all now temporary boarders waiting for their transitions. Representatives from law enforcement agencies and service dog organizations came in to evaluate them. Some of these dogs were good candidates for bomb or drug detection because their drive to follow their nose was too strong for guide work. Others, like Mandy, weren't confident enough to make their own decisions but were otherwise comfortable with the uncertainties of working in public spaces. A service dog organization gladly chose Mandy to train to assist a wheelchair user. Mandy's new trainer worked her on leash, not a harness, and was able to see when it was safe to cross the street. That worked for Mandy. She was only afraid of cars when she was responsible for making decisions about how to move safely around them.

Dogs who were found to be reactive to thunder, crowds, or the demands of working in public were adopted as pets. The life of a pet dog is way less stressful than that of a dog expected to work in public. Breeding staff made notes of these dogs, so as to identify and eliminate their reactive traits in the breeding lines.

Over their months in training, the dogs learned to work in quiet neighborhoods, in the business district of a nearby village, in the midsize city of White Plains, and finally, in downtown Manhattan. A dog whose only flaw was dropping his tail or pulling back his ears to show that he was overwhelmed in New York City could still be a great guide dog if assigned to a less stressful environment.

The staff kept each dog's limitations in mind when matching them with clients.

The dogs' needs were as important as those of the clients. Any dog might be momentarily distracted by birds, squirrels, other dogs, or people while they're working on harness. Some dogs test their limits by sniffing the ground. How they respond to correction differs. Some need to be told, "No," or "Stop that!" Other dogs mope when corrected and need to be praised for what they're doing well instead. As the admissions committee members got to know the human personalities of the clients they accepted, they talked with the trainers about how to best match those personalities with the canines in the class.

Guiding Eyes accepts clients of all ages and walks of life. They may be as young as seventeen or as old as ninety; some live in rural areas and others in the busiest cities. Some take their dogs when they go on weeklong backpack trips or perform in concert halls in front of hundreds of people. Others harness their dogs only to walk down the lane to fetch mail from the mailbox and to grocery shop and do other errands in town.

Clients and dogs are matched with dozens of factors in mind, including whether the client has children or pets, travels extensively, or teaches on a crowded campus. Sometimes clients have a list of specific traits for their ideal guide dog. If a client insists on a male German shepherd, for example, they might wait a year or more for their match. Only 10 percent of the dogs that Guiding Eyes breeds are German shepherds.

The admissions committee and the instructors talk through tentative matches so that, during the last months of training, the instructors can customize each dog's training to prepare them for the environments or special needs of the client. Every class has a few utility hitters—dogs who can work well with a variety of clients and environments. As matches are made, clients are scheduled for classes, and the admissions director gives them as much notice as possible. Clients receive no information about the dogs that trainers plan to match with them, and they do not meet their dogs until the third day of class. Instructors might make a last-minute change if a client shows up on campus with different needs than those that were obvious from their application. Sometimes a dog is released late in the training. No match would be considered certain until the dog and client had graduated and gone home together.

I learned later that the admissions committee voted to accept me as a Guiding Eyes student only after prolonged discussion. I didn't fit the mold of students accepted into any of the courses that they offered. The standard four-week program was meant to transition cane users to partnering for the first time with a guide dog. The ten-day accelerated ACTION program to which I had applied was meant for highly successful Guiding Eyes graduates returning for successor dogs. For less high-powered returning graduates, there was a three-week residential program. I didn't fit into any category.

My application cryptically said that my six-year-old, privately trained German shepherd guide dog had needed "a career change," which I knew was instructor-speak for "this dog is not suitable for guiding."

The admissions committee members argued over whether to admit me to the three-week program or the four-week program or reject my application entirely. Most guide dog trainers don't believe that a dog can safely guide without being specially bred and school-trained to do so. One member of the committee said that if I had been able to get by with a "pretend guide dog," I didn't need one from Guiding Eyes.

Graham listened and then politely disagreed with his colleagues' perspective. His opinion mattered most because, in addition to being a member of the admissions committee, he taught the ACTION program to which I had applied. Even though I wasn't a Guiding Eyes graduate, Graham had been impressed with what he'd seen in the video that the home interviewer had taken of me working Wylie in harness. It showed that I was competent working in harness and well attuned to my dog.

Home interviews are the second part of the Guiding Eyes application process. They include videos of the applicant navigating one of their usual routes using a white cane or their retiring guide dog. I had hesitated when the field representative who'd visited me in Florida had told me to put Wylie in harness and handed me a blindfold. I had never followed a cane or a guide dog completely sightless. When working with Oriel and Wylie, I'd used whatever vision I'd had, in addition to reading cues from the dogs. After Wylie had killed the cat, I'd asked him to work in harness rarely and only under the most predictable of circumstances. I never again had him at my university office. When I had him on harness in any situation, I worried that his prey drive might overcome his work ethic and that he would drag me along.

The interviewer explained that the video of me working under blindfold with Wylie would give the admissions committee a way to assess how I navigated when my vision was at its lowest. I would not be considered for the accelerated program without working the dog while I was under blindfold. I would not be considered for the regular program without a video of me navigating with a cane while under blindfold. Either way, I had to go under blindfold. We walked out the front door. I gulped, buckled Wylie in harness, and put on the blindfold. "Forward," I said, and felt Wylie pull into the harness. We walked through the front yard to the sidewalk. He stopped. "Forward, left," I said, directing Wylie to lead me down a sidewalk that was unlikely to have distractions on a weekday afternoon.

Graham noted my high stress when I started out with Wylie. I used a stream of verbal praise to hold his attention. "Good dog," I said. "Good boy." I carried treats in my right hand to offer if I sensed him becoming distracted. Graham's first thought: **She doesn't trust that dog.**

After less than a minute, though, Wylie and I settled into our usual pace, and I relaxed. Wylie seemed to be entirely focused on his work. Maybe he also wanted to make a good impression on the evaluator. I knew that a curb was coming up. Wylie stopped precisely at the edge of the sidewalk and waited for me to step down so that we could cross the quiet street. He stopped again at the up curb, and we strolled down the sidewalk. I felt Wylie appropriately detour around the bushes and palm fronds that stuck out into the sidewalk and then step back again into the line of travel, targeting the curb ahead. **Good job**, Graham thought as he watched.

Suddenly, Wylie veered right, turned off the sidewalk, walked across the grass strip to the street, and stopped. "What is he doing?" I wondered. I reached out my hand tentatively and touched the side of a car. Now I understood. A week ago, Wylie had led me in harness to meet a friend who had parked her car in that spot. We rarely walked down this street, and so Wylie had been trying to figure out why we were here now. He thought he had found the answer when he saw the parked car. "It's okay," I said to Wylie, smiling at his logic. "Good boy."

I pivoted 180 degrees, saying, "Wylie, turn," and, then, "Forward." When my shoes touched the sidewalk, I said, "Wylie, go right and forward please." Wylie did. Graham saw that my response to Wylie's error was strong and respectful of my dog. It convinced Graham that I was a good enough guide dog handler to be admitted to ACTION.

The other members of the admissions committee were unsure if I could tolerate even ten days of life on campus. I wasn't sure either. As a professor, I was long accustomed to setting my own rules and working on my own schedule. More recently, as a department chair, I'd grown used to making decisions for faculty and students, not having them made for me. I learned later that the admissions committee members agreed to admit me on the condition that I would be sent home if they had doubts about my suitability once I arrived. It wouldn't be the first time that a student had left Guiding Eyes without a dog.

In December, I opened the nine-by-twelve-inch envelope from Guiding Eyes with the same anticipation and relief that I had felt when opening my acceptance letters to college and graduate school. A big envelope meant good news; a letter-sized envelope meant a polite rejection. I laughed at the two large orange luggage tags that tumbled out from the pages of large-type printed instructions. The Guiding Eyes logo adorned the tags, ensuring that my bags would get to campus even if I got lost.

When the acceptance from Guiding Eyes arrived, I realized how afraid I had been of a rejection. I had gone from being suspicious of guide dog schools to being anxious to be accepted by Guiding Eyes. In my ethics classes, I taught my students that decisions are always made in uncertainty. When I have chosen one of several potential actions, I remind myself that I am more often partly wrong than I am completely right. I appreciate learning from my mistakes and surrendering to the uncertainty that comes with realizing that there might be a better choice. Surrendering to the unknown makes me curious, creative, and vulnerable. I had failed with my plan to rely on privately trained guide dogs. I was ready for a new approach.

As I waited to be told when to report to campus, I thought about what might help staff members identify the dog that best matched me. I sent a stream of emails to the admissions director, with updates about my lifestyle as they occurred. I wanted them to know everything they needed to find me the right dog. Ultimately, my emails landed on Graham's computer.

Graham decided I would need a resilient dog. I spent most of the year teaching in St. Petersburg, Florida, with summers and some holidays in the wilderness of western Montana. I also traveled extensively throughout the US and sometimes abroad to give lectures or conduct workshops. I had finally let go of my California consulting and the twice monthly cross-country commute. Still, I would expect the dog to hop off commercial flights ready to work and adjust to new time zones as easily as I did. We would have to work our way through crowds and chaos. Then I needed the dog to lie quietly at my side while I taught or attended meetings.

During our months in Montana, the dog could expect to cross paths with deer, elk, moose, and bear as we hiked or hung out at my house on the hill. Graham needed to choose a dog who would thrive on a lifestyle more intense than most people could tolerate.

In January, I learned that Graham had scheduled me for the accelerated class in March. The timing could not have been better. Seven of the class's ten days fell during my university's spring break. I designed a learning activity for my students to complete on the one class day after the break that I would still be at Guiding Eyes. I got permission from my university to go to guide dog training. I waited and wondered.

Although I didn't know it at the time, Graham had already picked Alberta for me. She worked joyfully; she was quick to learn and respond. She had a big personality but was small enough to fit comfortably in the legroom of an airplane seat. She did as she was asked but also eagerly improvised. When learning how to guide her instructor up and down a set of stairs, for example, after a dozen rehearsals she veered away from the steps, instead leading her instructor to the ramp that ran alongside them. She stared at it meaningfully, as if to say, "I think that using the ramp will be easier for both of us."

Graham wanted Alberta to have a smart, creative handler who would appreciate a dog suggesting modifications. It was no surprise to Alberta that everyone told her that she was great. The dog was a true extrovert, energized by activity and praise. She also had an excellent "on-and-off" switch. She walked briskly through a crowd one minute and lay quietly at her instructor's feet the next. Graham hoped that her ability to turn off in this way might have a calming effect on me.

The weeks rolled by. Soon it was February—time for Alberta's class to have their final evaluations. The evaluation consisted of each dog leading a blindfolded instructor for an hour straight, with Graham following and giving directions. The team would need to cross at least eight streets and would encounter at least one challenge that required intelligent disobedience. During the first half hour, Graham warned the instructor about obstacles coming up and helped them judge traffic flow, just as the instructors would direct the new students as they learned to work with their dogs. The team also worked escalators and elevators. Graham sent them on a zigzagged route through a department store, in which the dog had to avoid the store racks, a formidable challenge—their poles extended above the dog's field of vision at just the right height to bruise the handler's elbow or shoulder. Then they worked through city streets, with the dog guiding the instructor past pedestrians, trash cans, other dogs, trucks unloading, and buses pulling in and out of stops.

For the last half hour, the blindfolded instructor and dog were on their own, just as a new client and dog would be after graduation. The evaluator told the instructors to go forward for eight blocks and then go down a set of stairs to enter a subway station. Graham would not intervene unless the dog or instructor was in danger. If a blindfolded instructor gets lost on the route, is startled by blaring horns, or thinks that the dog has made a mistake, they need to work through it without removing the blindfold. The dog's new handler will sometimes feel stressed and uncertain as well.

During the evaluation, Graham observed each dog's technical skills, but he also noted their comfort level and connection with the instructor. Alberta seemed to genuinely care what her people thought of her. She passed all tests perfectly.

A quick conversation between Graham and the instructors confirmed that all but two of the dogs were ready to meet their new partners. This late in the training, dogs should not lose track of where they're heading, get distracted, or guide a handler too close to obstacles. But sometimes dogs go rogue. They sniff the ground to scavenge for dropped food. They fail to back up when approached by a moving car. Or, as an extreme example of testing boundaries, they might commit the greatest sin of guide dog work: stopping suddenly to pee or poop while on harness. Rather than being released, a dog who acts out during the final blindfold test is passed back for additional training with a different instructor.

The final blindfold test is emotional for instructors, regardless of how each dog performs. They're proud of their dogs' successes and puzzled by the occasional failure. Their intense six-month training period with these dogs has come to an end. Even the most experienced instructors get teary. Graham rewards the instructors with their own favorite high-value treat: pizza.

In the two weeks before I arrived for my class, Graham kept Alberta with him full time. Most days, he worked with her in White Plains. With Graham under blindfold, they practiced crossing streets and ignoring distractions. Graham thought that Alberta's guide work was impeccable. When they went to the shopping mall to practice avoiding obstacles, she remembered—better than he did—which door they used to enter the mall. When they finished their work going by all the stores and shoppers, up and down the escalators, and he told her, "Go back," she returned them to the same door, using the shortest route, and then led him flawlessly to where he had parked the van.

The one fault Alberta needed to overcome was her sophisticated approach to scavenging. She no longer dropped her head while guiding to pick up a half-eaten burrito on the sidewalk. Instead, she had learned to delay gratification so that she could grab food when her instructors least expected it. While Graham sipped coffee and caught up on paperwork at his favorite coffee shop, Alberta lay quietly under the table, scanning the area for fallen food. She seemed relaxed, but she was plotting. She knew exactly how far her leash would extend. As soon as Graham gathered his papers and said, "Alberta, let's go," she zoomed to the piece of muffin or bagel she'd spotted within range. She instantly returned to Graham's side as she swallowed the food, satisfied and ready to work. She was proud of her strategy. Graham was frustrated. By the time he realized what she was doing, it was too late to stop or correct her.

Back on campus, Graham developed his own strategy to break Alberta's scavenging habit. He dropped pieces of bagel under the table in the student lounge or in the dining room and then brought Alberta into the room on harness. He told her "down" and "stay" so that she was lying near the food Graham used for bait. Graham sat in a chair next to her at the table and waited for a few minutes. When he stood up and Alberta started to dash to the food, he intercepted her by saying, "Touch"—a command that required her to bring her nose to his hand. The first few times, she glanced at the pieces of bagel on the floor, but her training won out, and she obediently touched his hand. "What a good girl," Graham said, rewarding her with a salmon treat that was even better than the bagel. He made a note to teach me how to entice Alberta with high-value treats in environments where she was likely to scavenge. My classmates and I would arrive on Sunday.

CHAPTER 8

IN THE VALLEY OF THE BLIND

"How do you identify?" I asked Pam one evening at home, soon after she had completed her degree. People around us wondered how to define our relationship and pressed for information. Pam and I were both annoyed by their assumptions. We agreed that we owed no explanation to anyone but one another. The life that I shared with Pam seemed so multifaceted and unique that I gave up looking for a label. After the violation I felt by Paul's infidelity, his leaving, our divorce, I appreciated a relationship that lacked conventional boundaries and expectations.

Pam paused thoughtfully. "Jewish," she said with a smile. "And you?"

I laughed at her deflection. "Legally blind, I guess," I said.

"About time," she responded.

We sat silently for a minute. Pam had spent her life telling people she was Jewish. I was new to presenting myself as legally blind but was growing increasingly comfortable with that identity. Pam was the first person close to me who both knew the extent of my visual impairment and seemed untroubled by it. When she couldn't read my body language, she didn't hesitate to ask, "Tell me what you see." My answer helped her understand my experience. For my part, I didn't hesitate to ask, "Can you help me, please?" Usually, she said yes. If she said no, I learned to evaluate how much I really needed the help I'd requested. When Pam and I walked down the street, I seldom used the white cane. We held hands—sometimes because I needed her help and sometimes simply because we were enjoying our companionship.

I saw the point she was making about labels. The two of us could be ourselves, together and separately, without telling anyone what that meant. Sometimes, Pam felt like my sister or cousin. She knew me better than I knew myself. Other times, she felt like my best friend who I could always count on. Still other times, she was my closest colleague, as we traded drafts of our writing for the other to edit. In all dog-related matters, Pam was my mentor.

After the semester in Berkeley, Pam was offered a job in California. We talked about our connection and about our separate career needs. At the end of 2012, Pam moved west to live on her own. Neither of us tried to predict the future; we knew that somehow we would stay close.

Early in 2013, as the date of my Guiding Eyes course approached, I tried to prepare for the experience. The school's instructions told me I would be spending several hours each day outside, working with my new dog. I filled a suitcase with clothing appropriate for camping in the Arctic. Then I tucked in extra gloves and socks. When I compared the early March weather in New York with that in Florida, I tried to imagine how I could pay attention to anything aside from the cold.

On Sunday, March 3, I flew into LaGuardia. As I walked off the plane, I expertly unfolded my white cane into its full height and followed the blurry bunch of exiting travelers down the jetway into the gate area. Moving my wrist side to side, I swept the cane in a small arc. The cane's red tip nosed the floor a few feet in front of me. I had learned to keep the arc no wider than my shoulders, so as not to trip people walking by. The arc was still wide enough that the cane was likely to bump into an unseen rolling suitcase before I did.

I chose a brown smudge to follow, which I guessed to be a man wearing a leather jacket, but I continued to listen for where the rest of my flight companions were heading. I didn't want to follow my unknowing helpmate into the men's room or to his connecting flight. At some airports, like LaGuardia, the people from the flight were likely to walk toward the baggage claim and ground transportation area. In other airports that are major Delta hubs, like Atlanta and Minneapolis, there was an even chance that the passenger I chose to follow might be on their way to a connecting flight. According to the Guiding Eyes directions, I was to find my way to baggage claim, where a staff member would meet me and then take me to campus.

As the crowd slowed down and bunched up and a low mechanical hum became audible, I knew we were nearing an escalator. I stepped tentatively onto the moving stairs, feeling for the center of the step before placing my foot down. I moved quickly to the right so that the people walking down the escalator wouldn't push me off balance. I kept my right hand on the railing, feeling it curve down with the stairs. I heard echoes wafting from activity in the large open space below. No doubt. I had found baggage claim. When the railing began to flatten out, I began feeling with my foot for the stairs to flatten out as well. The nudge of the end of the escalator signaled me to step off.

Then I heard a woman's voice: "Deni, I'm from Guiding Eyes." I smiled and turned left, walking a few steps toward the voice, able to make out a young woman with blond hair standing to the left of the escalator. She introduced me to the two other students who had arrived and were waiting with her, suitcases in hand. The staff member went to the luggage carousel to pick up my suitcase, leaving us to introduce ourselves and share what had led us to Guiding Eyes. For all of us, it turned out, it had been a recommendation from someone we had reason to trust.

The staff member stepped in front of me. "Your suitcase is at twelve o'clock," she said.

Even without the Guiding Eyes tags, I would have recognized my red suitcase. I had dressed it in its usual high-visibility travel clothes: a neon yellow handle cover and a yellow-striped luggage strap. "Yep, there it is," I said. "Thank you." I reached in front of me where she had positioned the suitcase and moved it to my left, out of everyone's way.

Soon, another young blond staff member and two more students joined our group. "We're all here," said one of the staff members. "Let's go." We five students extended our white canes and followed the staff members. We each used one hand to sweep the cane in front of us and the other hand to roll our luggage slightly behind us, careful to keep our cane arcs narrow and to keep our suitcases close so as not to entangle with one another. The staff members walked side by side ahead of our cane-decked group. They kept up a steady banter, which helped us judge our distance from them and follow their lead to the van. No one asked for more assistance. We were all good at navigating without guide dogs. Otherwise, we wouldn't have been accepted by Guiding Eyes.

It was a forty-five-minute drive to the Guiding Eyes campus. The van drove through the gates and stopped at the dormitory. As we got out of the van, staff members called each of us by name. Miranda, my escort and the class supervisor, called mine: "Deni Elliott, follow me."

As we entered the building, she walked a few steps ahead to make room for me, my white cane, and my rolling bag. Miranda led me down a hall and said, "When you're at Guiding Eyes, please trail the right wall. That way, we avoid collisions with people walking in the other direction." I moved more to the right, tapping the intersection of wall and floor with my cane. Miranda chatted about the rooms that we passed, her voice keeping me oriented to her and to the space around us.

"Stop here," Miranda said. "Your room is on the right." She crossed in front of me, and I pivoted right. "Reach up to the middle upper part of the door and you'll find the raised number. You're in Room 11." The numbers were big and dark and bold against the white door. "I have enough residual vision to see the numbers," I said. I didn't want anyone to think that I was **that** blind.

"Our default at Guiding Eyes is to assume that no one—clients or staff—can see at all. You'll have an easier time here if you do that too," Miranda said. "It's great that you have residual vision. Your instructor will take that into account in your training, but don't expect anyone else to treat you as though you can see." I tried to wrap my mind around that.

I couldn't imagine what it meant for people to assume that I was totally blind. I was used to people thinking that I had more vision than I did. I had never been in a situation in which people expected me to see less. I had also never been in an environment in which I needed to assume that other people could see even less than I could.

Miranda continued with her orientation. "If we didn't stop at your room, we'd pass three more dorm rooms on your right, and then the hall widens out. The other side of this hall is lined with dorm rooms as well. Once you get to the end of the hall, you can go in three directions. Trailing the right wall, you'll know that you're at the intersection because wall and railing end. If you turn right, you'll come to a staircase in another six steps or so; that leads up to the second-floor dining room. Make sure to announce yourself before starting up the stairs. If you're without an instructor, the rule is one person on the stairs at a time.

"If you continue straight down the hall instead of turning right, you immediately enter an area with chairs lined up on both sides of the wall. On the right side of the wall, there are fewer chairs, because after four chairs, you come to a counter that has a big roll of poop bags and containers of dog treats. We call this area the student lounge. Once you walk through the student lounge, you come to stairs that lead up to the Guiding Eyes administrative offices.

"If you turn left where the hall widens out, you can walk straight to an outside door. If you stop after about three paces, you will find the coffee room on your right. There's no door to that room. The coffee room is where you find drinks and snacks outside mealtime and company almost all the time. Students and staff hang out there.

"You have an hour to unpack and get settled. Then, come to the student lounge where we'll have our class meeting. Now, I'll show you your dorm room."

I hadn't even stepped into my room yet and I already felt overwhelmed, trying to remember all the landmarks that Miranda had described.

Miranda handed me my room key and waited silently while I found the lock in the doorknob and inserted the key. She walked ahead of me into the room, then stopped as I pulled my suitcase in. The door closed behind us.

"We're in a short hall," she said. "There's a switch on the left side of the door for the ceiling light. Then an opening that is closet space with a shelf up top. Extra pillow up there. A horizontal pole with hangers at shoulder height. A plastic container with dog food on the floor of the closet space and two dog bowls on top. One for water. One for food. No door on the closet.

"Then the bathroom is on your left. There's a door that's now partly closed. Light switch inside the bathroom to the left. Toilet to the left and then the shower. The sink is out here in this hallway, but we'll come around to that. The shower is opposite the bathroom door. Towel bar on the right wall with towels hanging on it."

I stood still, mesmerized. Instead of darting my eyes to peer beyond the shadows that obscured my vision, I visually trailed Miranda's description of the room, letting her words help me sort out what I could see. No one had ever described a room to me before.

Miranda told me to walk forward so that I could notice where the short hall ended and the room opened wide. I ventured a few steps and felt the corner on my left. "Reach up on the wall a little farther," she said. "You'll find the intercom button and a pull string." As I touched it, she said, "Use that to call staff in case of an emergency. You'll hear announcements coming from the intercom as well. We use it to make sure everyone's up on time."

"The control for the room temperature is next to the intercom. Put your fingers on it and you'll find the buttons. Up for warm. Down for cool."

"On the far wall we're facing, you'll find a nightstand with a lamp, a phone with big numbers and Braille, and a clock with large digital numbers. Then a double bed. Then a crate for your dog. Then the corner for the outside wall.

"Walk across the room with me, and I'll show you how to adjust the blinds on the window. It's a good idea to keep them closed for privacy when you're in the room. The windows in the administration wing are directly across from you.

"Next to the window, you have an outside door. We call that the 'park' door. You will use that door when you take your dog out to go potty. When you go out the door, turn right toward the parking lot. You'll find gravel on the right of the sidewalk. Starting next week, you can use that graveled area for parking your dog. This week, we want you to come to the communal park area at scheduled times so that you learn the dog's routine for peeing and pooping. We'll show you the communal park area later, when we do the class tour. Both of your doors lock automatically, so remember to take your key when you go out. Your room number is on the outside of both doors."

My mind's eye tagged along as she continued to verbally tour the room.

"You'll find a hook on the back of the park door to hang your dog's harness. The wall across from the bed also has some hooks where you can hang your coat so it's handy when you take your dog out. Then three pieces of furniture that are pretty much the same height: a small refrigerator, followed by your desk, and then a dresser. There's another lamp on the desk.

"Then we're back to the short skinny hall we came in. Your sink and counter for toothbrush and such are on your left. Then you have a closet with no door opposite the one that I first showed you. There's a laundry basket on the upper shelf. You have a shoulder-height horizontal pole to hang more clothes. The floor space in this closet is empty." She slapped her hand on a door and said, "Here is the door that opens from your room into the hallway.

"So," Miranda said, concluding her tour, "we'll see you in the student lounge in an hour?" She opened the door, walked out, and closed it before I could respond.

I sat on the bed, feeling unusually calm. I felt none of my usual new-environment anxiety. This strange room didn't feel so strange now that someone had described it to me. I walked with unusual confidence to the short hall to get my suitcase. I lifted it to the bed and unpacked, knowing without searching that the dresser was directly behind me and the closets were to my left.

I compared this welcome with my usual hotel check-in experience. The first challenge was always finding the front desk. If I stood still in the entrance, eventually someone would offer to help. At the desk, I'd give the clerk my name, hand over my credit card, and tell them that I was visually impaired. I'd learned that my white cane or the privately trained guide dog at my side didn't always provide enough of a clue. I explained to the clerk that if the key method was insertion, my key card needed to be clipped so I could use it by feel. "Please hold the key in your right hand as though you're inserting it into the door," I instructed. "Now clip off the right corner of the card nearest the end you insert." Sometimes, doing this took two or more employees and multiple attempts, and a line of impatient guests would form behind me.

My next unusual request: "May I please have someone help me find the room?"

It usually took a few minutes to identify an employee willing to serve as my guide. They often seemed as uncomfortable as I felt, saying nothing as I juggled suitcase and cane or dog and followed them to the elevator, trying to identify small landmarks for future reference, like a large floral arrangement on a side table.

When we reached the room, I asked the employee to wait while I confirmed that the keycard had been marked accurately. I unlocked the door; I asked for help finding the door number. I pulled the tip I had previously stowed in my pocket, thanked them, and stepped into the void. Now alone, I banged my way into the unfamiliar space. Light and shadow danced into the kaleidoscope in front of me. I turned on every switch I touched. I tried to open every door, eventually finding bathroom, closet, and sometimes a locked door between my room and the one adjoining. I reached for dark spots on the wall, hoping to locate the thermostat, doubting that I'd be able to see the controls well enough to use it. My knee located the edge of the bed. My hip found the dresser. My shin found the ottoman that stood guard in front of the armchair.

But at Guiding Eyes, thanks to Miranda, I knew precisely where to find everything in my room.

I walked the length of the room between the park door and the hallway door, noticing that my footsteps were louder in the short hall. The air felt thicker there too. Since I wasn't distracted by any new-environment anxiety, I had the headspace to use my nonvisual senses to help map out the space around me.

I stood still with the sudden realization that, here, my fragmented vision was enough. At Guiding Eyes, I wouldn't need to explain what I could see, what I couldn't, and why. This was like my time at Bergin College, but with a campus totally focused on making it easy for people with visual impairment to navigate. I had always assumed that my professional success had been dependent on pretending to have more sight than I did. Now I wondered how different my life would be if I felt safe to ask others for information that would save me time, trouble, and bruises. I quickly finished unpacking, put on my coat, and stepped outside the park door with my cane, eager to explore more of this magical world.

Graham was in his office when a staff member worriedly informed him that his client was out wandering the campus alone. He watched me from his second-story office window as I methodically walked down the paths that I found. I swept my cane in front of me until I came across something significant: a building, parking lot, a patch of artificial turf.

I heard water in a creek and realized that I was on the edge of a large green space with trees and lawn. I decided not to venture there, not sure if the green space was on or off campus. I didn't want to start my first day getting lost or being late. My goal was familiarity. I believed that the more comfortable I felt in the setting, the better my lessons would go. I was surprised not to come across other new students doing the same thing.

As Graham watched, he hoped I would be pleasantly surprised when I realized that I had been matched with a dog who was also an overachiever. He tried not to get attached to that thought, however. He knew from experience that strong-minded students sometimes just couldn't accept the dog that Guiding Eyes staff had picked for them. Usually, those students were sent home with no dog.

He thought of Linda, an ACTION client who had returned to Guiding Eyes for her second guide dog. The training staff knew that Linda had a strong personality and needed a dog who could handle the crowds and traffic in Chicago, where she led her high-pressured professional life. Her first Guiding Eyes dog had been independent, confident, and adaptable, and hadn't required much from her in return. Graham noted that Linda had been impatient with the idea that a new, young dog would need guidance from her that differed from her previous guide.

Staff had matched Linda with a yellow Lab named Jenny. Jenny couldn't tolerate much correction—she put her head and tail down if anyone spoke sharply to her—but she had shown that she was rock-solid in a city environment and would do anything for a food reward. Linda and Jenny should have been a perfect match. Graham was puzzled that Linda didn't show much enthusiasm when she met

Jenny. He left Linda and Jenny alone to get to know one another. Within an hour, Linda opened her door, calling into the hall for an instructor to help her. In the first days of class, there is always a training staff member or two monitoring the hallways. "Please find Graham for me," Linda asked.

When Graham got to her room, Linda said that Jenny had jumped on the bed. Linda didn't allow her dogs on any furniture in her home. Graham patiently reviewed the instructions that he had given Linda earlier: Keep your dog on leash for the first day. Your dorm room has a crate. Use it. Say, "Kennel up," and the dog will walk into the crate and stay there until called.

Under Graham's supervision, Linda followed Jenny's lead well during the first few days, but dog and handler didn't seem to be making an emotional connection. Jenny needed Linda to be enthusiastic. Linda gave Jenny treats to reward good behavior, but only when Graham reminded her to do so.

During the next day's work, Jenny misjudged the width needed for her and Linda to clear a mailbox, causing Linda to lightly brush against it as they walked past. It wasn't unusual for a dog working with a new handler to initially miscalculate their combined width. Graham had them turn around and walk by the mailbox a few more times. Jenny consistently cleared the mailbox with enough room for two, as she did with every other obstacle after that.

As Graham drove the van of students and dogs back to campus that afternoon, Linda told the others that Jenny had run her into a mailbox. Graham felt angry. That wasn't fair. The dog had made a common new-team error and had learned from her mistake.

They had been back on campus for less than an hour when Graham was again summoned to Linda's room. "She jumped up on me," Linda said. "I can't have that. I wear nice clothes."

"Linda," Graham said, "Jenny is trying to find ways to connect with you. She wants to be close to you, but you're keeping her at a distance. Jumping up is not unusual if a dog feels ignored. What are you doing to make Jenny feel loved?" Linda promised to do better.

Their work the next day was nearly flawless. Toward the end of the afternoon, Graham told Linda that she and Jenny looked like they'd had years of experience together instead of just a few days. Then, while Jenny was guiding her, Linda stumbled over a hole in the sidewalk—her foot wobbled but she didn't fall. Graham explained that Jenny hadn't been able to see the hole from her vantage point, so she couldn't have known to avoid it. In the van on the way home, Graham clenched his jaw as Linda told the others that Jenny had let her fall into a hole.

When they got back to campus, Graham pulled Linda aside. He told her that her work with Jenny was exceptional for this early stage. He also voiced his concern that she didn't seem interested in creating a relationship with Jenny. He told her that Jenny was feeling stressed by Linda's lack of interaction. Linda said that Jenny was much different from her previous dog. She would work harder at building the relationship.

The next day, Linda again found fault with Jenny. The dog continued to work, but now she licked her lips and tucked her tail between her legs. Graham could see that this match was not good for the dog.

Linda and Graham talked again that evening. He listened while she laid out complaint after complaint about Jenny. When she was done, he asked, "Do you want Jenny to be your guide dog?"

Linda said, "No."

Graham told Linda that it was time for her to go home. Linda handed him Jenny's leash and said that she would pack. Jenny looked up at Graham and wagged her tail sadly as if to say, "I tried." Graham asked other staff members to help Linda with her travel arrangements, then walked Jenny back to the kennel.

Graham felt relieved. Before he handed Jenny over to the kennel staff, he hugged the dog and told her that she had done a great job. The dog gave him a happy full-circle tail wag and a lick on his cheek. He promised to find her a perfect partner. A few months later, he did just that.

Graham worried that, like Linda, I might have unrealistic expectations for my new guide dog. Alberta reminded him of Jenny—a highly resourceful dog who needed to be appreciated, not scolded. If I failed to meet Alberta's needs, Graham wouldn't hesitate to send me home without her.

Back at the dormitory, I walked down the hall, trailing the wall with my cane to the student lounge. I was a little early for the meeting and was happy to find some classmates there. I joined the group as they were introducing themselves. Our class included a professional chef, an artist, a college student, an accountant, a software designer, an occupational therapist, and a handful of retirees. I was the only professor.

We talked about our vision loss. Some people had lost their sight suddenly, through illness or in surgery. Others had been totally blind since birth. My progressive blindness felt gentle in comparison.

We quickly realized that the classmates among us who functioned best without sight were also the youngest: take twenty-six-year-old Asher, a blind-from-birth accounting student who was getting his first guide dog. He boasted that he already knew his way around the building—he used triangular spatial relationships, he said, to determine location. When he realized that he'd lost most of us with this technical description, he said, "Let me show you."

Asher said that he had already explored the coffee room, just around the corner. "Come with me," he said. I, and a few others, followed Asher as he confidently led the way. Unlike the rest of us, Asher was not tapping a white cane. He navigated without a cane and with zero vision.

As we entered the room, Asher tapped his hand on the doorway, then on the coffee machine, then on the table. "The door, the coffee machine, and the table form a triangle," he said. Then he tapped the door, the vending machine, and the table. "The door, the vending machine, and the table form a different triangle. You can hear the different sounds of the surfaces as well as the different sizes of the space between the objects. All

I do is remember the sound of each object and triangle to find everything again. I'm told what I do with my hearing is just like people remembering what they've seen," he concluded with pride. I was amazed at how simple he made these complex calculations sound.

Asher also used echolocation to make sense of enclosed environments. He clicked his tongue as he walked down the hall. The clicks echoed off the objects around him: a chair in his path, a door. Echoes have their nuances and helped him identify obstacles and differentiate the hallway from a doorway, or a wall from a table.

He said he had taught himself to click when he was a baby trying to find his toys. When he clicked his tongue, a toy bounced the sound back, whereas open space did not. Asher had felt no sense of loss around his blindness until he grew old enough to understand that other people had vision. Although he wondered what colors and nature might look like, he was comfortable with his own style of getting around. Once I got past imagining his parents' heartbreak at learning that their newborn son did not have functional eyes, I was astonished at how Asher's brain had wired itself for sightless life.

Another classmate, a totally blind college student who was studying computer programming, told us about the new technologies that were helping people with visual impairment find their way around airports and cities. Many of our classmates were already familiar with these travel apps and argued among themselves about the relative merits of iMove compared to BlindSquare or Loadstone or Trekker. I listened carefully but understood none of it. It would be several years before I would be coordinated enough to listen to a GPS app while also following signals from my guide dog as I navigated an unfamiliar city.

Those of us who were partially sighted talked about what we could see. One person had a small circle of vision in the center of each of her eyes. She could read if she moved her head to follow the type on a page, but her vision was limited to an area smaller than a place setting at a meal. Another classmate who could distinguish only between light and dark said this was often worse than nothing at all, because bright light created glare as it bounced off the translucent fog coating his visual field. One student talked about smears over her visual field. Another described having slivers of sight. I said that I could see color, movement, and shapes in between amoeba-like gray and black splotches. If the book was close enough and the light bright enough, I could read. That was the most dependable my vision could get.

Someone had discovered that there were Braille editions of Scrabble and other board games in the upstairs reading room. "I don't read Braille," I said. It turned out about half of our group didn't.

"No problem," a classmate said. "Those who don't know Braille can pair up with those of us who do."

I laughed with surprise and delight. I had arrived at a place where those who were most blind could navigate the best, and where reading Braille was more useful than vision. I realized how wrong Erasmus had been when he'd written, "In the valley of the blind, the one-eyed man is king."

Guiding Eyes culture rests on two guiding assumptions: Everyone is blind, and everyone is capable and independent. The campus, inside and out, had been designed to be navigated without sight. My classmates and I knew that we were all either legally or totally blind, as that was the minimal qualification for admission to Guiding Eyes. None of us could see more than about a fifth of what a fully sighted person could see. We knew that some staff members, including president and CEO Tom Panek, were also blind. Staff members walked past us with guide dogs; we didn't know who was blind or who was a sighted trainer instructing a young dog. We tried to guess which staff members had usable vision. Ultimately, the only staff members we could agree were fully sighted were those who drove the Guiding Eyes vans.

Our conversation turned to our ideal guide dogs. "I want a big male black Lab," said one.

"I've been waiting a year for a female German shepherd," said another.

I shrugged, unwilling to conjure up a desire that could lead to disappointment. "I told Guiding Eyes that I wanted a dog with a sense of humor," I said.

"Your dogs will be exactly what you need them to be," Miranda said, joining the group. "You have other things to think about. This is only Sunday. Dog day is not until Wednesday. You have a lot to learn before you're ready to meet your dogs. Let's get started."

Miranda gave us a tour of the building, leading us first from the student lounge to Alumni Hall, where we would have lectures, obedience training, and playtime with our dogs. We returned to the student lounge. Then she took us into the coffee room, then through the opening on the other side of the coffee room to a hallway in the dormitory to the laundry room. I noticed that the doors, vending machines, washer, and dryer rippled with Braille, raised numbers, and raised letters. We returned to the student lounge once more. I realized that Miranda was teaching us how to use the lounge as our home base. She led us to the stairs up to the dining room. Miranda said, "Please announce yourselves when you come to a staircase. If someone is already on the stairs, they'll yell, 'Wait,' and then, 'Clear,' when they reach the landing.

"Class coming upstairs," Miranda announced. We followed her up the stairs to the dining room to meet our instructors.

"Deni, you're our only ACTION client this class," she said, "so you'll be working alone with Graham Buck. Gerri, Barbara, and I will split up the rest of the class between us. Shane, our apprentice instructor for the class, will take turns working with all of you."

Graham stepped directly in front of me. "Hello," he said.

I smiled at Graham, looking directly at his eyes. I knew where sighted people looked when they talked to one another. I couldn't often see the color of their eyes or their expression, but I knew where to fix my gaze and how to blink and cast my eyes in other directions briefly so it didn't look like I was staring. Over the years, as my vision had deteriorated, I'd instinctively become drawn to the more obvious movement of people's mouths. I fought that impulse because I knew that I would look weird to sighted people if I watched their mouths when we were in face-to-face conversation. Instead, I gazed at the dark sunken area where people's eyes lived.

Graham sounded professional. He told me that we wouldn't start working together until he'd brought me my assigned dog. Until then, he said firmly, I was expected to do preliminary work with the others, attend all lectures, and follow the same routine as everyone else.

I told him that was fine. I wondered, but didn't ask, why he thought he needed to explicitly tell me that I needed to do this.

Graham wandered off. I heard him and Miranda laughing with other students and thought they sounded more relaxed than when they were speaking privately to me. I wondered if they were treating me differently or if that was my own projection. I let that worry go, remembering a mantra that a colleague had shared with me years before: "What other people think of me is none of my business." I tried to remind myself that I could not control other people's perceptions of me, but I sometimes found that hard to live by.

"Hi," said a voice to my right. "I'm Kara Snyder." I turned to see a woman, shorter than me, with long brown hair.

Kara was a classmate and an artist. She lived in Pittsburgh and exhibited her work there and elsewhere. She was married and had a son. Like me, Kara had progressively deteriorating vision. At forty, she was ready for her first guide dog. Kara's voice bubbled with joy as she described her charmed life.

Kara and I bonded over having had functional vision until we launched our careers. "I got through my doctoral work before losing substantial vision," I said. We were optimistic about our futures, regardless of our vision. Kara described how she used high-intensity lights and computer enhancements to translate her mental images to canvas.

"What will you do if you lose all your vision?" I asked.

Kara paused dramatically. "Sculpture," she said with a laugh.

That night, the staff gathered for their first debrief. As Graham walked down the hall to meet the class instructors in the meeting room, he passed by the music room, where a student was playing Beethoven's Sonata No. 32 in C Minor on the piano for a group of classmates seated on cozy chairs and sofa. By the time Graham had sat down with Miranda, Shane, and the other instructors, the sound of the piano had given way to laughter, and then to a guitar. The students' early camaraderie was a good sign. Class was best when the clients enjoyed and supported each other through the rigorous training.

Graham knew that class was just as intense for the instructors as for the students—bonding was necessary for him and his colleagues too. All of them except Shane, the apprentice, had been through this before. They knew how to take care of themselves and each other. After six months of working this cohort of dogs toward the goal of graduation, the instructors were relieved that the end was in sight. Yet they found it hard to give up the dogs that they had come to know so well to people they didn't know at all. The dogs were ready to meet their new handlers. The instructors weren't yet sure if the clients were ready to meet their dogs.

Class time is a significant marker in the instructors' work cycle. They refer to class as being in "the bubble." The overall cycle starts with training a new string of dogs. Six months later comes the class with the students and their matched dog partners. The class for most students runs for three weeks, with clients who have never before owned a guide dog staying an additional week. Instructors live in the dorm for the full class period so that they are available to students 24/7. After graduation, when the clients and their new guide dogs return home, the instructors have a two-week paid vacation, during which they relax and get ready to start the process all over again.

During the class, the instructors disappear from friends and family and become immersed in the drama of creating a dozen new guide dog teams. "Sorry that I didn't return your calls or texts or emails," they'd say to friends later. "I've been away from my life for the past month." When instructors are in class, nothing matters as much as the health and welfare of the people and dogs they have brought together.

As the assistant director of training, Graham went home at night rather than living in the dorm. Still, for the ten days that he was training an ACTION client, everyone knew that his primary responsibility was the client and dog. The communications and marketing director wouldn't ask him to go to the city for a television appearance or send him to Albany to meet with a legislative caucus. The training director wouldn't ask him to drive to Manhattan to pick up a dog that was retiring. Graham was available to help other instructors when a client's problem had them stumped or when a client-dog match wasn't working out.

Over the years, guide dog instructors from various schools had talked with each other about how their pasts had influenced their career choice. Few guide dog instructors could envision themselves working in corporate America. They were drawn to a life that connected them with dogs who loved them unconditionally.

Some saw themselves in the intuitive, intelligent but stoic dogs that they taught. Some instructors also saw themselves in their clients. Many of the students came to Guiding Eyes from lives in which they were considered broken. Those clients lived with people who seemed to see only their limitations.

At Guiding Eyes, instructors expected the clients, like the dogs, to live up to their potential. Instructors had spent hours and days working under blindfold with the dogs that they had matched with these clients. They knew that working under blindfold was different from being blind, but the instructors had trusted their lives to these dogs. They expected no less from the clients. Instructors tried to make all decisions about dogs, clients, and the success of the teams based on three simple questions: Is it safe? Is it effective? Is it humane?

Traditionally, during the first-night debrief, the instructors discuss any students they've initially identified as worrisome. This time, there were only a few to discuss. This was unlike some classes in which students had personality clashes with one another or with staff. Miranda remembered one class when the escorts had discovered an incoming student panhandling in the airport. When asked, he said he had no job, no permanent home, and no money. They brought him to campus, but he was soon processed to return to his temporary home with no dog. No dog would be placed with a client without a reliable home or the financial resources to support it.

In this class, one young student was using language that made the instructors uncomfortable. He had told the others about how, when his hound dog didn't do as told, he "kicked the dog's ass." Miranda had pulled him aside to say while she was sure that he was kidding, he needed to tone it down. He couldn't talk to—or about—a guide dog that way. Sam, in his last semester of high school, was about to get his first guide dog before going to college. He was young and probably trying to sound macho. The instructors would keep an eye on Sam when he got his assigned dog.

Graham later told me that the staff also talked about me that night. The instructors said that they had each told me in their own way not to expect special treatment. Graham had said that they had made that point and now they should lay off. He pointed out that they were kidding themselves if they thought I wasn't getting special treatment. The **Tampa Bay Times** was sending a team to write a feature story on me and my new guide dog for their Sunday magazine. I was a successful professional in the community, and an editor who taught part-time in the journalism department thought I had a good story. Their Pulitzer Prize–winning reporter and a photographer would be arriving the next day to follow my initial process at Guiding Eyes. They were planning to be in my dorm room when I met my new dog and then leave and pick up the story again when I returned home.

"Just ignore them," the marketing director had said weeks previously when the instructors groaned at the news that a reporter and photographer would be following us around. "I'll make sure that they don't get in the way of your students' training." It made no sense to argue with her. Guiding Eyes staff members knew that the donations that would result from this publicity were too important for the CEO to say no.

At the first-night lecture, Miranda had told the class that a reporter and photographer would be hanging around for a few days. "They won't take pictures of you or use anything you say without your permission," I was grateful that she didn't identify me as the reason for the press.

Once the "worrisome student" discussion was out of the way, the instructors started their usual first-night banter, comparing this class with previous experiences. "Everyone here has had a pet dog. So, they do know one end of the dog from the other," Miranda said.

The instructors laughed, remembering more than one student over the years who'd had trouble with front and back. Years before, when Graham had been class supervisor, he'd waited impatiently in the lobby one morning for a student, Bob, who had yet to show up from his dorm room. The other students and their dogs were already loaded up in the vans for the drive to the school's training center in White Plains. Graham called Bob's dorm room on the intercom, trying to keep the impatience out of his voice. "Please harness your dog and come to the lobby," Graham said. "Everyone is waiting for you." Finally, Graham heard a door close. He looked down the hall to see Bob and his dog, Silas, walking toward him.

Graham could tell from a distance that there was something wrong, though he wasn't sure what. As they got closer, he saw that Bob had put the harness on the dog backward. The chest strap was wrapped around Silas's belly; the belly strap was buckled around the dog's neck. Graham wouldn't have thought that such a configuration was even possible. Bob was straining to hold the harness handle, which was standing straight up rather than following the line of the dog's back. Silas looked confused, but he wagged his tail when he saw Graham, trusting him to fix this. Graham smiled and made eye contact with the dog, silently willing Silas to be patient. The Guiding Eyes philosophy is that whenever possible, clients, as well as dogs, resolve their own problems.

"Ah, Bob," Graham said. "What is wrong with this picture?"

Bob reached down to Silas. At first, he was perplexed. Then he realized that the harness handle was pointing in the wrong direction. "Oh my god," he said. "What did I do? I put the harness on backward," he answered himself.

"Let's unbuckle all of the straps and start over again," Graham suggested.

Bob undid the straps and then gently lifted the harness and handle off Silas. He and Graham both laughed as the dog gave himself a big shake.

"The day can only get better," Graham observed.

As the staff meeting continued, Miranda gave the instructors their assignments for the next day's hall monitoring and dining room assistance. "Shane," Miranda said, "we have apprentices run the fire drill, but don't let Graham tell you how to handle it."

"How many years do I have to hear about this?" Graham grumbled, even as he smiled at the memory.

"Until we forget," Miranda answered.

"Okay, Shane," Graham said. "Here's the story. Back when I was an apprentice, I was assigned to run the fire drill. That was fine, but that evening was my only time off for two weeks. I had **plans**. When the fire bell went off, I made sure that the clients got out of the building and gathered at the appropriate spot. I was in such a hurry to leave that I forgot to tell them to come back in. After a few minutes, one of the senior instructors noticed them standing outside and realized I was gone. She told the clients to come in. They were out there for maybe ten additional minutes. No big deal."

"Except that it was snowing," said Miranda. Everyone laughed.

They paused for a minute. From down the hall, they could hear the talented student back at the piano.

"Do you remember Martha, the orchestral pianist who wanted an 'independent' dog when she came back for her second guide dog?" Graham mused.

"Oh yeah," Miranda said.

"Just before dinner one night, Martha was playing the piano," Graham said to the others. "Her new guide, a black Lab named Olive, lay quietly at her side. At some point, Olive decided there was something more appealing than Martha's music. The dog quietly left Martha and walked down the hall to the dining room. Kitchen staff had put dinner rolls in the baskets on the tables. Olive walked in, put her paws up on a table and helped herself to a roll. Someone saw her and yelled, "NO!" Olive dropped the roll and ran back down the hall. She must have tiptoed back into the room where Martha was still playing.

"As Martha was my ACTION student, a staff member found me to tell me what had happened. I walked into the music room and there was Olive lying next to the piano like a little angel. Olive wagged her tail to greet me. Martha heard me walk in and stopped playing. At first, she didn't believe it when I told her what Olive had done.

"'I got the independent dog I asked for," Martha had said, smiling and patting Olive. "'I'm going to have to keep a close rein on this one.'" The instructors' meeting ended.

Students would be woken the next morning at six.

Our lessons, layered hour by hour across Monday and Tuesday, became increasingly complex: Pretend that the instructor holding the harness and leading you around town is a dog. Don't forget to say, "Good dog." If the pretend dog seems distracted, help them refocus on where they are going by saying, "To the curb." If the pretend dog stops suddenly, try to figure out why the dog might have done that. When you figure out what the pretend dog is telling you, say, "Good dog." Here is a list of obedience commands that your dog knows. Practice them now with your pretend dog. You will do obedience every day while you're at school and you should do it every day at home too.

We also had lectures at least once each day—about guide dog law, how to kindly tell people to keep their hands off your dog, how yelling at dogs causes them to shut down and you must never, ever do that.

When the day's activities were done, most of us gathered in the music room to laugh, talk, and share our anticipation.

Wednesday morning finally dawned. Dog Day. We were as ready as the two-and-a-half days of intensive training could make us. We had memorized when to feed, when to groom, when to park, when to play. We had been given stiff new leashes and had massaged them to make them softer and pliable. This helped us both to prepare for our new dogs and to manage some of our nervousness.

Subliminal lessons wove themselves through every practical skill we were taught: It is safe to be blind. Your dog makes it even safer. Instructors do not ask more of us than we can do. Trust the instructor. Trust your dog. Trust yourself.

On Wednesday morning, the other students and I gathered for breakfast while our instructors met elsewhere one last time to discuss the client-dog matches. We picked at our French toast. Even the students who had gone through this before were silent. No one told stories of previous Dog Days. We each silently reevaluated how well or how poorly we had performed over the past few days. We each wondered if our instructors still believed we were worthy of their dogs.

We had heard stories about students being sent home without dogs. Sometimes it was because the student had become ill during the training. Other times the staff had decided that the student was unsuitable. Staff didn't talk to students about these failures. No one had any way of knowing if they were on the possible hit list. We huddled together, sipping coffee and counting the minutes until the 9:30 meeting, when we'd learn about our new dogs. We were afraid to leave each other, as though our strength in numbers would prevent an instructor from walking into the dining room and calling out a name. We knew that meant that the person called was being excused from the program. This was the staff's last chance to terminate a student's training before we met our dogs. Once we met our dogs, we hoped, the trainers would be committed to sending those dogs home with us.

Finally, it was time to leave the dining room. We had ten minutes before we were due to gather at Alumni Hall. I stopped in my dorm room to stretch and breathe and brush my teeth. Then I walked out of my room, down the hall, and into the meeting room. "Deni here," I said. At Guiding Eyes, this is the type of announcement that one makes upon entering a room.

I was answered by the sound of hands tapping on empty chairs. This, again, is a Guiding Eyes tradition, designed to help people who cannot see find a place to sit. I moved toward the spontaneous drumming and heard Kara call, "Deni, I saved you a seat next to me." I walked toward her. "This side," she said, tapping to indicate the empty chair on her right. I sat down next to my new friend. Artist and ethics professor, we faced our new futures together.

Kara squeezed my hand. Miranda said the matching would begin.

The wave of anticipation that washed over me took me back to childhood memories of Christmas morning. In my family, each person was handed a present, and then we went around and opened them one at a time so that everyone could share the moment. I remembered the delicious agony of holding my present in its crinkling wrapping paper until it was my turn to open. So it was the morning of Dog Day. In a few minutes, instructors would announce the name, sex, breed, and color of each of our assigned dogs. When everyone had heard this information, we would go back to our dorm rooms and wait for our instructor to bring our dog. Clients' names were called out in random order. No one knew who would be next.

Graham called my name. "Deni," he said, "you will be meeting a female yellow Labrador retriever. Her name is Alberta." I responded with tears of joy, of gratitude, of confusion. I had been handed a wrapped present with no way to guess what—or in this case, **who**—lived inside that description. Alberta. I wondered why she had been given that name.

"Kara," Miranda said, "you are getting a female yellow Labrador named Haven."

Kara and I wrapped arms around one another, laughing and crying. This was really happening. We were getting our dogs. "Haven," I said, rolling the sound on my tongue. "She will be a safe haven for you," I whispered to Kara.

We got up, sweeping our canes for what we hoped would be the last time. As we filed out the door, Shane handed each of us five high-value salmon treats.

I got to my room and sat on the side of the bed. I waited. Rehearsed. When Graham arrived, I was to give the dog the five treats, one right after the other, and praise Alberta by name.

I tried to identify my complicated feelings. Excitement fluttered in my stomach, gratitude filled my heart. I worried about what would happen if the dog didn't like me. The five treats grew sticky in my clenched hand as I practiced saying, "Good dog, Alberta. You are such a good dog."

In our lecture the night before, Miranda had explained that handing the dog a sequence of high-value food rewards is called a jackpot. She said, "We want the dogs to feel like they have hit the jackpot in meeting you. You reinforce their interest in getting to know you because you know their name and tell them, 'Good dog.' That is what they want to hear.

"Sit on your bed or chair when the dog comes in," Miranda said. "Your instructor will hand you the dog's leash and leave. You can let the dog explore the room, but keep them on leash for right now. Do not let the dog get up on the bed. Don't sit on the floor. If you start your relationship with the dog with bad habits, they will be harder to break later.

"Try to keep the dog focused on you. Call the dog. Tell your dog to 'Get close.'

"When you say, 'Get close,' the dog will sit between your legs with their head facing out. Massage your dog's ears, throat, shoulders, and chest. That will help the dog relax. If the dog rolls over, rub belly, chest, and throat. This is a very good sign that the dog is ready to trust you. Massaging the dog also helps you to know your dog's size and shape and how all the pieces come together.

"Stay in your dorm room with your dog. Someone will come to your door around 11:30 to escort you and your dog to the dining room for lunch. You will not have a harness yet, so you'll heel with your dog. Your escort will serve as your sighted guide. Your dog knows how to heel at your left side while you hold the elbow of your sighted guide on the right. At lunch, you'll start learning how to help your dog stay quietly tucked under the table.

"After lunch, your instructor will help you park your dog, and you'll have your first chance to work with your dog on harness."

I tried to remember all the dos and don'ts. I sat on the side of the bed nearest the door, hearing footsteps in the hall as instructors led dogs to other clients. I loosened my grip on the now mushy treats. Footsteps stopped, and I heard a knock on my door.

"Yes! Come in!" My heart pounded.

Graham walked in and handed me a leash. "Here is Ms. Alberta. Her hair is the same color as yours, and she seems very happy to meet you." By the time he finished his sentence, Alberta had placed her front paws on my thighs. I bent toward her and rubbed my right hand over her head and shoulders. She reached to touch her nose to mine. I gave her one of the treats that was sticking to my left hand, which she took gently. Then another.

I slid from the bed to sit cross-legged on the floor. I was breaking a rule, but I didn't care. I wanted to feel all of this magical dog. She swirled in my arms, a flurry of tongue and fur and tail. Alberta seemed as intent on touching every inch of me as I was on touching every part of her. I gave her treats three, four, and five. Now that my hand was empty, Alberta sniffed the residue, sighed, and flopped down into the circle of my crossed legs. She rested her head on one of my legs and thumped her tail rhythmically on the other. Graham quietly left the room.

My head bowed over Alberta's, my tears dropped onto her muzzle. "Alberta," I said. "Thank you for coming into my life."

I would never understand why my journey to this dog had taken so long. Everything about her felt exactly right to me.

CHAPTER 9

A TEAM OF THREE

"Curl your left hand around the harness handle, fingers down," Graham said. "Can you feel your dog?" I could. Alberta's wagging tail and anticipatory breaths were sending vibrations up both sides of the harness handle to where my hand curled on the five-inch, leather-coated steel rod that connected those two sides. She felt like an engine revving up.

"Just tell her 'Forward,'" he said calmly, with a smile in his voice, "and we'll be on our way."

I hesitated and cocked my head, trying to make visual sense of the blurry kaleidoscope before me. When I'd first explored the campus, I'd made it only to the edge of the Guiding Eyes nature path. Now I was there with my dog. Lawn and trees stretched out in front of us in undulating shades of green. The wide, dark ribbon that extended out from beneath my feet was certainly a paved path. I caught the scent of snow gone sour from months on the ground. Despite the sun, I shivered in the cold. After nine years in Florida, I was overwhelmed by the Northeastern chill, even with my down jacket and wool gloves.

I wasn't ready for this.

I tried to clear my mind.

"Forward," I said, hoping that I sounded confident to Graham and Alberta. The dog leaped ahead, pulling hard enough into her harness that I had to speed up to match her pace. My left hand was full of harness handle and the folded-up excess of the six-foot leash. There was also a second leash for Graham to hold; before we had started, Graham had put my left hand on Alberta's collar to show it to me. The dog led our parade with assurance, seemingly oblivious to all the duplicative leather. Graham and I walked on either side of her, parallel to each other and to the dog's back legs.

At first, the enormous energy I'd felt when Alberta pulled into her harness made me think that she would have preferred to walk even faster, but I noticed that, as I took steps, she paused, a paw at a time, attempting to match her pace to mine. I knew I wasn't making that easy. I was alternating between moving quickly to try to keep up with her and hesitating, worried that I might trip or that Alberta might make a sudden move and knock me off balance.

To even out my own pace, I started silently counting my steps. Focus. One, two, three, four. Every step moved me out of my own head and into the dog's rhythm. The more I relaxed, the steadier the dog felt. I stopped worrying about what might lie ahead. As we continued to walk, I noticed a slight side-to-side movement in Alberta's gait. "I feel a little rocking while we are moving forward," I said to Graham. "It reminds me of cantering a horse."

"Good," he said.

After a moment of silence, he said, "We have some obstacles coming up ahead. Don't tighten up. Just follow your dog."

I dropped my shoulders away from my ears, as if responding to my yoga teacher. Alberta stepped closer to me, nudging her body against my left leg. She gave me a gentle push, shifting us a few steps to the right. Then she gave me a soft pull, and we flowed back into our original direction. **Cool**, I thought.

We zigzagged right and then left. Alberta led me smoothly around objects before I could even identify what we were avoiding. Each time, I felt her readjust her body afterward so that she picked up the same path that we had been traveling before the obstacle. "Good girl,"

I murmured. I could tell that Alberta was multitasking to make everything work. She paid attention to my pace and tried to match it. She noticed obstacles and pivoted around them. She remembered where we were heading in the first place so that she could continue guiding me in that direction.

"You are about to reach an intersection," Graham said. "She'll be looking to you for direction."

"Wait!" I said. I stopped, trying to process this new information. I felt guilty as Alberta screeched to a halt. I realized that my voice had sounded sharp and desperate. I stroked the dog's head. I told her that I hadn't meant to yell.

"'Wait' was the right command, if you're not sure of where you want to go," Graham coached. "But you gave the command at the wrong time. As you can tell, you stopped your dog in her tracks. You are about six feet short of the intersection—not where you want to be to make a turn. So, now give her a double command, 'Left, left,' or 'Right, right,' so she understands that you want her to go forward until you reach a point that she can turn the direction that you have asked."

"Left, left," I chose at random. Alberta walked forward three paces and then pivoted to face left. I felt her tuck her rear end behind my left leg and then pull forward in the direction I had asked. The pressure that she put on the back of my leg told me when to turn with her; her forward movement into the harness prompted me to walk in a straight line with her again. "Wow, good job, Alberta," I said, impressed. Alberta rose up a bit in her harness as I praised her, proud of her perfectly executed left turn.

She's showing off, I thought and smiled. I liked that Alberta responded to my praise. Even more, I liked that she had the confidence to be pleased with her own performance.

Alberta slowed down for a few paces and then stopped. "Forward," I said. When she still didn't move, I reached my right foot out and felt an elevation in the path. Then I heard water flowing underfoot. I realized that Alberta's front paws were on the incline of a ramp that bridged running water. I stepped out with my left foot. We walked over the bridge, and then Alberta stopped again. Before I could figure out why, Graham reached down and unsnapped his leash from Alberta's collar. "You two are ready to solo," he said. "Don't worry, I'm right behind you." I hesitated, feeling lost.

"Forward," I said. Alberta didn't move. I reached my right foot and felt a step down. "Got it," I said to Alberta, then stepped down with my left foot. "Forward." She put her paw on the step below, timing it precisely with my foot. We walked down two steps in perfect cadence, as though we were performing a well-rehearsed dance routine. Then she stopped again. I guessed that we were at another intersection.

"What if I give her a direction and the path doesn't turn that way?" I asked Graham.

"Let me give you a little orientation," he said. "The path turns left and right at the intersection we're at now. If you turn right, that will take you back toward the dorm. All you have to say is, 'Right,' and 'Forward.' If you want to keep walking through the nature path, which is what I want you to do, then tell Alberta 'Left' and 'Forward.'

"If you try to walk straight from where you are," Graham continued, "you will walk off the path and down a little incline. The grass is still icy, so you and Alberta would probably slide into the creek. The water that you hear flowing is under a thin layer of ice that you would break through. Not a good choice for our first walk together.

"The good news is Alberta knows that going forward is not a good idea. So, if you say, 'Forward,' she'll stand still and wait for you to make a better choice."

Good dog, I thought. I said to Alberta, "Left, forward, please."

I felt Alberta's butt against the back of my left leg. We turned left, curved around another obstacle, and then Alberta stopped again. "What now?" The path seemed to be continuing smoothly ahead of us. I glanced back toward Graham. "Figure it out," he said. "Your dog is trying to tell you something."

I reached my right foot out. No curb or step. I reached down into the darkness below my truncated visual field. "Found it," I said. A pole was blocking my path at knee level. The right end of the pole, held by a V-shaped post, extended beyond the sidewalk.

"This is a post-and-rails jump that you might remember from riding horses," Graham said, "but we don't allow guide dog teams to leap over obstacles in harness. Now that you know what you are facing, tell Alberta, 'Forward' and let her decide what to do next."

"Forward," I said. Alberta immediately turned us to the right. She led me off the paved path and onto a patch of grass, crunchy with snow. She looped us around the end of the pole and continued walking down the path. "Let's stop, Alberta," I said, forgetting the command I was supposed to use. She did. I reached down and stroked her ears while I processed her navigation choice. "Good job, Alberta," I said.

To Graham, I said, "I'm guessing the pole was sticking out beyond the path on both sides. Alberta made a good decision to guide me to the right. If she had gone left, I might have bumped my leg into the pole as we rounded it. When she chose to go around to the right, she put herself between me and the pole sticking out."

"That's exactly what she did," he said. "Wow!" I said in amazement. I wondered how she had figured that out.

We continued down the nature path, walking around obstacles on the ground, at ankle height, at waist level, and in between. We walked back over the ramp that bridged the icy stream and down the steps on the other side. We turned back and walked up the stairs and down the ramp. If Alberta vetoed the direction that I asked for, she waited for me to come up with an alternative suggestion. Finally, I had a mental map of the paved loop and intersecting paths that made up the campus nature walk. I was filled with respect for the diabolical minds that had designed this obstacle course to be as complicated as possible for people with low or no vision. I was also cold and tired. My brain was full.

"Time for a break," Graham said. "Tell Alberta 'Right, right,' and she'll go that way at the next paved opportunity. That will lead us to the door by the student lounge. Let's go in, warm up, and get some coffee. You and Alberta deserve a rest."

I said, "Right, right," and a few steps later, we turned. Alberta stopped when we encountered a stretch of the tactical bumps placed on the sidewalks at city street crossings and at all intersections on the Guiding Eyes campus. I called those strips "Braille for the feet." Alberta didn't need me to tell her that the bumps meant that we should stop so that she could check for traffic. She stopped automatically. I said, "To the door."

Alberta walked me across the street, stopping with her front paws on the up curb. I could feel the angle of the harness handle change as she stepped up. I stepped up to join her. With another "Forward," she began walking again. I assumed that she was heading to the door. "Wait," I told her. She stopped. Coffee sounded good, but I wanted to attend to Alberta's needs first.

I turned to Graham. "I want to give Alberta a chance to pee before we go inside," I said. "Is there a water bowl for her in the lounge?"

Graham said, "No and no."

I felt scolded but said nothing. "Forward," I said and followed Alberta's lead. She took a few steps and then stopped. I reached out and found the push bar to open the door to the building. "Good dog," I said. But before I could open the door, Graham spoke.

"Just so you know," he said, "when Alberta stopped at the door, she pointed her head up and forward to show you where to put your hand to open the door. When you two come to a door, first put your hand on the top of your dog's head. Follow the line of her nose, and she will show you the door handle or doorknob and indicate if the opener is on the right or left side of the door. On this door, with a push bar all the way across, it is easy to figure out how to open it. It is more difficult to figure out where to push or pull when you are confronted with a door that has only a single handle or knob. That's why Alberta shows you where to push if there is a single handle or knob. If she were a taller dog, she would touch the opener with her nose for you."

"Wow," I said, again in awe. I hadn't known dogs could do that.

Alberta and I followed Graham into the student lounge. He and I took off our coats and sat at the table. Graham poured us coffee. "The cup is at twelve o'clock," he said as he sat it on the table. I was glad not to have to search for it.

Alberta dropped to the floor, stretching her front paws under the table to rest them on my feet. Soon, she dropped her head on top of my feet as well. She had chosen to doze where she wouldn't lose track of me. Graham noticed and said with approval, "She's bonding with you."

Graham then spoke to what was still on my mind. "I know it seemed harsh to you that I wouldn't let you take care of your dog," he said, "but our dogs are trained to park—have their potty breaks—at regular times, five times each day.

"Sometimes there are emergencies. You've already seen how hard Alberta works to communicate with you. If she really has to go RIGHT NOW, she'll find a way to let you know. When she does, take off her harness immediately so she doesn't pee or poop with it on. Conscientious guide dogs like Alberta are mortified if they can't wait another second and end up relieving themselves in harness. But, if they do get into the habit of doing it on harness, it's a difficult habit to break.

"For your sanity and hers, keep her on a schedule for parking, eating, and drinking. Unless you're hiking in the desert, she gets water when you feed her breakfast, again at her dinner, and in the evening, a couple of hours before you go to bed. That's it. If you stick with that routine, she'll know what to expect and when. You'll know when she needs to relieve herself. Soon, she'll remind you that it's time for one thing or the other. Dogs have great internal clocks."

That made sense. I felt my anxiety thaw. Graham seemed open and gentle. He reassured me. It would take me a while to learn what Alberta had to teach me, but Graham acted as though I was up to the challenge.

I was curious about Graham and why he'd chosen to work at Guiding Eyes. I wanted to learn how Alberta had been taught all the skills she'd demonstrated this afternoon. I withheld my questions, afraid he might find them inappropriate for a student to ask the first day with her dog. Instead I sat quietly, enjoying the warmth of my mentors: one at the table, the other on my feet.

Too soon, Graham declared our break over, and we headed out again. This time we walked past the nature path and out through the back gate of the campus, where we practiced our skills on a quiet road in the neighborhood. Alberta guided me past homes with wide yards on Colonial Street, where the lack of sidewalks was an intentional aesthetic and good for dog training too. We walked in the street, Alberta's left paws grazing the curb that separated lawn from paved road. Graham trailed behind us, ready to explain any dog cue that I didn't understand or quickly heed.

After another hour, I felt exhausted and exhilarated by this new experience: a long, ongoing dialogue with my dog. Alberta processed my requests and then decided if they were possible. I quickly came to understand her responses, even if her answer was, "We can't do that." I felt her lateral push or pull when she moved us around obstacles to the right or left. When we came to an intersection, I noticed that she danced in place impatiently while waiting for me to decide which way I wanted to go. In this first day of training, I'd gotten only the faintest glimmer of what it meant to partner with this dog, but I was beyond impressed with what she knew and how hard she was working to communicate with me. I was drained from the mental gymnastics of translating Alberta's guide-dog-speak and trying to send her clear messages in return.

I also felt embarrassed. I had convinced Guiding Eyes to accept me into their accelerated training program for experienced guide dog handlers. Now that I was beginning to realize all that I didn't know about working a school-trained guide dog, I felt like a fraud. I worried about what would happen when Graham inevitably confronted me about what I was supposed to know but could not demonstrate.

Underneath it all, I felt curious. Alberta had shown me in a single afternoon how different partnering with her would be from my previous experiences with Oriel and Wylie. Oriel and Wylie had been trained to perform specific tasks like stopping at a curb. Alberta had the big picture.

Before I had even buckled Alberta's harness around the dog's chest for our first work session, Graham had known that my first days of working with Alberta would be challenging for all three of us. He was struck by the contradiction between my wanting to work a guide dog that blatantly displayed my disability and my practiced habit of presenting myself as fully sighted. Graham couldn't tell which one I wanted. The answer, though irrational, was both. Graham didn't confront me with this contradiction, but he carefully watched how I managed my conflicting desires, ready to call off the training if my ambivalence confused Alberta.

From the first moment of our first work session, Graham had realized that I wanted to understand every detail of this guide dog. When he'd handed me the harness, he'd expected me to immediately slide it on over Alberta's head and shoulders. Instead, I ran my fingers down its length, comparing it to the harnesses I had used with Oriel and Wylie. Alberta's harness had leather loops that sat at the dog's shoulders, allowing the handle to move freely within the loop. "It's similar to the design I used with my privately trained dogs," I said, "but I like the quick-snap connectors."

"Thanks," Graham answered. "I designed those. Handlers need an easy way to release the handle without taking off the soft part of the dog's harness, like when they're on an airplane. If you kept this twenty-inch-long, rigid handle attached to the strap that goes around the dog's shoulders and belly when you sat in your seat on the plane, it would tangle in your legs and make it impossible for the dog to squeeze under the passenger's seat. Taking the whole thing off is not a good option. In an emergency, you need to quickly connect the dog to the handle. The harness back strap also stays on the dog for identification. 'Guiding Eyes for the Blind' is embossed on the strap, in case the dog ever gets separated from their handler."

I listened, nodded. Then I held out the harness in my left hand and a treat in my right. "Alberta," I said, with great excitement, "get dressed please."

"Good dog," I said as she nosed into the harness and crunched into her Charlee Bear treat. I buckled the harness under her belly. As I laid the handle down softly, I noticed that it hovered slightly above Alberta's back. "What a good dog," I said, smoothing her fur to lie flat under the soft straps that encased her belly and back.

Then I said to Graham, "I'm ready."

Graham appreciated the logic of my giving Alberta a verbal cue when it was time to put on her harness. Once Alberta learned, "Get dressed," she would come running when she heard it, nose into the harness, and be ready to be buckled in for work. Graham knew that the other instructors had already told the clients not to teach dogs "off-list" commands at this stage. He decided to let this one go.

Then he noticed that excess leash was dangling next to Alberta's ear, distracting her and getting in the way of her vision. He remembered that, in the video from my home interview, I'd bunched up the leash in my left hand along with the harness handle, and he recognized this as one of my bad habits. He wondered why I didn't clip the excess leash to the working ring near the dog's collar. That would have shortened the leash but kept it loose enough that it wouldn't compete with the harness for the dog's attention. There would also have been less leash for me to hold. Most handlers extend the leash its full six feet only when the dog is off harness and needs some space to pee or poop. Once again, Graham swallowed his words. He decided against offering advice before I had taken my first step with the dog. He made a mental note to look for a shorter, three-foot traffic leash in the equipment room.

"Let's do this," he said. "Tell her **Forward**."

After the first hour of work, Graham was pleased that I was in awe of Alberta's abilities. When Alberta moved her body in a way I didn't expect, Graham could see by my face that I was working to figure out what she was trying to communicate. He heard me praise Alberta with a tone of wonder. Graham unhooked his instructor's lead from Alberta after only fifteen minutes. As the day went on, he found there was less he needed to say. He decided that Alberta and I were a good match but needed many hours of practice together. His goal was for us to walk between fifty and seventy miles in harness over the course of the ten-day ACTION class.

By midafternoon, Graham told me we were done for the day. "You need to absorb what you learned today. You and Alberta both need to relax and take a nap. I'm going back to my office to take care of other work."

Alberta and I returned to the dorm room. I opened my laptop to connect with my office, appreciating the unexpected hours of work time. After a while, I realized it was 4 p.m., time for Alberta's late-afternoon potty break. I harnessed her and had her guide me out through the park door. "Left, left," I said randomly, waiting to see where we'd end up. We walked off the path and up a grassy slope. I removed her harness, unfurled her leash, and said, "Get busy." Alberta sniffed the grass and then squatted to pee. As I waited for her to finish, I was surprised to hear Graham say, "Hi, Deni." He was running over to us, pulling on his parka.

I smiled at him but kept my attention on Alberta. When she stood and walked over to me, I asked her, "Are you done?" I held out the harness and said, "Get dressed, please." She walked into the harness and waited for me to buckle her in. "Good job, Alberta!" I said and gave her a treat.

I turned back to Graham. "I didn't mean to be rude," I said, "but I'm trying to teach her a routine. I ask if she's done when she gets off harness to go potty. If she isn't eager to walk back into the harness, I assume she isn't done yet. I'd then give her time to finish up her business. What's up?"

Graham said a staff member had come to his office and told him I had taken my dog out to park on the school's front lawn. "She was worried that you were lost," he said calmly but firmly. "I doubted that, but you seem to have forgotten a few rules. The first couple of days, you need to take your dog to the communal park area to relieve herself. It's 4 p.m., the right time, but you're in the wrong place. Shane will be wondering where you are. Please swing by there on your way back to the dorm so that you and Alberta are accounted for. In the future, do not let your dog relieve herself on the front lawn of the administration building."

"Oops, sorry," I said. "See you later."

Graham mused about how each of the teams of three that he had formed—instructor, dog, and client—were different. The three must bond before the dog and client are ready to become a team on their own. Alberta's guiding skills were excellent. I was treating her as an intelligent, sensitive coworker. And it was good that I was praising Alberta and focusing on relating to her rather than waiting for

Graham to intervene. That helped Alberta learn to look to me rather than to him for support and encouragement. Graham could see that I was also worried I might do the wrong thing. He categorized me as a sensitive puppy who would shut down if criticized. He liked that I paid close attention to him. Nevertheless, I was demonstrating a pattern of forgetting or ignoring rules that I found arbitrary, which meant that he needed to keep a closer eye on me. He knew that I was the weak link in our team of three.

The next morning, Graham drove Alberta and me to the school's training center in White Plains. I chatted with him from the front passenger seat, reaching down occasionally to pet Alberta, who was curled at my feet. Once Graham parked the van in the lot behind the center, I got out and waited a beat before giving Alberta permission to jump out too. She charged into her harness as I held it out. She had been training in White Plains for months. "I know this place," Alberta seemed to say. "Let's go!"

White Plains was a perfect city for training new guide dog teams. It is home to about sixty thousand people and has a downtown with office buildings, bars, and restaurants clustered in a five-block square. There is a shopping mall with elevators and escalators, and residential areas that encircle the downtown. The sidewalks and streets were often crowded, providing endless opportunities to practice working around obstacles. The Guiding Eyes training center was a large old house that had been modified to provide a comfortable all-day training center for a dozen students and four instructors at a time. It had a handful of offices, a commercial kitchen, a diner-style eating area with a half-dozen booths and a few four-top tables, and a variety of lounge areas where students could relax and visit or work on their laptops while they waited their turn to work with their instructors.

Graham, Alberta, and I walked in the back door of the house and into the large front room. My classmates were all there with their dogs, along with three instructors: Miranda, Gerri, and Barbara. The students were talking and laughing with one another, excited by their first opportunity to train here. The dogs picked up on the excitement and scuffled playfully with each other. Miranda raised her voice to be heard. "Pay attention to your dogs, and keep them close to you," she said. "Once you find somewhere to sit and be quiet, the first teams can get out to work."

"Follow me," Graham said to me, quickly ushering Alberta and me through the crowd and out the front door to the sidewalk. As I was Graham's only ACTION student, I wasn't sharing my instructor with any other students. "You can check out the training center later," he said. "We'll be back here for lunch. You can hang out with your classmates then. Tell her, 'Forward and left.'"

I did so, encouraging Alberta the whole time. "Good dog." "Good girl." "Good job." I looked down at her, trying to keep an eye on my dog with whatever my residual vision could offer. Alberta wagged her tail and gazed up at me as we walked. When I saw her look ahead to find the upcoming curb, I praised her for that. I noticed that every time I spoke to her, she looked up at me. Did she need more reassurance?

Within a few blocks, Alberta began to hesitate, as though unsure of what she was supposed to do. With each hesitation, I became more effusive with my praise. Graham sighed, knowing that my praise was confusing the dog and he would have to give me some one-on-one verbal instructions. When working with a new guide dog team, Graham's preferred teaching style was to let something go wrong and then commiserate with the dog and client while they figured out together how to solve the problem. If they got tangled up walking through a door, for instance, Graham waited silently for them to disentangle themselves. Intervening in such a situation would only teach them to be dependent on him rather than on each other. Sometimes, he had no choice but to take control. Now, he knew he had to do something. Too much was going wrong here, and it was undermining Alberta's confidence.

At the next curb, Graham told me to wait. He said, "Alberta is doing a good job of guiding, and you're doing a good job of following her lead. So, save the praise until Alberta comes to a full stop at a curb. Be quiet and let her work."

I complied, but it was an effort. How was Alberta supposed to know that I was happy with her work? Graham noticed that now both Alberta and I seemed uneasy. "Let's get some coffee," Graham said.

We stopped at a coffee shop a few blocks from the training center and sat at a table against the window. Graham said that this was a frequent training stop. Teaching a new guide dog team was more than walking together on harness, he explained. The dog also needed breaks—and practice in staying out of the way in crowded restaurants. The client, meanwhile, needed time to process the lessons. We were here now, Graham said, because he needed to understand what was going on inside my head.

I reached down to make sure that Alberta's paws and tail were tucked under the table. I unzipped my jacket and wrapped icy fingers around a mug of coffee. I listened.

"I can tell that you're good at taking care of your dog," Graham said. "We are in a crowded coffee shop and your first instinct is to make sure that Alberta's parts are tucked out of the way so that she doesn't get stepped on. That's exactly what you should do here. But she doesn't need your help when she's guiding you."

I tilted my head, unable to read his facial expression, but feeling more curious than offended.

"Your constant praise is making her unsure of herself," Graham said. "She gets distracted from her work when she sees you looking down at her or hears you praise her. Dogs are quick to read people's facial and vocal cues, and Alberta is more perceptive than most. She's trying to figure out what you want of her. You've told her, 'Forward,' and she's doing that. So, she wonders, 'Why are you still talking to me?' She wonders if you want her to stop so that you can give her a treat or pat her head. She wonders if you're asking her to do something new, like change direction. Alberta is trying to make sense of all your chatter while trying to guide. That's making her hesitant about moving forward, which is what you have asked her to do."

I blinked back tears. Even my attempt to encourage the dog had been wrong. "I just want her to know that she's being a really good dog," I said.

"Alberta is a wonderful guide dog," Graham agreed. "There are times that she will need your reassurance, but not today in White Plains, where she's worked a hundred times and you both have me right behind you. You'll have years to let her know she's wonderful. When she's focused today on getting you from Point A to Point B, she doesn't need your praise."

"Let me be honest with you," Graham continued. Now he sounded annoyed. "I'm confused about what you know and what you don't. I can tell that you're always thinking about what Alberta needs. That's great. But when you do something, like that constant praise, it makes me wonder what you really know about guide dogs. We haven't talked about your experience. Your application said that you worked two guide dogs over the last ten years?"

I nodded, feeling exposed. "They were privately trained," I said. "My previous dogs were trained to wear a harness and keep me from running into obstacles or tripping up or down curbs or stairs. Until I got to Guiding Eyes, I thought that was all a guide dog did. I see now that Alberta is different."

"Every guide dog school and trainer has their own way of doing things," Graham said. "It's okay that you don't know how a Guiding Eyes dog works. That's what you're here to learn. I need to ask you some basic questions, though, so don't get offended."

I nodded and then smiled. "It's a deal," I said, "as long as you don't throw me out of school for not knowing the answers."

"Got it," Graham said, smiling in return. "Here's something you should know, Deni. We instructors misunderstood who you are. We expected you to come here sure that you already knew everything that we had to teach you. Now I think that you came here knowing that you have a lot to learn. I think you are afraid that we'll decide that you are not skilled enough and we will send you home without a dog. That's not the way it is. Everyone at Guiding Eyes, including Alberta, and including me, will do everything that we can for you to succeed. We are on your side. Keep up the work you're doing," he said, "and you won't have to worry about us sending you packing. I can tell that you adore Alberta and that she adores you. Did you know we picked out Alberta for you two months before you came to school?"

"Really?" I said, with surprise, wiping away a tear. "Alberta's perfect for me. How did you know she was exactly what I needed?" I felt special, knowing that Graham had matched me to this wonderful dog months ahead of time. "Your personalities are alike in ways you don't yet understand," Graham answered. "But right now, you need to get on the same page as Alberta and me." I nodded and leaned in to listen.

"Let's start with targeting," he said. "Do you know the touch command?" I hesitated. Graham told me to make a fist, reach down toward Alberta, and say, "Touch." Alberta immediately pushed her nose into my fist. "Good dog," I said.

"Yes," he agreed. "And now you know how to always find your dog. Just say, 'Alberta, touch' and she will come running from wherever she is and bump your fist with her nose. We use a fist for 'Touch,' as there is no other hand signal that looks like that.

"In advanced training, we teach the dog to visually focus on a target ahead of the handler. If we are working on streets and sidewalks, she targets the curb or intersection up ahead. You already know how she stops with her toes at the curb or at the tactile bumps on the sidewalk. If, when you are walking, you talk to her, she will look up at you and can't stay focused on her target."

Of course. That made sense. I should have known that.

"When in doubt, just say 'Touch' if you need her close. Tell her 'To the curb,' if you need her focused on moving forward. 'Touch' and 'To the curb' are the two most fundamental guide dog commands."

"Now I get it," I said.

"Are you two ready to get back to work?" Graham asked.

I paused, knowing that I was again about to color outside of the lines.

"In a minute," I said. "I'd like to use the bathroom before we go back to work. And I'd like to start shaping Alberta's behavior to help me find bathrooms when we're out. 'Find the bathroom' is one of the commands I taught my privately trained dogs. So, if you don't mind, please lead us to the restroom. I'll give Alberta the command 'Find the bathroom' and then ask her to follow you. Don't worry, I won't distract or reward her until we get to the restroom door."

Graham cautiously said, "Okay." We stood up.

"Alberta," I said, "find the bathroom." Graham led the way, and Alberta and I followed. When we reached the women's room door, I used my right hand to follow the upward line of Alberta's head and nose to the door handle.

"Yes," Graham said. I smiled with pride—he was praising me with the same word and enthusiasm that he used with Alberta.

While Graham waited for me, he thought about how much he enjoyed working with students who already knew something about guiding. This was the first time he'd seen a client ask a dog to find a public bathroom. He had never thought to teach guide dogs to do that, but he realized now that it would be easy for them to learn. Public bathrooms have a distinctive smell; even to people, the men's room smells different from the women's. The dog could learn that smell and find it, regardless of where she was.

We exited the coffee shop. "Deni," Graham said, "I need you to trust me. I think you'll get a better feel for what Alberta can do if you're not trying to use your residual vision. I'd like you to work under blindfold." He took a new blindfold out of his pocket, still in its cellophane wrapper. "It's common around here. People in White Plains are used to seeing a pair of instructors working a dog with one of them under blindfold."

"Oh please," I said, catching my breath at the shock of what Graham was suggesting, "not the blindfold! I hated wearing the blindfold during my home interview. Please don't make me wear a blindfold." I'm sure my shock surprised Graham as well. After being blindfolded for my application evaluation, I should have expected to spend time under blindfold while working at Guiding Eyes. I didn't expect it. I was used to eking out every usable visual impulse I had to try to make sense of my environment. A blindfold closed out the entirety of my visual experience, not just the path that Alberta was leading me down.

I must have sounded as panicked as I felt. "Okay, no blindfold," Graham said. "Let's try the closed-eyes approach. That's completely under your control. First, I'll ask you to do ten steps with your eyes closed. Then, if you're ready, we'll try twenty. I'm right behind you. I promise not to let you run into anything. Alberta's got this."

We walked ten steps while I kept my eyes closed. Graham counted the steps out loud. Then we did the twenty steps. Then fifty. I realized that Graham had stopped counting the steps out loud. I relaxed into Alberta's gently rocking gait and kept my eyes closed for blocks at a time. Although I had no visual cues, this was the safest I'd felt walking down a city street in years. Alberta stopped reliably at the down curbs, guided me through crosswalks in front of idling traffic, and stopped in front of every up curb, waiting for me to find my footing before we stepped onto the next block. I flowed with Alberta around pedestrians, trash cans, and sandwich-board signs. By the time we had completed a mile-long route back to the training center, Graham told me that Alberta and I were moving at a comfortable 3.5 miles per hour. I felt proud that I literally could do it all with my eyes closed. And I understood the reason behind letting go of any vision. My job was not to navigate White Plains. My job was to learn to trust my dog to get me where I needed to go. I needed to change my focus. I now knew that I would absorb more from the dog and the environment if I focused on what my dog was telling me than if I tried to use what little vision I had to stay in control. I was willing to walk under blindfold with Graham and Alberta when Graham next requested that I do so. Right now, I was ready for a lunch break with Kara and Haven.

Kara and I sat in a booth at the White Plains training center diner, where the dining room staff were serving lunch for the clients and instructors. Our dogs were sprawled out at our feet and in the narrow aisle. After a morning of constant movement and learning, I happily surrendered to sipping soup and feeling pleasantly penned in by dogs and people. I had no reason to move. Laughter and conversation flowed around me as Jerome, one of the dining room staffers, vigorously debated with a student about the March Madness brackets.

"I need a nap," I whispered to Kara.

"Me too," she said. "Our dogs have the right idea." I realized that every dog in the diner was lying still amid the storm of conversation, laughter, and food passing over their heads.

The next day it snowed enough that the instructors declared a snow day, and we stayed on campus. It was one of the few days that I spent with my classmates. I attended the evening lectures with them. We had all three meals together, but during the days, I was almost always working alone with Graham and Alberta.

The morning's group lesson had clients and their dogs scattered across the floor of the large Alumni Hall. Learning to put boots on our dogs was an appropriate lesson considering the day's weather, but it turned out to be the dogs' least favorite activity. With or without normal sight, it's not easy to tell the front of the boot from the back or loosen the straps to slide the boot on and then adjust it for a snug fit while the dog is jerking her foot away. It was fun being with my classmates, struggling and laughing alongside them. We encouraged each other and finally begged the dogs to lie still while we secured a boot on each foot. Our instructors watched but didn't intervene or offer suggestions. A return to my childhood.

Once the boots were on, some of the dogs comically high-stepped as they walked around one another with the unwanted encumbrances on their feet. Alberta did a little of that but then got distracted by the abundance of treats that had fallen to the floor in the process of the students getting footwear on the dogs. Alberta grabbed and swallowed all the treats that she could reach and tested the length of the leash to see if she could reach a few more.

"Deni." Graham suddenly appeared next to me and whispered in my ear. "I know you are totally infatuated with your dog. And she is with you." I nodded and hugged Alberta close. "But, you know, Deni, your dog is not perfect."

"What?" I responded in mock surprise. "Alberta let me get four boots on her, and now she's helping clean up the floor. What more do you want from this dog?"

"Her cleaning up the floor **is** the problem," Graham said. "Alberta's scavenging is a problem. She can work past any human or animal distraction, but it's hard for her to avoid dropped food."

"Hmmm," I said jokingly. "Yes, that is a serious problem." With everything this incredible dog could do, I thought he must be kidding. He wasn't.

"Take off your dog's boots, and come with me," Graham said in his instructor voice.

I took off Alberta's boots, put on her harness, and followed him out into the hall. Alberta wagged her tail expectantly, ready for more fun and more rewards. She and I had both been enjoying this relaxed snowy day.

"Deni, I've got a bag full of Charlee Bears," Graham said. "I'm going to drop a few on the floor and then tell you and Alberta to go forward. I'll put my foot over the treats I've dropped so that Alberta can't grab them. If she tries to stop to look for the treats, tell her no, and tell her to go forward. When she walks four or five steps past the treats, I'll tell you to stop. Then give her a high value treat from your hand." Graham handed me a half dozen of the salmon bits that the dogs particularly loved.

Alberta and I worked past the Charlee Bears on the floor. Graham made every pass a little harder. Soon Charlee Bears were scattered at our feet like autumn leaves. Alberta guided me across the hall, ignoring the treats on the floor without a pause. When we stopped, she looked up at me expectantly, waiting for the salmon treat. I gave it to her.

Inside Alumni Hall, the boot lesson ended, and the rest of the students and dogs streamed into the hall. "Keep their heads up," Graham told the students. "I have scattered Charlee Bears all over the floor. Give them treats from your hand for not picking up the treats off the floor." Every moment at Guiding Eyes was a teachable one.

On Saturday, the fourth day of my training with Alberta, Graham again drove us to the White Plains training center. When we arrived, all was quiet. Graham suddenly remembered that the city's Saint Patrick's Day parade was being held that day. "I have no idea why the parade is a week early this year," he said, but now he understood why none of the other instructors or students were here. The streets would be full of people, horses, and huge floats with blaring horns. Graham said we would go elsewhere to train.

I argued that we should stay. We had a few hours before the parade would begin, and navigating around people standing on the sidewalks and putting up chairs and claiming their space for the parade would be good practice. There were likely to be pet dogs to work around as well. "Great natural distractions," I said, quoting one of Graham's favorite lines. "If at any point Alberta seems stressed, just direct us down a side street to move away from the crowds." Graham agreed, and we headed out.

Alberta seemed invigorated by the excitement in the air. I moved fluidly in step with her, offering only occasional praise. "You've got this," I said as we wove our way around groups of people on the sidewalks. Once we arrived at a corner, I rewarded Alberta with food and praise. As people streamed out of the bars with mugs of beer in hand, Graham moved closer to Alberta and me, making it clear to passersby that we were a team of three. Alberta moved with confidence, her swift, sure movements broadcasting her message: "We are coming through. Stay out of our way."

I marched proudly with her down the sidewalk, feeling Graham's protective presence hovering around us. Sometimes he moved ahead of us to open a path. Sometimes he coached me from my right elbow. Other times he silently brought up the rear. It belatedly occurred to me that my suggestion of working through the crowd had made Graham's job tougher. His caution and care enveloped Alberta and me. I could tell that he was watching me, monitoring the crowd, and trying to predict what would happen next, all at the same time.

Suddenly, a shadow crossed in front of me from the left—someone was reaching down to pet Alberta. Alberta swung us to the right to avoid the arm. Without stopping, I said, "Please don't touch her. She's my new guide dog and needs to stay focused." Once we'd walked past, I realized proudly that Alberta and I had handled that one on our own.

We dodged small children and more than a few pet dogs. After several more successful blocks, Graham told me to turn left—toward the training center, away from the growing crowd. I smiled at Graham and thanked him for his hard work. "Now," I said, "I know that Alberta and I will be fine together." Graham agreed. Our team of three was transforming, as it should, into a team of two.

CHAPTER 10

TEACHER, STUDENT, PARTNER

At 6 a.m., music blasted from the intercom in my dorm room. It was the wake-up call for me and Alberta, who was asleep in her crate next to my bed. Today's tune was the 1968 hit by the Rascals, "It's a Beautiful Morning." I smiled at the overly appropriate lyrics.

Indeed, we were learning to trust our new guide dogs to lead the way. As instructors encouraged us past our mistakes, we repeatedly heard, "It's okay." For most of us, the morning wake-up song became the day's earworm.

As the song ended, Miranda's cheery voice filled the room. "Good morning, students. It's time to get up and park your dogs." By now I had shaken off sleep, pulled my parka and boots on over my pajamas, opened Alberta's crate, and gotten her into her harness. She wagged and pranced as she led me through the park door, into the freezing morning air, and down the long sidewalk to the communal dog-relief area. Alberta stopped when her toes brushed the edge of the artificial turf that defined the area. She waited for me to remove her harness and relax my hold on the leash so that she could range a full six feet. I greeted the other students shivering along with me. Each dog staked out their own piece of turf. We humans listened to the play-by-play of the dogs' activities, provided by the apprentice instructor, Shane.

Alberta sniffed the morning air, walked a few paces, turned, walked a few more paces, turned again, and then squatted. Shane said, "Deni, Alberta is peeing. Praise her, but give her time to poop. She has that look."

"Eric, your dog is pooping. Reach over to him so you can feel how his back is hunched over and shaped like a C. Praise your dog and reinforce what Pico is doing. Say, 'Good dog, get busy.'"

On Shane's cues, we praised like an out-of-sync cheerleading squad. We shivered and prayed that Shane would soon say, "Harness them back up."

"It's been ten minutes," Shane said finally. "That's enough time for the dogs to decide if they are going to go."

This was the last day that a Guiding Eyes staff member would clean up the relief area after our dogs were done. "Picking Up Poop You Cannot See" was the topic of the coming evening's lecture. I hoped that someone would then explain why the training staff referred to the dogs' potty breaks as "parking your dog." The reference "park" seemed confined to dogs relieving themselves. "So, it's not like they are 'parked' like a car when they are not actively working," I mused. "I don't get it." The metaphor did not work for me.

In the morning cold, the dogs waited patiently for our novice hands to slip the harnesses back over their heads and find the buckles. With "Back to the room. Forward," the dogs eagerly guided us to the dorm, anticipating the kibble we would be dishing out for breakfast. Alberta ate so quickly that I didn't bother to remove my coat. Then it was back outside for the after-breakfast ten-minute potty break, giving the dogs a final chance, before the day commenced, to do whatever they hadn't done before breakfast—or do it again.

It was only my awareness that this was Alberta's last chance to relieve herself until the afternoon that kept me from judging Guiding Eyes for imposing this brutal routine on us, requiring us to park, feed, and park again—all before coffee.

The halls were off-limits from bedtime until the 6 a.m. wake-up call. We were not allowed to go to the coffee room earlier than that because our movements would wake the other dogs, triggering them to expect to be taken outside ahead of schedule.

Guiding Eyes structured our life 24/7. We were told to keep lights on at least until we had taken the dogs out to pee for the last time, at 9:30 p.m. Totally blind people might not care if the light is on or not, but dogs do. They are used to "lights out" signaling time for bed.

Between training sessions, we groomed and played with our dogs on a schedule. "Dogs thrive on routine," Miranda said. "Be fair to the dog. If you are inconsistent with your dog, your dog will throw inconsistency right back at you. Your dog needs to know what to expect from you if you expect the dog to consistently guide you."

Sunday was a day of rest, but apart from that, our days at Guiding Eyes were packed. Get up with the dogs at 6 a.m. Park and feed and park again. Breakfast in the dining room at 7:15 a.m. sharp. Coffee. Lots of coffee. At 8:15 a.m., take the harnessed dogs to meet the vans and drivers. Load up for the half-hour ride to the Guiding Eyes training center in White Plains or whatever training venue might be planned for the day. For the next three hours, walk increasingly complex routes through city traffic. Take a lunch break with other clients and instructors. Complete three more hours of work on harness, maybe navigating an enclosed shopping mall and learning to ride escalators. That's just as intense as the city streets, though not as cold.

By the time we returned to the dorm at 4 p.m., took the dogs out to park, fed them dinner, gave them water, and had them guide us up the stairs to the dining room for our own dinner, we were all dog-tired ourselves. Few of us were used to walking five-plus miles every day with the intense level of concentration required to learn how to handle a new guide dog. Even clients who'd had guide dogs previously needed to learn how to communicate with their new dog. Each dog has their own "tell" for when they're approaching a curb. Each has a unique way of signaling that they are picking up their game to navigate a crowded sidewalk, walk past a pet dog, or meet some other challenge up ahead.

I couldn't know the full range of sensory experiences that Alberta was bringing to our partnership, but I understood that she was using all her capabilities to help us navigate to my destination. My job was to become fluent in her unique dog-speak dialect. Otherwise, I wouldn't be able to understand the directions she gave me.

The instructors translated and amplified the dogs' signals and taught us how to communicate clearly back to our dogs.

My classmates and I were also getting a sense of our own performances by listening to how our instructors referred to us. We were called "students" or "clients," sometimes "handlers," and occasionally "partners." As the lessons progressed, we were called "students" less and "partners" more. "I got called partner twice today!" someone would announce with pride as my classmates and I gathered for dinner at the end of the day. The instructors had been giving us directions and corrections from the moment we'd ventured out of our dorm rooms in the morning. Unless we had an evening lecture, the stretch from dinner to "lights out" was our time to talk with each other about the day's achievements and disasters.

We knew the dogs were not magic wands that would cure our visual impairments. But when one of my classmates told the rest of us that federal and state laws categorized guide dogs as "tactile accommodations" and "medical equipment," we all groaned. Those descriptors did not come close to the reality of these exquisite dogs or the relationships that our instructors were helping us build with them. Guiding Eyes preached the importance of bonding with our dogs and fulfilling their legitimate needs. We learned to treat our dogs with the same respect that we would show to human coworkers. The dogs expected no less.

One evening, when we first sat down to dinner, I heard an instructor call from another table, "Deni, Alberta's rear end is sticking out into the aisle. Someone's going to trip over her." I resisted the impulse to nudge the dog under the table, knowing that any physical action from me would result in a reprimand from the instructor. I remembered the line from one of our lectures: "Do not physically manipulate your dog." It was one of the school's foundational rules. "If you move your dogs," the lecturer had said, "they will expect you to be responsible for keeping them out of danger instead of them taking care of that on their own. As you probably won't see when your dog is in the wrong place at the wrong time, remind your dogs to recognize and correct their own mistakes."

So instead of sliding Alberta on the smooth floor farther under the table, I said, "Alberta, get close, please." She crawled farther under the table and curled up between my feet. "Tail too," said the instructor. I felt Alberta curl her tail around her body. "Good girl," the instructor and I said together. Reflexively, the other students reached down to feel around their chairs to make sure that their dogs were safely stowed away too.

Guiding Eyes instructors knew from experience that if a student handled a dog roughly at school, it would only get worse if they were allowed to graduate and take the dog home. These dogs had only ever known kindness and compassion from the humans around them. Far better to dismiss the client during class than to rescue a neglected or abused guide dog later.

When the kitchen staff members served us dinner, they used analog clock references to describe our plates. "Meat at noon. Potatoes at three o'clock. Green beans at nine. Your salad is in a separate bowl at ten o'clock. Your iced tea is at two."

Asher started the evening's conversation as we each found our way around our plate. "Did you learn escalators today?" he asked the group. He was answered with a round of assents.

"I felt free," Asher said. "Riding the escalator with only the dog's leash in my hand. It's the first time in my life that I have been on an escalator without a person holding me or trying to steer me up or down or to the side. Or being told that I can't ride escalators because I can't see. I knew there had to be a better way. A dog is it."

We applauded Asher's experience, and together we reviewed the escalators skills that we had practiced that afternoon. When I heard the noise of an escalator, I was to face it and tell Alberta, "To the stairs." I could verify the direction of the escalator by lightly touching the handrail on the right. If it was moving toward me, that meant that Alberta had stopped in front of the escalator that was heading the wrong way. I needed to find the corresponding escalator whose handrail was moving away from me. When I was ready, I was to let go of the harness and step on the escalator in front of Alberta. The dog would immediately hop onto the step behind me and stand still. I was to keep the leash loose between us.

As we rode, I would put my right foot to the right of Alberta, creating as wide a stance as possible on that step to keep other people from trying to pass us. This might frustrate other people, but their hurry is not my problem. It was my job to protect Alberta from being bumped or knocked off balance. As I felt the railing flatten out, I would also feel Alberta preparing herself for the transition back to solid ground. Guide dogs learn to hop on and off the moving stairs with care so that they don't catch their toenails as the stairs flatten out on the circulating belt.

The most important thing to remember when riding the escalator, our instructors told us, is not to fall. If you must fall, however, let go of the leash so that your dog can safely hop off the escalator without you.

Everyone was tense while learning to work escalators with a new dog. We had heard the horror stories of dogs getting paws caught in the circulating belt at the escalator exit. The dog cannot be freed until the machinery is turned off. The dog is often severely injured, sometimes requiring the paw to be amputated. Even if the injury is not that serious, the dog is often so traumatized by the experience that they need to retire from guide work.

Some people refuse to ride an escalator with their guide dog altogether. There are guide dog schools that refuse to teach this skill, convinced that there is no way to do so safely. But those of us who have ridden escalators in subway stations in major cities, both in the US and internationally, know that there are also risks to not riding the centrally located, well-lit escalator. Elevators that serve as alternatives may be hard to find or may be in isolated, unsafe areas. If the elevator is out of service and the guide dog is not trained to ride escalators, the handler can't get to street level. Working with a guide dog is not without risk.

That evening, we had the all-important lecture "Picking Up Poop You Cannot See." During the lecture, we learned the origins of the phrase, "Park your dog." It has been part of US guide dog culture from the opening of the first US guide dog school, The Seeing Eye, in 1929. The story goes that the school's trainers referred to the slab of concrete where students took the dogs to relieve themselves as "the park." They'd known that some clients might be offended by a direct reference to the dogs' biological needs, and so they coined a verb to go along with the place.

"It's time to park your dog" and "Your dog is parking" are now part of guide-school lingo throughout the United States. The common dog relief command, used by Guiding Eyes and many other schools, is, "Get busy." As puppies, they learn to go where and when they're asked, be it on concrete, asphalt, gravel, grass, a pee pad, or a newspaper. They learn that "Get busy" means that, if they don't go now, their next chance may not be for a long while. During the lecture, my classmates and I learned best practices for parking our new guide dogs. Regardless of our lack of vision, we were to employ three key concepts: predictability, proximity, and perceptibility.

Predictability. A regular schedule makes guide dogs happy, and it helps their handlers predict when they will poop. If they don't poop during the first morning park, they are likely to go at the second park, right after breakfast. If they don't poop again at the 4 p.m. park before dinner, they certainly will at 7:30 p.m., or at the last-chance park before bedtime at 9:30. Nevertheless, we learned to carry extra poop bags just in case. Sometimes, for no apparent reason, the dog will poop twice in the same park session or will poop during three different parks in one day.

Proximity. The only way that a visually impaired handler will know if their dog is pooping is if the dog is on leash and close enough that the handler can feel how the dog is moving. Guide dog puppies are taught that people will touch their backs as they relieve themselves. Each dog has a unique way of moving while getting ready to poop. Some pace. Others sniff the ground, turn, and sniff again. Some do what instructors call "the dance": they walk in circles around their handler, requiring that the person either twirl with the dog or continually shift the leash from their left hand to their right until the dog finally stops and hunches over to poop.

When the dog stops, the handler touches the dog's back. If the dog's back forms a straight diagonal line heading down from shoulders to tail, the dog is peeing. A rounded back means that the dog is pooping. When the handler has confirmed that the dog is pooping, they stand by the end of the dog's tail, placing feet parallel to the dog's back feet. Once the dog finishes, the handler's feet will be about twelve inches from where they can expect to find the poop on the ground.

Perceptibility. When I felt Alberta step away from the pile, I was to hold the leash in my right hand and reach down with my left, mittened in a poop bag. Based on where Alberta had been hunched over, I would know that the pile of poop was about twelve inches from my toes. I was to scoop up everything that I thought was there, then use the back of my bag-covered hand to check around for anything soft and warm that I might have missed. When I was sure that I had it all, I would slip the bag off my hand, encasing the poop within it. Then I'd tie it at the open end, ready to throw it away.

Once students knew the procedure, we were given the freedom to park our dogs independently, as long as we stayed on the five-times-a-day Guiding Eyes schedule.

After the lecture, I realized with a start that I was due to fly back to Tampa in just two days. I'd started class at the same time as everyone else, but my accelerated track meant that I had only ten days of training on campus, compared to the others, who had twenty-one or twenty-eight. As eager as I had been to take the accelerated course, I now regretted it. Why had the admissions team agreed to let me do this? I had barely learned how to read Alberta's signals. I forgot whether to step out with my right foot or my left. And, as I had learned earlier that day, I was a complete failure at dealing with strangers.

When my classmates, who usually gathered at the same table, all sat down for dinner that night, I said, "I want to share my disaster of the day."

Graham had taken Alberta and me to a high-end grocery store so that we could practice working through the unique distractions of that type of space. Graham trailed us, occasionally telling me to turn right or left or go straight. We practiced dodging people, shopping carts, and produce displays.

Suddenly, a woman stepped in front of me. Alberta and I were barely able to stop before we ran into her.

"What a pretty dog," she said. "What's his name?"

I caught my breath and stuttered, flustered, knowing that we weren't supposed to give our dogs' names to strangers but not knowing what to say instead.

"Ah, ah, ah—" I blurted out. "Alberta."

"**Alberta**," the woman said, "you are a very good dog." I felt Alberta turn in her harness to look up in surprise at this stranger who knew her name and called her a good dog. I stood speechless, not sure what to say, or to whom. Alberta shouldn't be taking her focus off me and looking up at a stranger. But it wasn't fair to correct her. It was all my fault that the woman had called her by her name to begin with.

Graham appeared at my side, ignoring the stranger. "Walk with me,"

Graham said firmly. "Deni, tell your dog 'Forward,' **now**."

Alberta and I followed Graham into a quiet corner of the store. "Don't ever tell strangers your dog's name," Graham said, upset with me rather than with the woman who had gotten in our way. "Yeah, right, I know that," I said sheepishly. We left the store and drove back to campus in silence.

On the way back, I thought about how the school's instructors had violated their own commitment to operant conditioning. With the dogs, they tried always to tell the dogs what TO do rather than what NOT to do. They rewarded good behavior and, if possible, ignored the bad. I felt bad in response to Graham's stern DON'T, but I couldn't figure out what I should have done. I'm sure Graham or the other instructors had told all of us how to deflect a stranger who asks for our dog's name, but I had forgotten what we were supposed to say. I was suffering from information overload.

At the dinner table, I said, "I told Graham that I'm not good at making up lies on the spur of the moment. I get flustered. I turn red. I don't know what to say."

"Other people can be such jerks," a student across the table said.

Kara, ever the peacemaker, said, "I'm sure that the woman who stopped you didn't know she was doing anything wrong. People admire pet dogs all the time and ask their names. They don't know that calling our dogs by name or praising them distracts them from their jobs."

"I could say that I can't tell them the dog's name because she's working," I said. "That's true but takes too long, requires too much thought, and feels rude."

Sue, who was training with her third Guiding Eyes dog, said, "Last time I was here, the class sat around and came up with aliases that we could remember to use if someone asked our dog's name.

The dog named Bear got the alias Grizzly. Nissan became Auto. Fargo became Dakota. Everest's other name became Nepal."

"Now, that could work for me," I said. We tried on different aliases for our dogs: Scholar became Student; Yahtzee became Game Boy. Major became Minor, and Gabriel became Angel. By the time dinner was over, Alberta had been given the pseudonym Province—a clever reference that would be easy for me to remember.

That night, with my last full day of training looming, I couldn't sleep. The next day, when I met with Graham in the lounge for the morning's lesson, I knew I had to be honest with him. "I can't take Alberta home yet," I said. "You know that Wylie hated airports and airplanes. I don't know what I did to make him so neurotic about flying. You saw how badly I handled the woman in the grocery store. Graham, every day I'm afraid I'm going to do something that breaks this fabulous dog."

Graham was silent for a moment. I braced for him to tell me that I was right and that I should leave today without Alberta.

"Deni," he said, "you and Alberta have come a very long way in the little time we've been together. You two communicate better than you know. Do you remember yesterday when we worked the train platform?"

I nodded. The stress of that session had been part of what had kept me up all night. We had gone to Peekskill train station to help prepare Alberta and me for navigating public transportation when we traveled.

"We worked up the stairs to the elevated platform," Graham said. "I had Alberta walk you to the end while she was between you and the train tracks. I told you to turn to walk back to the stairs. Now you were next to the drop-off where the trains run. Alberta was not in between you and the tracks. An express train came through while you were walking back. I could tell you were unnerved."

I nodded again. In fact, I had been terrified. I don't like walking on bridges or elevated platforms. That train station had had both of those things and a speeding train passing by besides.

By the time Alberta and I had walked past the express train and reached the stairs to head back down to street level, I felt disoriented. A breeze from another passing train wafted at my back. I felt air rising beneath the open platform. "Left to the stairs," I said to Alberta, hoping that Graham was close by in case I missed the step and fell. Alberta turned sharply to the left, tucking her rear behind my left leg as she always did. I let go of the harness handle and stopped to take a breath.

"When you reached the stairs," Graham said, "I knew you wanted my help, but I watched you instead of coming to your rescue. You let go of the harness and took a deep breath. Alberta gave a full body shake. She was saying to you, 'Come on, shake it off, we're fine.' Then she reached up to touch your left hand with her nose."

"I remember that!" I exclaimed. "When I felt her nose on my hand, I realized she was there for me. I relaxed and picked up the harness handle, ready to walk down the stairs."

Graham said, "Then you two walked down the stairs to street level in complete sync with one another. Alberta did what I call the 'coronation walk.' She timed her steps precisely so that she put her paw down when your foot touched the next step. You followed her lead. She focused on you. I've never seen a guide dog team perform better."

I wiped tears away and smiled. "So, do you think we'll be okay?"

"Yes," he said.

I decided to make a big ask. "Would you please go with us to the airport and

come to the gate? That way I'll know if I'm doing something that will makes airports or flying difficult for Alberta."
I waited while Graham thought about it. Apprentice instructors and kennel assistants were usually the ones to ferry clients back and forth to LaGuardia, not the assistant director of training.

"Yes," he said. "I can do that. But only if you stop worrying about 'breaking' this dog. You could never break Alberta. She's already a part of you."

Graham drove us to the airport, got a gate pass, and walked with us to the jetway. Graham reassured me that I was handling Alberta just right. Then he took a private moment to say goodbye to her. They knew each other better than I knew either of them. They trusted one another more deeply than I could then imagine. The envy I felt surprised me.

Graham gave Alberta his final words of encouragement just as pre-boarding was announced. I did not have words to express the gratitude that I felt for Graham and Guiding Eyes. I hugged him, said, "Thanks for everything." Then Alberta and I turned to hurry down the jetway.

On the plane, I mulled over how ten days had changed my life. Alberta communicated better with me than most humans I knew. I could trust the choices she made for both of us. The only person I felt I could depend on as much as Alberta in terms of my limited vision was Pam.

Enhanced by this dog, I felt more patient with my limitations than I had been when I flew to New York. Traveling back to Florida, I decided that I was done trying to make my visual limitations minimal or invisible. Now that I thought about it, Pam had counseled me years before to stop minimizing my needs.

As was often the case with my decision-making, when I finally reached an inevitable conclusion, I recognized that the choice I was making could have been made years before and prevented anguish or expense. Rather than beat myself up yet again for being a slow learner, I listed the requests I would make at work. I wanted text-to-speech for my computer and would not worry about what other people thought when my computer spoke to me. I would ask friends to tell me in clock-face, blind-friendly language where I could find my water glass in a restaurant. I no longer felt that I needed to handle anything alone. When I was uncertain, I could count on Alberta to push her nose into my hand or nudge my leg, reminding me that we were in this together.

CHAPTER 11

DENBERTA

Three years after we graduated from Guiding Eyes, Alberta and I had a partnership so seamless that friends called us "Denberta." They rarely noticed me giving Alberta a command or her giving me a cue. Our communication became so subtle that it felt subliminal to me. When asked for specifics, I had to think back to parse the scene that had raised the question.

"Alberta paused to let me know that we were at the edge of a down curb."

"She stepped up at the first stair, then waited until she felt me step up and get balanced. Then she took the next step up."

"When I told her our destination, she gave a tug on the harness to let me know that she understood and needed no further instruction."

"She pushed me to the right so that we walked around rather than into the group of students hanging out on the sidewalk."

"She nudged my leg with her nose when we got to the meeting to let me know that I owed her a treat because she got me there safely."

"She put her paw on my knee to let me know that she had to go outside to pee RIGHT NOW."

I respected Alberta, her abilities, and her constant creativity. Even when she convinced me to break the rules.

Our day started with claws clicking on the bedroom floor. A half hour before my alarm went off, Alberta danced in place next to the bed. She let out a loud Labrador yawn, which was sure to stir me from sleep. Then she stood silent. I had been sleeping on my right side, facing her. By then, I was more awake than asleep. She sat, her tail sweeping the wood floor in anticipation. I felt her breath, her eyes on me.

"Okay," I mumbled. "Come up."

Alberta leaped onto the bed, somehow levitating her fifty-two pounds so that she landed gently and precisely against the side of my body, creating a human-canine spoon. She curled her back into my belly and then stretched out to her full length. She tucked her head under my chin and flexed her back toes on my knee. She nosed my neck, slurped her tongue once across my chin. I curled my arm over her side. Alberta's tail wagged her greeting: "Good morning. I'm sure happy to be here with you." Her tail slowed, and her breathing deepened. Sleep reclaimed me. We snoozed together until it really was time to get up.

"Don't let your dog on the bed," had been the first Guiding Eyes rule that we'd broken, and that had happened gradually over time. When I brought Alberta home, I expected her to sleep in a crate. Before I went to Guiding Eyes, I set up a dog crate in the corner of my bedroom as the school instructions said. I furnished the crate with a cushioned mat covered with a blanket to match the quilt on my bed. I scattered toys inside the crate for my new guide dog to discover.

As I got ready for bed that first night home with Alberta, I told her to "kennel up." Alberta dutifully walked into the crate to let me know that she understood what I had asked her to do. Rather than flop down in the crate as she had at Guiding Eyes, Alberta turned and walked out. She lay down on a scatter rug next to the side of the bed. We considered each other for a minute. Well, if that was where she wanted to sleep, I decided it was okay with me. No one told me she was required to sleep in the crate as she had at school. Even there, I had left her crate door open at night.

At home, Alberta's crate sat unused night after night and through parties and thunderstorms and any other time Alberta might seek a "safe place." Generally, she wanted to be by my side. When I didn't want her underfoot as I was cooking or welcoming company, I said, "Alberta, please go into the bedroom and **stay** there." She did as I asked, often picking up her squeaky bear or a Nylabone from her toy basket on her way.

After a few months, I disassembled the crate and put it in the shed. When I worked in my home office, Alberta napped on the dog bed there. When I streamed movies in the TV room, she sprawled on the dog bed in that room. I bought her a third fluffy oversized dog bed to replace the crate at the foot of my bed. She was happy to sleep there rather than on the rug next to the bed. I was comfortable with the half-hour cuddle as part of the morning routine.

Most mornings, we walked the mile to my university office. Alberta briskly led me down the sidewalks, maneuvering us around any palm fronds or tree branches that leaned into our path. I learned not to carry dog treats in my pocket when we walked to school. If Alberta knew treats were handy, she nudged me every time she did something she determined treat-worthy, like avoiding obstacles or successfully taking us across a street. It would take too long for us to get to school if I stopped to immediately reward all her good choices. I decided that if I could wait until I got to the office for my second cup of coffee, she too could wait until then to get treats for her work in getting us there.

I was continually in awe at all that Alberta understood. Once she got to know our usual routes, she no longer needed to be given immediate directions like

"Turn right," or "Go forward." All I had to say was, "To the bank," or "Dean's office, please," or "We're going to the library." When she heard her favorite destination—"Let's go home!"—she picked up the pace and eagerly led me toward playtime and dinner.

One afternoon, as we were walking home from a day at the office, Alberta suddenly stopped mid-stride. She placed her foot down softly and stood still. I knew that my job was first and foremost to do what Alberta was telling me to do: wait.

Then I needed to puzzle out why Alberta was insisting that we not move. We were on the sidewalk, so there was no car traffic to worry about. I heard nothing to indicate a moving bike or a runner.

If there had been a low-hanging branch in our way, Alberta would have detoured us off the sidewalk, onto the grass, and then back.

If there had been a larger obstacle, she would have walked into the street and then curved back to the sidewalk, as she had the morning after a hurricane, when the walk to school had been littered with tree branches, fronds, and other debris. My residual vision would have allowed me to see enough to know if something big was blocking our progress even if I couldn't identify the object. The only thing I could make out was a handful of twigs on the sidewalk. Alberta easily could have woven us through that tree litter.

"Hup up, go forward" I said to Alberta, urging her to get moving. She huffed, puffed, and snorted. She danced in place. She refused to walk forward.

Then a twig on the sidewalk began to move. It was a foot-long black snake. It calmly slithered into the shrubs to our left. We waited at a respectful distance to make sure the snake was safely out of the way. Then we waited a little longer for my heart to stop pounding. "Good dog," I told Alberta, stroking her ear. She was ready to continue walking home.

"How did you figure that out?" I asked. I understood why Alberta had stopped instead of detouring out to the road. The snake had taken up too much territory for Alberta to feel safe going around it on either side. I wondered, but never figured out, why Alberta had decided to stop for a snake when she didn't stop for dogs, cats, squirrels, or birds. Snake training had not been part of the Guiding Eyes curriculum.

Then there was the afternoon we got caught in a brief but intense tropical storm. We had just finished an errand in town and were walking back to my office at the university. In seconds, a slight mist and breeze turned into a torrent of rain and wind, soaking my hair and clothes. "This is why we keep towels at the office," I told Alberta as we walked on. We had only another block to go.

At the intersection just a stone's throw from my office, Alberta refused to cross the street in front of us. At the curb,

I said, "Go forward." Instead, she pivoted to the left, stopped and then refused to move forward in the new direction. I could hear the water rushing wide, deep, and fast through the storm gutters on both streets. Alberta's message was clear: we can't cross safely through the torrents of water running down the streets.

Rain ran down my head and back as I pondered what to do. Alberta abruptly made a U-turn and led me back in the direction from which we had come. Mid-block, she veered to the left, guiding me under the roof of a parking garage that I hadn't known existed.

Once we were under the roof, Alberta turned to face the sidewalk, flopped into a soggy down position and sighed. She had decided that we would wait out the storm right here. Five minutes later, the sun came out. Steam began to rise from the wet pavement. Alberta stood up and shook the rain from her coat. The torrents in the storm gutters were now just a trickle. She wagged her tail as she led me across the street to my office.

When Alberta deviated from what I asked or made a detour on a regular route, I was always curious about what she had noticed that I hadn't. If I couldn't figure it out, I tried to find a passerby who could tell me what was going on. There was always something. Construction that had closed the sidewalk ahead. A truck being unloaded that would have blocked our progress down the block. A window washer's scaffolding taking up space on the sidewalk where we would walk.

Alberta liked her time off harness and off leash. In the late afternoons, we often heeled off leash across the cul-de-sac from my home to the waterfront park. There she could play with other dogs, explore the half-mile beach, or take a swim in the bay. Ever aware of her purpose in life, Alberta devised a way to guide me safely from our house to the park even though she was out of her harness. As we walked out of our front yard, she stayed at my left side, her head raised so that I could reach down and feel which way her nose was pointing. My fingers grazed her head until we had safely crossed the street. Then I said, "Free dog," which told her it was okay to leave my side.

When I carried my paddleboard across the street, which took two hands, she nosed my leg to let me know that she was right there next to me. As soon as her feet touched the water, she was happy to relinquish her responsibility. She enjoyed swimming, and she liked riding on the paddleboard even more. It was not unusual for a curious dolphin to swim by, looking up quizzically at the dog riding on the front of the board. I could paddleboard in the small cove in front of my house without fear of getting lost. A tall wall of mangroves marked the outer edge of the area where we played.

I found a new activity that we could enjoy together, separate from our work. We started taking Wednesday night classes at the Dog Training Club of St. Petersburg in a dog sport called rally. In rally, dogs and handlers navigate a course that includes a dozen or more separate activities to be performed in a forty-by-fifty-foot ring. The ring has numbered signs at floor level, each with words and symbols describing the exercise for dog and handler to complete. The sign may instruct the handler to have the dog sit, down, stay, heel, turn in a circle, or jump over a low hurdle while the handler passes by. Rally requires dogs to respond quickly to what is being asked of them, and handlers are encouraged to praise their dogs as well as give direction. When I'd had more substantial vision, I had trained a dog for the beginning level rally competitions, so I knew how the sport worked.

By the time Alberta and I started rally class, I no longer had enough vision to find the 8½″ x 11″ laminated signs in the ring or see them clearly enough to understand the instruction. Without assistance, I would trip over the signs, safety cones, jumps, and fences.

Jan Erickson, who also trained her dog in rally and taught classes at the club, volunteered to serve as my sighted guide. Jan had years of experience showing dogs and teaching classes. Helping guide Alberta and me in rally was a new challenge for her.

The novice-level exercises were easy for Alberta. She already knew most of them from her Guiding Eyes training and our own daily obedience work. "Right turn." "Call dog front. Finish right." "Heel." "Fast." "Figure eight." Jan walked on my right side, calling out the directions on each sign. On my left, Alberta walked off harness on a loose leash.

The first week, Alberta didn't understand that rally was not a route with a particular destination. Alberta seemed baffled as to why I was asking her to do these silly things, like suddenly sit or walk around in a circle. As she knew her job was to weigh the wisdom of my requests, she hesitated when I gave her a command. Jan and I could not explain to Alberta that she was not expected to guide. We encouraged her to play along with us, praising her for doing as I asked.

In our second week, Alberta got it. She suddenly understood that the rally ring was a special place designed for her enjoyment. Alberta saw that when I felt lost, I reached for Jan's shoulder. It finally made sense to Alberta. In rally, Jan was in charge. Alberta was free to play.

Alberta put her own twist on our structured playtime. When Jan gave us the command, "Fast," Alberta stag-leaped. When I asked her to sit at my left side, she spun in the air, landing next to me. I described Wednesday evening as Alberta's bowling night—her chance to hang out with dog friends between opportunities to show off during her individual minute-long sessions in the ring.

Jan convinced me that Alberta and I should enter rally competitions sponsored by the American Kennel Club (AKC). After a call to the AKC, I got a letter of accommodations allowing me to have Jan accompany me in the ring to read the signs and provide needed direction. If I wasn't sure of Alberta's position, I could put my left hand down and ask the dog to touch.

Before each competition, Jan and I walked the course with the other competitors to learn the order of exercises that the judge had laid out. That's when Jan planned her strategy of how to best guide Alberta and me. She walked in front of me, at my side, behind me, or occasionally, several feet away. Jan choreographed how our team of three moved together so that she didn't block the judge's view as Alberta and I moved smoothly through the numbered exercises.

When it was time for Alberta and me to take our turn in the ring, the other handlers gathered, hushed, and watched. Most had never seen the dance of visually impaired handler, dog, and sighted guide. When Alberta heard the judge say, "Exercise finished," she knew that we had completed the routine. She leaped in front of me and sat as I requested. Her audience clapped. Alberta's tail never stopped wagging. We had found her sport.

Ribbons piled up in a bowl on my office desk, and new toys filled Alberta's toy basket as we consistently placed first, second, or third. Soon, we were only a show away from completing AKC's top title, Rally Advanced Excellent.

The University of South Florida, St. Petersburg, is a compact campus of fifty-two acres that curls around Bayboro Harbor. With only four thousand students and fewer than five hundred full-time faculty and staff members, it wasn't long before more people on campus knew Alberta's name than mine. They learned through my continual gentle reminders not to distract Alberta by calling her name and admired her from a distance. My school turned out to be the ideal place for Alberta to become the poster girl for guide dogs. Literally.

When the campus's fiftieth anniversary approached in 2015, Sophia Wisniewska, the university chancellor, brokered a deal with 3 Daughters Brewery to whip up a special batch of Bayboro Blonde Ale for the festivities. She and Jessica Blais, the university's vice president of communications and marketing, chose Alberta as the Bayboro

Blonde who would appear on the beer labels and posters celebrating the event.

The artist sketched Bayboro Harbor in the background. Alberta sat large in the foreground, wearing only a smile and a collar from which a fiftieth-anniversary tag dangled. No guide dog harness. We didn't want anyone to think that she was drinking on the job.

My students loved watching Alberta work. They asked questions about how she had learned her skills. I told them that once Alberta understood that she would be praised for thinking critically and creatively, she continued learning on her own. Since I praised my students for the same thing, they decided Alberta had made me a better teacher.

One day, while I was lecturing and writing on the white board, I dropped the eraser I had been holding in my left hand. I continued to teach, deciding that I could find the eraser later. Alberta had other ideas. She got up from where she had been resting under the table, picked up the eraser, and then nudged my hand with it. After I took it from her, she quietly returned to her spot—with no direction, praise, or treat. The students and I both admired the consistent attention my four-legged assistant provided.

When we were halfway through our three-hour seminar and it was time for our break, Alberta began to fidget under the table to let me know. I didn't need to check my watch to know that Alberta's time sense was right. During the break, I took off Alberta's harness, and she was free to wander among the students, accepting petting and praise. The students asked me questions to help them sort out how and why Alberta acted so differently from the pet dogs they had left at home when they came to campus. The students' eagerness to understand the special training that guide dogs received led me to ask them if they thought students might be interested in forming a club to do puppy sitting for guide dogs in training. They eagerly said yes.

While puppy raisers provide stable homes for potential guide dogs in their first year or so, a college campus offers a unique setting for socializing the puppies. The people on campus range in age, dress differently from one another, and navigate campus on foot, on bicycle, on skateboard, or by wheelchair. Students or faculty are as likely to cluster in impromptu meetings on the sidewalk as they are to hurry off to a class. Dining halls and residential halls are hubs of noises and enticing smells—all things that guide dog puppies must learn to ignore. The library and classrooms provide quiet settings in which the pups can learn to lie unobtrusively under a desk or seminar table while their person is busy.

Southeastern Guide Dogs, a guide dog school only thirty miles from the St. Petersburg campus where I taught, was the obvious nexus for the campus puppy sitting club. With the help of a Southeastern board member, student leaders got the program started. When local puppy raisers had doctor's appointments, jury duty, or other obligations that kept them busy for longer than is good to leave a puppy in a crate, the student club was there to help.

Puppy raisers dropped off their charges at an easy to park spot on campus with water bowl, food, toys, and poop bags. Each puppy was assigned to a team of two students who decided the visiting puppy's schedule together. Some of the pups were old enough to go to class with students and rest quietly for the length of a class. If the puppy was too young or rambunctious, one student took the pup to play on the lawn or in a dorm room while the other student went to class. The puppies got practice learning to settle quietly in the library while their sitters studied or completed assignments. They learned to ignore other people their sitters might encounter. The puppies left campus more confident from their experience. Students were eager for more.

The next step was obvious, even to the dean of students. I approached him cautiously to ask if we could experiment by having a few carefully chosen students raise guide dog puppies in one of the residence halls. He enthusiastically approved, allocating students living space that would be most accommodating.

The Puppy Love Living Learning Community opened at the start of the 2016 fall semester with student puppy raising volunteers assigned to live in four-person suites on the first floor of one of the residence halls. The assigned hall had a door at the end that opened to a grassy area perfect for housebreaking the youngsters. While each puppy had a primary raiser who took the puppy home on school breaks, all suitemates pitched in to take care of the pup on campus.

Having the "Puppy Suites" at one end of the building made it less likely that a whimpering or barking puppy would disturb other students—and less likely that a student with allergies would be inconvenienced by the dog's presence. Of the twelve living learning communities on campus, Puppy Love was the first to fill.

Alberta led me briskly through the terminal at Tampa International Airport as I searched for our gate. The TSA agent had said, "Turn right after you pass the food court." When I smelled hot dogs and too-sweet cinnamon buns, I directed Alberta, "Right, right."

Alberta gave a brief tug on the harness handle, letting me know that she had heard my direction. She slowed as she watched for an upcoming intersection. She threaded us between a rolling suitcase and a wandering toddler, then turned right. "Good girl," I breathed.

"Find the counter," I said next, sweeping my gaze to search for a large light-colored rectangle in the kaleidoscope of color and movement before me. Now Alberta's tug on the harness was intended to keep me moving. She knew this airport and could find the counter at the gate without my help. I relaxed and followed her lead, ready to check in with the agent for our pre-board.

A deep-throated growl lurched me to a stop. Before I knew what was happening, Alberta leaped diagonally in front of me, yanking me to my right, away from the blur of black fur that was snarling and lunging at us from the left.

To be sure that we were safe, I coaxed Alberta a few more feet to the right. Then I leaned down, cupped her head in my hands, and stroked her ears to calm both of us. I thanked her for her quick action. I took a deep breath. Shaking with rage, I turned toward the person who was restraining the growling dog. "That dog is a threat to public safety!" I thundered in anger and fear, hoping to get the attention of everyone around us. Regardless of what kind of assistance animal the owner claimed the dog to be, it had tried to attack Alberta and me. It was a threat to public safety and did not belong in an airport.

Calmer now, Alberta and I walked to the counter. The gate agent said she had seen what happened. "You're at the right gate," she said, "and don't worry. That dog's not on your flight." I told her that I was grateful that the aggressive dog was not on my flight, but I asked her to call security. That dog should not be allowed to board any airplane. The agent demurred. "The airport is worried about getting sued if we question anyone's disability," she said. It was time for me to pre-board. I chose not to fight that battle this time.

In the years since Oriel accompanied me on her first flight in 2000 and Alberta saved us from the vicious dog in 2016, no-pet zones had changed from an occasional service dog assisting a person with an obvious disability to a kennel full of competing interests, including pet dogs not trained to do anything that accompanied people who didn't have disabilities. Gate agents allowed passengers to board with animals plucked from a seemingly limitless menagerie, including a duck in diapers and a tarantula in hand.

The onslaught of inappropriate animals made gate agents and bystanders suspicious of Alberta. Instead of the easy acceptance that I had grown used to while traveling with Oriel and even Wylie, I was repeatedly asked if Alberta was a **real** guide dog.

In the US, people accompanied by dogs in no-pet zones are not required to carry proof of disability. They are not required to carry proof that the dog is disease-free or vaccinated. They are not required to carry proof that the dog has been tested for its ability to act appropriately in public settings. With no proof required beyond a person's claim of disability and the person's claim that their service animal can perform one or more assistive tasks, people have been allowed to fraudulently gain access with dogs that threaten public safety.

To protect the civil rights and privacy of people with disabilities, gate agents in airports and other no-pet areas were allowed by the Americans with Disabilities Act to ask only two questions: (1) Is the dog a service animal required because of a disability? (2) What task or work has the dog been trained to perform? These questions allow anyone willing to lie to pass off their pet as a service dog. Ironically, the questions violate the privacy of people with disabilities while failing to protect the public. When I respond to these questions by saying that my dog leads me around obstacles that

I cannot see, I have been compelled to self-identify as blind.

After Alberta and I were threatened by the snarling dog at the airport, I decided that I should use a polite form of activism to address the problem. When I am aware of other dogs near me in no-pet zones, I strike up a conversation with the dog's handler and ask what tasks or work the dog does for them. Usually, the person ignores me and walks away. Sometimes, the person I ask admits that their dog is not a service dog. I remind them politely that we are in a no-pet zone.

Along with staying alert for the possibility of an attack from an inappropriate dog, Alberta and I developed our own air travel rituals for our frequent travel. With the help of a Guiding Eyes follow-up home trainer, I taught Alberta my routine at Tampa International Airport. First, we found the Delta ticket counter. I checked my luggage. Then up two floors on the escalator to the concourse where the Delta gates could be found.

When we got off the escalator and I said, "Alberta, please find the E gates," passersby were impressed to see her turn precisely in the right direction. But since we only ever flew Delta Air Lines, Alberta was showing off her excellent memory, not her reading skills.

At the security check, Alberta led me to the counter near the walk-through metal detector. She pointed up with her nose to the X-ray screening belt where I needed to place my backpack. Then she pivoted us ninety degrees, walked a few steps, and stopped at the edge of the metal detector.

"Hi," I said to the TSA agent who I knew was standing nearby. "I will tell my dog to stay. I'll walk through the detector on my own. When you tell me you're ready, I will call my dog. When she walks through, the metal on her guide harness will set off the detector. Someone will need to pat down the dog." Then I smiled. "That's the dog's favorite part." The TSA agents seemed to appreciate my explanation of the process that worked for Alberta and me and my reassurance that Alberta would respond appropriately to their security check.

After the metal detector and pat-down, Alberta and I turned back to the belt on which people's belongings had ridden through the X-ray machine. "Find mine," I said. She did so, putting her front paws on the belt in front of the bin that held my backpack.

A quick stop at the dog relief area in the terminal and we were off to find our gate.

I reserved the bulkhead window seat to give Alberta and me the most space. I used the few extra minutes that came with pre-boarding to remove Alberta's harness and then buckle a vest over her shoulders that said GUIDE DOG. The vest had identification in a pocket and was more comfortable than her wearing the harness. Generally, the people assigned to sit next to me were okay with the dog at my feet. "This is my guide dog," I said when I heard them settle in the aisle seat next to me. "If she gets in your way, let me know, and I'll slide her back against the window." Alberta never got in the way, but my spiel reassured business travelers that they wouldn't be brushing dog hair off those expensive trousers.

I held a crispy dog treat until the plane accelerated for takeoff, then handed it to Alberta. Crunching the biscuit eased any ear pain caused by air pressure change in the cabin and gave her a predictable high-value reward for the good work she'd done. Lulled by the motion and the drone of airplane engines, Alberta dozed at my feet for the duration of the flight.

Outbound, we often connected with another flight at one of Delta's hubs—Atlanta, Minneapolis, Detroit, or Salt Lake

City. When I got off the plane, I needed to take Alberta to the dog relief area and then proceed to our next gate. I followed the "meet and greet" Delta employee I had requested. Alberta had no problem using the dog relief areas within the terminals, although the facilities differed wildly. In some airports, they were well lit and ventilated, featuring Astroturf, concrete, sinks for washing human hands, and hoses with sprayer wands to clean up after the dog. A few were converted closets, containing nothing but a pee pad on the floor with maybe some replacements stacked nearby. Regardless, Alberta seemed to shrug and get down to business, as we all do when the only choice is a porta-potty.

When we landed at our destination and the cabin door was opened, Alberta wagged her tail with happy curiosity, her nose high in the air to catch familiar or unusual scents. Once off the jetway and in the gate area, I said to Alberta, "Let's find baggage claim." Alberta used her canine scenting skills to find it, drawing on abilities that we people have no way of understanding. If we were in a large airport that was unfamiliar to us, I asked the gate agent for directions to baggage claim so that I had some sense of where we were heading, but I let Alberta choose the route. I no longer had to follow a blurred fellow passenger, hoping they would lead me to the right carousel.

When we arrived at the carousel, I asked Alberta to find the suitcase. If she seemed uncertain, I knew that the suitcase had not arrived. Eventually, Alberta sat by the side of the moving belt, sniffing the air with eager anticipation. As our suitcase came within grabbing distance, Alberta stood and nosed forward, leaning in to point her snout at my suitcase. Even if other pieces of luggage were the same size, color, or shape, only one carried the smell of her dog food, treats, toys, and my clothes. As

I reached, she backed up so I could lift the suitcase off the belt without hitting her. The bright yellow luggage strap confirmed for me that Alberta had gotten it right. She always did.

Alberta was more comfortable helping me out in unfamiliar airports than any human companion with whom I had traveled.

One of the joys of being a Guiding Eyes graduate is participating in the grads-only online discussion group. We talk about dog food recalls. We talk about health and training issues. We talk about the rude sighted people we've encountered. When someone says their dog is retiring, we empathize with their sense of loss and grief. When Guiding Eyes matches the grad with a new guide dog, we offer our congratulations to the team. We share the wish that Guiding Eyes could "brain dump" the information learned by one guide dog into the next. After years of working with one partner, it's daunting to think about how to connect with a new young dog.

We delight in how our dogs are similar but so very different. We ask each other silly questions. One day a graduate asked the group: If your dog was a punctuation mark, which one would they be?

One grad said that her dog would be an exclamation mark. Eager to work! Eager to play! Eager to see their favorite people!

Another pegged her dog as a question mark. "She's always asking me, 'Can we go outside?' 'Will you play with me?' 'Is it time to go home?' When we go somewhere in a car, she sniffs the air before getting out, asking, 'Now where are we?'"

A deafblind graduate said that her dog was both a question and exclamation mark. "My dog is curious and insistent, trying to solve the puzzle of what I'm asking her to do. If I don't communicate clearly enough for her, she noses me to say, 'Ask again.' Then she's excited when she gets it right."

Another dog, Regal, was dubbed an asterisk, "because she's a star."

Within seconds of reading the question, I knew my answer: Alberta was a comma. She created space between me and any obstacles in my life, keeping me safe in her clause.

CHAPTER 12

LETTING GO

Some vacations are better without dogs. Even if the dog is Alberta.

In the early spring of 2016, I eagerly accepted Pam's invitation to spend a week with her at another friend's beachfront condo in Kauai. Lying on the beach, playing in the waves, and snorkeling sounded like heaven to me. But I knew such a trip would be hell for Alberta.

It wasn't the travel. With her rabies vaccination, health certificate, microchip, and an additional titer test to confirm that she didn't have rabies, I could have taken Alberta with me to Hawaii without her being quarantined. The problem was that Alberta's idea of fun at the beach wouldn't work for the state of Hawaii or for the ultraclean, ultramodern high-rise condo where Pam and I would stay.

When Alberta and I go to the local dog beach on the Gulf of Mexico, here's how it goes: Alberta runs in the waves as they crash on the shore for a half hour or so. If I go into the water, she swims in circles around me. Then she wanders to the beach and rolls in the sand, rubbing it thoroughly into her coat and skin. Then she is done, ready to go home. I rinse her off at the dog shower and towel her off before we get in my friend's car. I spread the towel on the floor of the car so that she doesn't get it too sandy. Once home, she drinks a gallon of water, begs me to feed her because swimming makes her hungry, shakes more sand and water out of her coat, and flops down on the cool tile, still panting from heat and exertion. (Unless she has consumed too much salt water. Then she urgently needs to go outside first because she has diarrhea.) Then, she sleeps for a couple of hours.

Sand seeps from her body during her nap, leaving a perfect silhouette on the floor when she rises. None of this would go well with the interior design of the offered condo. As the condo had a "no pets" rule, I could not leave her alone there. Taking her out to relieve herself would require me to get dressed, ride the elevator down five floors, and find a spot away from the condo entrance for Alberta to pee and poop.

On the beach, Alberta would also not be legally allowed to get off harness to frolic in the waves or play in the sand. If I walked her into the water on harness, that would be work, not play, for her, and the salt water would rust the harness's metal buckles. Alberta would not be happy lying next to me in harness on the beach while I baked in the sun and listened to the waves crashing.

Alberta and I were a perfect guide dog team. I was happy to care for her needs in return for all that she did to keep me safe. But right now, I was ready for time away from all my responsibilities, even Alberta. I looked forward to late nights drinking wine and playing Scrabble. I wanted to sleep in and enjoy a cup of coffee in the morning before doing anything else. I needed a break.

I also had a solution for Alberta's care. I had built new friendships in the Southeastern Guide Dogs community. Kathy Saunders, the Southeastern board member who had helped me create the Puppy Love Living Learning Community, had become a friend. She often came to speak at my freshman seminar on canine-human relations, discussing real-world examples from her years of raising guide dog puppies and training other puppy raisers. Kathy had introduced me to the development officer at Southeastern, Larissa Daigle, who had offered to dog-sit for Alberta when needed. Alberta, as a dog trained by a guide dog school, could accompany

Larissa to work. I knew that Alberta would have a good week without me.

A few weeks before the trip, Kathy drove Alberta and me for a visit to Southeastern so that the dog's first exposure to the school would be with me. To my surprise, from the moment she stepped out of the car, Alberta recognized Southeastern as a guide dog school. As I buckled her into her harness, she sniffed the air and wagged her tail eagerly. Through the harness handle, I recognized the quiver of anticipation I had felt from her the first time we'd worked together. She was restraining herself. She was working hard to behave perfectly. The ease that we had developed through our familiarity with working together was gone.

When I said, "Forward to the door, please," she led me briskly to the administration building door, then stopped, pointing with her nose to the door handle. I thanked her and pushed open the door. Once we entered the lobby, I stopped. Alberta stood at my side, shoulder precisely six inches in front of my knee, watching, wagging, but not moving an inch. She could have been modeling for a guide dog ad. Kathy followed us from behind and noticed Alberta's spruced up guide dog behavior.

Kathy chatted with the receptionist, who buzzed us in through yet another door. "Graham would be proud," I said to Kathy. "Alberta's showing off how she can be the perfect guide dog." I didn't know how Alberta had figured out that this was a guide dog school. Do guide dog schools have a signature smell? I had been appointed to the Guiding Eyes Graduate Council a year after I brought Alberta home. I recognized Alberta's "I'm at guide dog school" behavior from our twice-a-year trips back to Guiding Eyes for Graduate Council meetings.

When we entered Larissa's office, Alberta stood still while I removed her harness. She waited for the release words, "Free dog," before she began greeting the people and dogs in the room. She greeted Larissa first, whom she knew, and then politely stopped in front of each of the two other people there, allowing them to pet her. She touched noses with the two dogs in the room and inspected their toys. Finally, Alberta decided that she was off duty and could really enjoy herself. She danced around the room with a rope toy dangling from her mouth, asking, "Does anyone want to play tug?"

Larissa showed us to the dog paddock where Alberta would join the employees' dogs at lunchtime to run and to play with one another. Alberta and I had already visited Larissa at her home and seen the backyard saltwater pool where Alberta could enjoy supervised swims in the evening after they returned home from work.

Larissa and Alberta spent a day and a night together to make sure that they were both happy with the arrangement. When that went well, we sealed the deal. Alberta seemed happy to be back at Larissa's house when my assistant, Chaz, and I dropped her off on our way to the Tampa airport so that I could catch my flights to Hawaii. I left unworried and eager for my vacation.

When I flew home, Chaz picked me up at the airport and drove to Larissa's house. I couldn't wait to get my hands on Alberta. I'd had a wonderful time, but a week was a long time to go without touching my dog. When I sat on the floor, Alberta circled in my crossed legs and opened arms just as she had the morning we'd first met at Guiding Eyes. She told me about her week in grunts and yips. Larissa interpreted. In between Alberta's quick kisses and enthusiastic body wiggles, I learned that she'd liked playing with the employees' dogs, all of whom were retired guide dogs. Larissa said that the dogs played complex games of keep-away, pretending to run in one direction before heading in another. They had made up another game in which they hid toys from one another.

Throughout the week, staff members had come by Larissa's office to admire Guiding Eyes Alberta and comment on how much she looked like a Southeastern guide dog. The two schools had exchanged breeders and training strategies for many years, so it was no surprise that Alberta resembled a Southeastern guide.

Alberta had loved her evening swims, whether she was alone or with people. I wasn't surprised to hear that Alberta had always waited obediently at the side of the pool for Larissa to say, "Okay, you can swim," before jumping in.

I was proud of my girl. She had had a wonderful time. Larissa said that Alberta was welcome for a sleepover at any time.

"By the way," Larissa said, "Dr. Conrad, our veterinarian at Southeastern, said that she is a lovely dog in perfect weight and condition. He also said that you should have her right eye checked. He noticed some redness there. I also thought something looked a little off one time that I saw the sun shining into that eye."

The next day, I dutifully called Alberta's vet, Dave Landers, for an appointment. Dr. Landers was also vet to the St. Petersburg police department's K-9 squad. Alberta and I both knew that he understood working dogs. I wasn't worried. She could have been hit in the eye by a dog shaking a tug toy. Her eye could have gotten irritated from the saltwater pool. Larissa said that she had not seen Alberta rubbing the eye, so whatever it was wasn't causing her any discomfort.

"Conjunctivitis," Dr. Landers pronounced. No big deal. Two weeks of antibiotic eye drops and she would be fine. Her vision seemed perfectly normal.

"Good thing," I said with relief. "One of us needs to see well."

A week later, we were back at the vet's office for our follow-up appointment. Dr. Landers examined her eye again. He still saw nothing of concern, but he said that the eye was still red. He asked me about the dosage of drops I was giving her.

"I'm doing what you told me," I said, "two drops in the affected eye three times a day."

"You're probably running low on the drops," he said. "I'll be right back." He returned with a new bottle, removed the plastic packaging, and handed it to me. "Here," he said. "Why don't you give her a dose now?"

I took the bottle and paused. "Is this a test?" I asked.

"Yes," he said gently, "I guess it is. I'm not sure if you can tell whether you're getting the drops in her eye."

I held Alberta's head. After a week, she was used to the routine. She held still while I held her eye open with one hand and squeezed two drops into her eye with my other hand.

"Good," the vet said and waited.

I sighed. "Even if I got both drops in this time, I see your point," I said. "Because of my fragmented vision, I'm not seeing the whole process. If I'm looking to make sure that her eye is open, I can't see the tip of the dropper. If I'm looking at the dropper to count the drops, I can't see if her eye is open."

Sometimes I still felt ashamed of my visual impairment. This was one of those times. "I can't even take care of my own dog," I said.

"Don't you have an assistant, someone who drives you and helps you out as you need it?" Dr. Landers asked gently.

"I do."

"Well, your helper needs to be in on this one," he said.

I worked out Alberta's eyedrop schedule so that Chaz could help. I'd hired him as my assistant after Pam had moved, when I was looking for someone to help me run errands and provide a hand around the house. A mutual friend had recommended Chaz, who'd recently retired from his full-time job. Chaz was there for me, even when I didn't know I needed his help.

In our early days of working together, he mostly chauffeured me to the airport or around town. After a while, he decided that it was also his job to make sure that I looked good when I left the house. When he came to the house to pick me up, he came in, looked me up and down, and sometimes gave unsolicited advice. "Top, yes. Skirt, no. You need leggings with that top. And a necklace." I'd sigh and change clothes. Chaz could better judge how I would look to others than I could.

Now when he came to the house in the morning, we had a new routine.

Chaz called, "Ms. Alberta, come for your treatment, dear." She sat still at his feet. I held the dog's eye open. He got the drops in the eye. Mission accomplished.

A week later, we were back at Dr. Lander's office. Her eye was still red. He recommended that we see Dr. Miller, the local canine ophthalmologist. We made an appointment for the next day.

I called Graham and Guiding Eyes. I wanted them to know about Alberta, certain that they had dealt with this issue many times. The Guiding Eyes chief veterinarian, Dr. Sandler, repeated what Dr. Landers had said. It didn't sound serious. Dr. Sandler said that he would be available during Alberta's ophthalmologist appointment in case Dr. Miller wanted to consult with him.

Dr. Miller watched me remove Alberta's harness and take a deep breath. I told him that Dr. Sandler was on standby. I held back tears as I sat on the floor and wrapped my arms around

Alberta to hold her still. Dr. Miller rotated on his low rolling stool between a shelf of instruments and the dog. The doctor was silent as he examined her eyes except to identify the tools or test as he changed instruments. "I'm measuring pressure here." "This is a slit lamp." "This is a fundoscope to look at the interior lining." "This instrument shows me the inner eye."

Tears rolled down my cheeks as I felt Alberta wince at the bright light in her eyes. I had been through enough eye exams to know how uncomfortable that felt. Then he rolled back on his stool a few feet and looked at both of us. Alberta panted. I held my breath. "She's got a tumor in her right eye," Dr. Miller said with compassion. "I think it's a uveal melanoma."

"What does that mean?" I asked. "How do we fix it? Laser treatment? Drugs?"

"No," he said. "The dog needs her eye removed."

"Please call Dr. Sandler," I said. There had to be another answer.

"I'll be right back," he said. As he walked out, Chaz saw us from the waiting room through the open door. He walked in. "Good news?" he asked hopefully. "No," I said, wiping away tears. Chaz returned to the waiting room.

Dr. Miller walked back in, cell phone in hand. He closed the door, put the phone on speaker and introduced himself to Dr. Sandler. They spoke in medical shorthand. "Unusual" was one word I understood—hearing it surprised me. "Enucleation" was another word I recognized—that I didn't want to hear. I knew they were agreeing that Alberta's right eye should be removed. If the tumor was benign, Alberta could live a long and happy life with one eye. She could not, however, continue to be a guide dog.

Dr. Miller handed me the phone. I felt soothed by Dr. Sandler's voice.

Every Guiding Eyes graduate meets Dr. Sandler when they take their guide dog in for a final checkup before leaving the school. As I'd been serving on the Guiding Eyes Graduate Council, Alberta saw Dr. Sandler on our semiannual visits. Council members got the benefit of having Dr. Sandler examine our dogs when we met on campus.

"Deni," Dr. Sandler said, "you can work Alberta for another two or three months if you want. But keep in mind that this is a fast-growing tumor. She didn't have it when you were on the Guiding Eyes campus a few months ago. I would have seen it when I did my usual vet check of the Grad Council dogs. Over time, the tumor will obscure her vision. As the tumor grows, it will cause her pain."

"I won't do that to Alberta," I said. "The least I can do is to make sure she gets through this as easily and quickly as possible."

"I'd like her to come back to Guiding Eyes," Dr. Sandler said. "We'll have the surgery done by a veterinary eye surgeon at Cornell. That way we can monitor her recovery. We also need to run genetic tests. If Dr. Miller is right about the kind of tumor she has, this is only the second dog in the history of Guiding Eyes to have that problem."

Dr. Miller knew the surgeon at Cornell and agreed with the choice. Guiding Eyes offered to send a staff member to St. Petersburg to fetch Alberta, but I was not willing to end our relationship in that way. I would go to Guiding Eyes with her.

There was no way to explain to Alberta that our work together was ending. She rested her head on my knee as I cried and shared the news with family and friends. I grieved, wondering how I would ever get through this. In the week before she and I returned to Guiding Eyes, fifty of Alberta's friends joined me in giving her a retirement party. They wrote notes to Alberta and to me in a hand-bound book.

As I packed for our trip, I said to Alberta with as much enthusiasm as I could muster, "Hey, sweetheart, we're going to Guiding Eyes." Alberta wagged her tail at the familiar sound of the words, the suitcase that included a few of her toys, and in anticipation of another adventure together.

Our flight into White Plains was late. Graham was there to meet me, but his reception was cool. Distant.

"Are you okay?" I finally asked, while we waited for Alberta to find my suitcase on the baggage carousel. "No," he said in a tone that both Alberta and I knew meant: don't push.

"I'm angry. I'm frustrated," Graham said. "I'm like, 'Why?' This is so unfair. How did we go from conjunctivitis to Alberta needing her eye removed? Why is the universe doing this?" I realized that Graham was coping with his own grief.

"Oh," I said, relaxing my shoulders as Graham had taught me to do when I felt stressed. "I'm glad you're not mad at me."

"You?" he said, "I'm not mad at you. I feel like Guiding Eyes and I have let you down. You and Alberta were the perfect match. I know this is devastating for you."

Guiding Eyes instructors don't have much experience with what Graham called "catastrophic events." The school graduates approximately 140 guide dog teams each year. As the dogs usually work for seven or eight years, there are approximately one thousand Guiding Eyes teams actively working at a time. Only two or three handlers each year go through the trauma of having their guide dog relationship end abruptly due to accident or illness, or the dog being attacked by someone's inappropriate pet. Otherwise, the dog naturally slows down with age and becomes less enthusiastic about working. The handler reaches out to Guiding Eyes. Together, the handler and admissions staff plan to retire the dog in the months ahead, and to match and train the handler with a new young guide.

When Graham parked his vehicle at Guiding Eyes, I found my room—the same one I had been assigned three years before, when I first met Alberta and had been assigned for every Graduate Council meeting I attended. I remembered how startled and grateful I'd felt that first day, when Miranda had given me a verbal tour to help me know where to find everything.

I dropped my suitcase, fed Alberta, and parked her in her usual spot. Then I had her guide me to the coffee room, where Graham had told me that pizza and beer would be waiting. Graham was there when I arrived. Other staff members came in, put their hands on my shoulder, and said nothing. They greeted Alberta with enthusiastic petting, saying, "Welcome back!"

I nibbled at pizza, sipped a beer. I gave up trying to have a coherent conversation. As much as my friends at Guiding Eyes wanted to comfort me, and as much as I needed their comfort, we all knew that none of us had any words to make this better. I returned to my room and invited Alberta up on the bed to sleep the whole night with me. I held her tight and counted down the hours we had left together.

The next morning, Shane, who had been an apprentice when I met Alberta, knocked on the door. He had stayed on at Guiding Eyes as an instructor and had become my friend.

I hesitated at Shane's knock, reliving Graham's knock on the door three years prior when he'd brought Alberta to meet me. When Graham had opened the door and Alberta had walked into the room, I'd been filled with anticipation. This time I opened the door dreading the future for Alberta and for me. "Hi," Shane said sadly. He hugged me and whispered, "I'm sorry." Then Shane turned to the dog with enthusiasm and said, "Alberta, look at you!"

Alberta wagged her tail. She made eye contact with Shane, anticipating, as always, something good to come. I gave Alberta a tearful, final hug and attached her leash to her collar. Shane looped Alberta's harness over his arm, took the leash, and said, "Let's go, girl." Alberta walked away with Shane, tail wagging, head held high. Then they disappeared into the fog before me.

CHAPTER 13

CATCHING SIGHT

An hour after Shane and Alberta left, I extended my cane and walked down the hall to the van that would take me to the airport. I returned alone to Florida, nursing the most profound loss of my life. This was different from my husband leaving me. It was different from when my father had died. Alberta and I had bonded at such an integral level that losing her meant losing capabilities I had come to identify as my own.

Alberta had surgery the next day. To everyone's relief, the tumor was benign. She'd lost her right eye, but she wouldn't lose her life. "Eventually," Dr. Sandler said, "she'll be fine."

The day after the surgery, Michelle Brier, a Guiding Eyes staff member and friend, brought Alberta home with her for a few weeks of rehabilitation. Michelle let her sleep on the bed, despite her drippy eye, so that she didn't feel lonely. When Michelle called her name, Alberta moved her head to scan the scene in front of her, initially unable to find the source of the sound. Her depth perception was gone. Michelle kept her in a cone collar to protect her eye from being bumped—Alberta was running into obstacles on her right side, where she suddenly had no vision. I cried at the ironic cruelty of Alberta learning how to live with visual impairment.

Michelle sent me videos and text messages that helped me cope with the reality of Alberta's loss and recovery. Every evening, Michelle took Alberta for a supervised swim in her pool. Finally, I could smile: in Michelle's narrated video, Alberta ran confidently down the water-covered steps that led into the pool. If she lost her footing, the water was there to support her. She swam to the end of the pool, turned, and swam back. Now Alberta was behaving like the dog I knew.

My nephew, Kurt, surprised me by asking if he could adopt Alberta. He and his wife, Casey, had moved into my Montana house as Casey embarked on graduate work at the University of Montana. Alberta and I had spent summers, sabbaticals, and semester breaks there. She knew the house well. She had walked every inch of the thirty acres that surrounded the house, and many miles of the abutting wilderness. Kurt and Casey had a boxer-Lab mix named Mack whom Alberta adored. I could visit Alberta and spend time with my family. Updates on Alberta would be just a phone call or text away. I couldn't have asked for a better new family for Alberta, or an easier transition for me.

Keeping Alberta with me was not an option. Graham and I agreed that she would not be happy living with me as a pet. I would have a new guide dog as soon as Guiding Eyes found a suitable match. Graham said that Alberta would become jealous and depressed when she watched me walk out the door with another dog who was doing her old job. Alberta was only five years old. I owed her a retirement home that would let her build a new life. I loved her enough to let her go. Kurt and Casey loved me enough to give Alberta a new role in our family.

Michelle flew with Alberta from New York to Missoula, with Delta's approval for her to transport a retired guide dog in the cabin. They sat in the bulkhead seat that Alberta knew well. The pictures, videos, and stories that Kurt and Casey sent helped reassure me that I had made the right choice. Alberta was happy hiking, swimming, and relaxing in an environment she knew, with people and a dog that she loved.

My time with no dog moved slowly. Dr. Sandler said that I needed to give Alberta at least eight weeks to adjust to her new life before I went to visit. I counted down the weeks. The school couldn't tell me how long I would be waiting to meet my new guide. I knew the admissions committee would have a tough time coming up with a dog who could replace Alberta. That dog was one of a kind.

In mid-July, exactly eight weeks after Alberta's surgery, I flew to Montana, glad for the moment that I didn't yet have my new guide. I needed time alone with Alberta. I was eager to be with her and to support her new role in our family. She was no longer my guide dog; she was Kurt and Casey's pet.

Kurt met me at the airport. I felt disappointed that he hadn't brought Alberta along but said nothing. I silently vowed not to give him suggestions for her care or to monopolize Alberta's time and attention. I needed to find my new role in our reorganized family.

Alberta jumped and yipped when we walked in the house. I sat on the living room rug, and as she circled in my arms, I gave her the full body caress that had become our routine greeting after time apart. Alberta showed me her new toys. She raced and played in the meadow with Mack while I watched and praised her.

When Kurt told the dogs that it was bedtime, I said nothing, both pleased and sad that Alberta followed Kurt and Casey and Mack upstairs to the main bedroom suite instead of heading downstairs with me to the guest room. I ached for the old relationship that Alberta and I had had. I also wanted her to have no doubt about where she now belonged.

Kurt and Casey and I hiked with Mack and Alberta up our favorite hills, and we sunned ourselves on rocks by glacial streams. Alberta didn't complain when we went out to dinner and left her home with the other dog. I thought that it was a good sign that she no longer expected to go everywhere with me. Her adjustment was going well.

On the last day of my four-day visit, a neighbor called Kurt to tell him that the gate that separated our property from the Forest Service road had been left unlocked. "I'll go lock it," I said. I knew the way to that gate in my sleep. It was the start of any walk into the million-acre wilderness that lay west. Cross-country skiing through the gate to the Forest Service road had been my favorite New Year's Eve ritual.

"Come on, Alberta," I said. "Come for a walk with me." She eagerly followed me out of the house and planted herself on my left side. We walked down the driveway. On this familiar walk, there was no reason to have her on leash. The road was private. If a neighbor's car or

Forest Service vehicle drove up the dusty dirt road, I'd be able to hear it long in advance. For now, we were totally alone.

"Go play," I said, gesturing to the multiple acres of meadowland that surrounded us. "Free dog." Alberta ignored my suggestion. She seemed perfectly happy walking at my left side, her head positioned so that I could reach it with my hand. It wasn't until we turned left out of the driveway to head up the hill and Alberta tucked her butt behind my leg that I realized she was guiding me, off leash and off harness, as she had in the past.

As we walked up the dirt road to the Forest Service gate, Alberta stayed glued to my side. I tried to find words that she would understand. "Alberta," I said, "you can't be my guide dog anymore. You're retired now. Go play."

Alberta continued to walk next to me. I locked the gate, then turned to retrace our steps. I could tell that Alberta was getting tired from her effort to guide me. Without her right eye, she couldn't tell where I was without touching me. I talked to her and rested my hand on her head to help her stay oriented. When we turned right into the driveway, her lack of depth perception caused her to turn into my path and get tangled in my feet. I lost my balance. Alberta and I ended up sitting together in the grass next to the driveway. "You are such a funny girl," I said, hugging her so that she knew I was fine.

Regardless of my words and tone of voice, Alberta knew that there was nothing funny about what had just happened. She hadn't been able to see me. She'd tripped me and made me fall. She'd shown herself that she could no longer guide me.

I got up and continued walking back to the house. Alberta lagged behind, head and tail drooping as though she was worried that she might trip me again. When we got inside, Alberta went up the stairs to her bed in the main bedroom suite. After a few hours, she rejoined the family but didn't come to me for petting. I waited until everyone else had gone to bed to start packing my suitcase for my flight back to Florida in the morning. Kurt would drive me to the airport, leaving Alberta on the hill with Casey and Mack.

The morning was a rush of showers and coffee and goodbyes. Kurt opened the front door to carry my suitcase to the car. Alberta was out the door in an instant, hurling herself into the car the moment I opened the passenger side door. She curled up on the floor. "No, Alberta, you can't go with me," I said. "Come on, Alberta, get out of the car." She refused.

Kurt guided her out of the car. She immediately jumped back in, lying down determinedly in the passenger foot space where she had always traveled with me. "Come on, Berta," Kurt said with compassion. "You are staying here. It's all okay." Finally, Casey clipped a leash to

Alberta's collar and gently led her back to the house. Kurt and I drove away. I hadn't expected Alberta's meltdown, but I knew what I needed to say next. "It's better that I don't see Alberta for a while," I said tearfully. Kurt agreed. I was grateful that he'd let me figure out the obvious on my own.

By the time we reached the airport, Casey had texted Kurt a photo of Mack snuggling with Alberta, front leg extended over Alberta's chest. As the dogs had never before slept entwined, it was clear that Mack was comforting her.

Two weeks later, Graham called. The trainers had picked out my new dog, a female black Lab. The dog had completed advanced training. Because the fall semester at my university would be starting soon, I opted for home training rather than training on campus at Guiding Eyes. Graham explained that Jim Gardner, the longtime director of home training at Guiding Eyes, wouldn't be able to bring her to Florida until September. For the month of August, then, my new dog would live with Graham and his husband, David. Graham said he'd work the dog in harness every day to fine-tune her guiding skills and house manners. When Jim gave me the date for his trip to Florida, I blocked out my schedule to work with him for up to six hours each day, for as many as ten days. Jim would help the dog and me become a team. I couldn't have asked for a more experienced home training instructor. Jim had more than ten years' experience leading the Guiding Eyes home training team. He had never had a dog returned because of a bad match. In accordance with Guiding Eyes convention, I would not learn the dog's name until she arrived.

I talked to Graham about the new girl as often as he would take my calls, eager for anything that he could tell me. "Well," he said, "she has a sense of humor." Graham sent me a video of the new dog and his own dog, a retired black Lab guide named Nate, splashing together in the marshy inlet near his home. The new dog ran circles around Nate, reaching to mouth the scruff of his neck. She threw water and sand in the air as she enticed him to chase her, and she splashed water and sand at Graham. "She acts like a puppy," Graham said.

Another video showed the new girl in Graham's office at Guiding Eyes, trying to get Nate to play. She grabbed toys and threw them in the air. When a Nylabone hit Nate on the head, Graham said in his no-nonsense voice, "Calm down." The dog stopped in her tracks and tucked her tail. She didn't like to be reprimanded.

A photo from Graham showed the dog in regal recline, her front legs stretched out, her back legs tucked in. I magnified the picture as much as I could. In contrast to Alberta's compact body and small ballerina feet, this dog seemed to have soup plates for paws, on legs that looked too long for her small body.

"And you're sure this dog is perfect for me?" I asked. Alberta had been confident and happy. This dog seemed like an overly sensitive gazelle-like goofball. "Trust me," Graham said. "You'll love her. I have her guide me all over town," he said. "She's a joy in the house. She follows the rules and wants to get along. She doesn't like it when people raise their voices. She takes criticism personally."

"It sounds as though this new dog matches you perfectly," Pam observed wryly in one of our regular phone conversations.

"How's that?" I asked. "Long legs and big feet?" I guessed.

Yep," she said, "along with being too sensitive to criticism."

Finally, Jim arrived with the dog. I was ready. The house was clean, the crate once again set up at the end of my bed, the food and water dishes waiting to be filled. A basket overflowed with toys, ready for exploration. The doorbell rang. I opened the door. Jim said, "Hi. We came straight from the airport." The dog didn't greet me at all.

"Let's go in," Jim said. "Then I'll introduce you two." Jim walked from the entranceway into the living room and sat on a chair. I sat on a corner of the couch near him. The dog sat between us, back against Jim's leg in the "Close" position, her face turned up to look at his. I could tell that she was taller than Alberta and sleek as a seal. Her black coat glowed with health. I sat quietly, waiting for her to notice me.

After a moment of silence, Jim said, "Deni, this is Koala. Her birthday is September 20. She'll be two at the end of this month." Koala looked at Jim more intently when he said her name.

"Koala," I said. "What a good dog." I unfurled my left hand to reveal five high-value treats. Koala sniffed my hand and stood up. She looked at my face and gave a slight wag of her tail. She accepted the five treats in rapid succession, then returned to Jim and sat facing him.

"Hmm," I said, more amused than offended.

"This dog is sensitive," he said.

"And aloof," I said.

Over the next hour, Jim talked with me about Koala. I learned what she ate, how much, and at what times of day. Jim told me when to provide water and how to keep her weight at its current fifty-two pounds. He told me about her training, and his feeling from the first time he'd worked with her that she was a very nice dog. Focused and responsive. We walked out into the fenced backyard together for Koala to learn her new relief area, with me walking her on leash.

Satisfied with things so far, Jim handed me a ziplock bag of kibble, a Nylabone, a dog comb, and a leash. "I'll bring the harness with me tomorrow," he said. "You'll be ready to work at eight," he added as he left.

"Well, Koala," I said, "it's you and me." Koala looked out the glass front door and watched Jim's car drive away. "First," I said, "I bet you're hungry. Would you like some dinner?" Koala's ears perked up. She wagged her tail. We walked into the kitchen. The Guiding Eyes "First Actions Have Consequences" lecture was on my mind. I needed to ask her to do now what I'd always expect of her at mealtime.

"Here's your mat," I said, pointing to it. "You need to sit and stay there while I make your dinner." She sat on the mat and watched me. I mixed two cups of the kibble and a cup of water and put it down on the same rubberized place mat where Alberta had eaten her meals. "Okay," I said. "Free dog." Koala trotted over to the bowl, recognizing the smell of the food she had eaten at Guiding Eyes and at Graham's house. As it had been hours since she'd last been fed, I wasn't surprised when she wagged her tail and emptied the bowl.

"Now, Koala, let's go outside again. Do you want to go out? And get busy?" I snapped her leash onto the collar. She followed me into the large backyard. Koala led the way as we walked together around the yard. "Get busy," I said. She peed and then stood, watching me. I unhooked the leash to give her the freedom to explore the fenced-in yard on her own. Instead, Koala raced to the door. When I opened it, I wasn't surprised that she ran to the front of the house, looking for Jim. I followed her in.

"Koala, you're staying with me tonight," I said. "Let me show you around." She followed me to the basket in my dressing room full of soft squeaky playthings, balls, and chew toys. "Look at this," I said and showed her a ball that blinked bright colors when squeezed. I threw it into the hall for her to chase.

Koala watched it go and stood still. Next, I tried a flat furry squirrel with multiple squeakers. "Do you want to play tug?" I asked. She turned her head from me. I dropped the toy in the basket and asked her to follow me into the bedroom. Her crate sat with its door ajar, a soft cushion, and more dog toys inside. She looked at it and then at me but made no move to explore it.

"Okay, Koala," I said. "I'm going to give you some time to check this place out on your own. Come with me to the office so you'll know where to find me." She followed me back to my desk. I sat in my chair, asked her to sit, and scratched her ears. I handed her a Charlee Bear from the bowl of treats on my desk. "Okay, Koala," I said. "Free dog. You're on your own." I turned to the computer, letting her choose her next move.

"Interesting dog," I dictated in a text to Graham. "I think that Koala is a

German shepherd in Labrador clothing. She doesn't warm up to strangers."

"That's right," he texted back. "You have to earn her trust."

"I'll get back to you if she lets me get to know her better," I said.

I turned my attention to my students' essays. Koala left the carpeted office and padded across the wooden floor of the TV room. I heard her walk across the tile floor of the kitchen, undoubtedly heading back to the front of the house to watch for Jim's return. Then, silence.

Ten minutes later, Koala hadn't reappeared. I looked for her. I didn't call her. I wanted to see the space she'd chosen when left on her own. She was not at the front door, nor was she lounging on any of the dog beds scattered throughout the house. She was not in the crate. I stood in my bedroom, thinking about where to look next. I was running out of ideas.

I wondered if Koala could have silently opened the front door and left to look for Jim. Then I heard a sound in the bathroom. I opened the shower curtain in the walk-in shower stall to find Koala stretched out inside. She was resting on her left hip, back legs tucked under, front legs reaching out. Toes to tail, she filled the space. She wagged her tail. I stroked her head, gave her a treat, and returned to my computer.

I understood better now. Koala was not the extrovert that Alberta had been. Alberta had pranced, waiting for people to give her the praise she knew she deserved. Koala appreciated acknowledgment but looked for quiet private spaces to think about things.

I thought about the last few days from Koala's point of view. After a month of bonding with Graham, he had dropped her off at the Guiding Eyes kennel. Jim, whom she knew slightly, had worked her on harness to get to know her, but soon took her from the kennel to the airport for her first-ever airplane ride. When they'd reached the Tampa airport, Jim had brought her to my house to meet me, a stranger. After a little more than an hour and lots of encouragement for both of us, he'd driven away. Alberta had met me at Guiding Eyes, in the company of dogs and instructors she knew well. Koala hadn't had that luxury. We were unknown to one another, thrust together like partners in an arranged marriage.

I didn't know why Koala chose the walk-in shower over the dog crate as her private safe space, but I decided that I liked this reserved dog of mine. I could take a shower in the morning. Other than that, she could hang out in the shower as she desired.

A few minutes later, after I had returned to reviewing student essays, I felt Koala's cold nose nuzzle my leg. I stopped working and faced her. I scratched her ears and told her that we would be just fine together. I turned back to the computer. She groaned and stretched her front legs across my feet as I finished grading an essay. Then I turned my full attention to her. She let me run my hands through her soft, thick coat while she stared intently at my face. I took a deep breath, knowing that I needed to let our relationship grow on Koala's terms.

The next morning, Koala and I were at the door when Jim arrived. We walked outside. I had Koala on her leash. Jim handed me the harness and said, "Let's go."

I put Koala in harness. She stood still and steady. No anticipatory vibration—just calm energy. She knew what was expected of her. She knew what was expected of me. "Go out your gate, cross the street, and then turn right," Jim said. I smiled. Our first route would be the one that I'd told Jim was my favorite morning walk.

I hadn't walked the waterfront since I'd taken Alberta back to Guiding Eyes. But she and I had walked this mile many times—every morning that we hadn't needed to go into the office. Because there was no sidewalk on the water side of the street, we'd walked facing any oncoming traffic with the dog tight against the curb, a practice that Guiding Eyes called "shorelining."

There were few cars down this quiet street in the early morning. I knew that Koala and I would not encounter any obstacles aside from a handful of parked cars belonging to people walking the beach or kayaking in the cove. Waves lapped gently at the shore to my left. Seabirds announced their hopes for breakfast as they flew past. It was a good walk to start the day.

When I said, "Forward," Koala didn't surge ahead into the chest strap as Alberta had. She led me with a light touch. Alberta had taken two steps for each of mine as we walked down the street. Koala's long legs let her stretch out to match the reach of my legs with hers.

I saw a large dark object ahead of me that I could identify as a parked car. I followed Koala, waiting for her to stop so that I could tell her to "go around." Instead, she kept walking, detouring us around the car. I said, "Koala, wait," and turned to Jim.

"Should I have her rework going around the car?" I asked him.

"Why?" he asked.

"Koala didn't pause to tell me she was making a detour. That's what Alberta did."

"They're different dogs," Jim said. "If Koala veers off path and you don't know why, stop and consider what's going on. Ask her to rework it only when you're sure she did something wrong. Otherwise, follow your dog. She is efficient. You are safe."

Koala seemed to recognize from the start that I knew what to do at my end of the harness. When we turned at the end of the waterfront and walked the half mile back to the house, I crossed the street to follow the sidewalk that snaked along the yards of beachfront houses. Koala seamlessly swung me around palm fronds that protruded into the sidewalk. She stopped squarely at each street crossing so that I could listen for traffic before telling her to go forward. As we started walking the last block back to the house, Jim said, "Tell her 'Left, left' so she knows that it's time to look for your front gate."

I could already feel Koala pulling me gently to the left when I gave the command. She turned and stopped at the gate. After I unlatched it, Koala led me to the front door and used her nose to point to the door handle. I rested the harness handle on Koala's back and opened the door. Koala stayed still until I lifted the harness handle again. We walked inside together. Then I removed her harness and said, "Free dog."

When Jim left us that afternoon, Koala did not watch him drive away. After a drink of water, she headed to her private room—the shower stall. I headed to the computer to catch up on work. Soon Koala was there with me, nuzzling my leg. I stopped working to tell her what a wonderful girl she was, the best dog ever. I stopped and blinked back tears, realizing that the last time I'd said those words, I had been talking to Alberta. "How could two different dogs be so right for me?" I wondered.

As I worked at the computer, Koala snoozed on the dog bed behind my desk. After a while, she stretched out on the rug next to my chair and put her feet on mine. Alberta had also used this gesture to keep track of me while she'd slept through my many meetings at the university.

After a few minutes, though, I realized that Koala wasn't snoozing. She was trying to tell me something. When I didn't respond to her, she groaned and stretched her legs out more forcefully. I felt her toenails flex into my foot. I checked the time. It was 5 p.m. Dinnertime for the dog. Koala's training of me had begun.

The next day, we walked the mile from my home to my office with Jim trailing behind. "Koala, we're going to the office," I said when we left the house. The quicker that Koala could learn verbal cues like "to the office," the less specific navigation I would need to provide.

Jim watched us stop for streets, pause at alleys, and ignore driveways, aside from the one with the car pulling out. I didn't count palm frond detours with Koala; she smoothly walked me around them without bothering to notify me first. She had this.

Once in my campus building, she led me to the elevator when asked and showed me that she knew how to use her nose to point to the elevator button. She sat calmly at my side as we rode up one floor. All was fine until we approached the door that led into the department's office suite. As soon as we turned to face the door, Koala backed up a few feet.

"No, Koala, let's go forward," I said. "To the door, please." She stood her ground, even when I gave her a quick tug forward on the leash. I turned to Jim, who stood near watching us. "What am I missing?" I asked.

"What do you mean?" he asked.

"Why won't she go up to the door?"

Jim was quiet for a moment. "Is the door right- or left-hinged? Then he answered himself: "Left. Do you prefer the 'side method' or 'pivot' to go through a left-hinged door?"

"Excuse me?" I said. I had no idea what any of this meant.

Jim tried a different tactic. "How did you and Alberta work this door?"

"I have no idea," I admitted. It had been four months since I had walked through this door with Alberta at my side. Now I was stuck out in the hall with my guide dog and instructor because I couldn't remember the right way to go through the damn door. Koala stood patiently, her harness handle resting on her back. I felt ridiculous.

Jim tried to jog my memory. "If the hinge is on the right, then you are automatically between the dog and the door. You and your dog walk through together on harness. No problem. That's what you did when you opened the door to go inside at your house. As you first put her on harness in the front yard, it didn't occur to me that you might not know how to get out of the house with your dog on harness."

That makes two of us, I thought.

"You go through differently when the door's hinge is on the left," Jim said. "The handler must always stay between the door and the dog. That way, it is impossible to accidentally close your dog in the door."

"Really?" I said, honestly surprised. "I don't remember ever learning that. I don't think even sighted people know what side of the door to find the hinges. How am I supposed to know?"

Jim said patiently, "Koala has learned to back up when the door opens toward her, anticipating how you are going to ask her to move around you."

"How did she know that?" I pressed. He took a breath but remained patient. "She learned that when she was in advanced training," he said.

"Really?" I said again. **How is that possible?** I wondered. **Why didn't I know that?**

"Okay," I said, "so the hinges are on the left."

"Left-hinged door," Jim said, sounding pleased that I was learning the lesson. "First, praise your dog for letting you know that you two have approached a left-hinged door."

"Good dog, Koala," I said, but I was distracted by what Jim was teaching me.

"As you don't remember the two techniques for getting through the door that swings open toward you," Jim said, "let's see what Ms. Koala prefers. Tell Koala 'Side,' drop the harness handle, and transfer the leash from your left hand to your right hand behind your back. She'll walk around your back to be on your right side."

"Koala, side please," I said, and moved the leash as asked. She immediately crossed behind me to the right.

"Now open the door," Jim said, "and say, 'Let's go.' You walk in before your dog."

I pulled the door open toward me. The left side of my body was next to the door as it opened. Koala stayed on my right and walked just behind me into the department's reception area. I was between the hinges and the dog. "Tell her to heel," Jim said, "and she will return to your left side." I did as Jim asked, and Koala responded promptly.

"Okay," Jim said. "Let's go back out in the hall and try the other technique."

I said hello to the bewildered receptionist. "We'll be back," I said, and turned to walk out the door.

"Wait," Jim said. He prompted me: "Where are the hinges?"

I thought quickly. "The hinges are now on my right side. When the door opens, it will swing out, away from me. The door handle is on the left. When we walk through the opening, I'll be between the door and my dog."

"Good," Jim said. "Notice that Koala is not backing up." I noticed that both Jim and Koala thought they were being more patient than I deserved.

Back in the hall, we readied ourselves to enter the office again. Koala backed up and I said, "Good dog, Koala."

"This time," Jim said, "tell your dog to stay, then let go of the harness. Turn to face her while opening the door. Keep your body between the dog and the door. Hold the door open with your shoulder so the door won't close on your dog. Tell your dog, 'Let's go,' and she'll walk through the door in front of you. Once you're sure the whole dog is inside, you can follow and move into the heel position."

Jim watched Koala pass through the door with me following. "I prefer the pivot method for you two," he said. "Koala will feel safer if you give her the extra space to walk completely through the door before you enter." I agreed, wanting both of them to approve.

For the rest of the day, Jim looked for doors that Koala and I would walk through. I struggled each time to figure out where the hinges were and how we were supposed to maneuver, but Koala never failed to tell me with her behavior what I needed to do.

The next day was devoted to more doors, and to escalators. Then we spent a day taking on all the complications that the shopping mall could throw at us.

The day after that, we introduced Koala to the Tampa airport. After only three run-throughs, Koala was able to lead me without direction from the drop-off area at the curb to the Delta ticket counter where we scored gate passes, then to TSA, then the inside security dog relief area, the Delta Sky Club, and the gates. She understood how to retrace our steps from the gate area to baggage claim. We put the suitcase that we'd brought with us on the carousel belt and practiced having her find it.

As the home training continued, we walked predictable routes and found new challenges for Koala and me to figure out together. She and I gained confidence. I grew to admire Jim for his ability to know exactly what areas I felt vulnerable in and needed more practice. I knew we were coming to the end of the home training when Jim told me to walk to my office with Koala. He would meet us there. It felt luxurious to work my dog without being followed. I had obviously passed some important tests.

The walk itself was a test that I didn't expect. Rather than meet me at my campus office, Jim had planned a traffic check. Two-thirds of the way to the university, Koala and I walked across the start of an alley that was heavily lined with shrubs. Koala's view of the alley was blocked until we stepped into the intersection. Then Jim backed his vehicle out from where he had been waiting and watching for us, his car roaring its intention. Koala was unflappable. She calmly backed up, pushing on the harness so that I backed up too. Jim sped down the street toward campus. Another test passed.

When we got to campus, Jim congratulated Koala and me. He said we were done with our home training. He would be flying back to New York the next morning.

"Would you mind if Koala and I come with you to the airport?" I asked. "My assistant can pick us up to go home. Koala and I will travel at least once each month through that airport, following the same routine of checking in with Delta, going through TSA, and finding our gate. I want Koala to feel totally comfortable working there, and I don't want her to wonder what happened to you. If she sees you leave at the airport, she will get it that this is a place where people come and go." Jim agreed.

"You two make a nice team," Jim said as Koala and I left him at TSA.

"You made that happen," I said. Koala and I **were** a team—a different kind of team than Alberta and I had been. The two dogs pulled different parts of my personality into our working relationships.

Koala was more analytical than Alberta, and she encouraged me to be more mindful of our partnership too. Alberta had been a risk-taker, ready for any adventure, from riding up a mountain peak in a gondola to being the first guide dog in the park ranger's memory to lead a blind handler through the Lewis and Clark caverns, four hundred feet below the ground's surface.

Koala was confident, but she didn't rush into new situations. The first time that she and I walked through Detroit's massively busy airport to catch a connecting flight, I felt Koala drag slowly in her harness and then stop. I knew this was not what a guide dog was supposed to do, but I could tell that Koala needed to process. I dropped the harness handle and led Koala by the leash out of the busy walkway. We moved next to the wall.

I crouched down next to Koala to get a sense of what she was experiencing at her level. People walked back and forth in front of us, dragging suitcases and weaving around each other, not following any convention of passing on the left or right. Just beyond the walkers, people rode on a moving walkway. Beyond that, a train that connected the terminals screamed to a stop and disgorged passengers. The deboarding passengers weaved through those getting on the train. To our right, a bank of escalators ran between the main level and the mezzanine above.

"Oh, honey," I said, "everyone gets overwhelmed here." Together, we watched the chaos for another minute. "Okay, ready?" I asked. Koala shook off any stress she was feeling, and we were on our way. Now she was fine.

When Alberta and I had first come home after meeting at Guiding Eyes for the Blind, Alberta learned that when she was finished eating, her job was to pick up her bowl and then bring it to me so she could place it in my hands. Then I could wash the bowl.

I taught Koala the same routine, but she added her own twist. Rather than pick up her bowl immediately, as Alberta had, Koala left the bowl on the kitchen floor while she trotted around the house looking for me. Once she found me, she raced back to the kitchen and grabbed the bowl to bring it to me. She'd decided that it took less effort to find me first than carry the bowl around while she looked to see where I had gone.

Alberta had taken any treat offered and hadn't hesitated to nudge me for additional food rewards. When Koala wanted a treat, she didn't beg. Instead, she figured out a task to do that might be treat-worthy. She came up with a new job one month into our new life together, when we'd returned to the house in the evening from the university. As usual, I removed my shoes after stepping inside. I unbuckled Koala's leash and harness and hung them in the front closet.

Koala had an idea. She raced down the hall to the bedroom and quickly returned, carrying one of my house slippers that I always put on when I got home. "What a clever girl," I said. "Good job! But I need the other one." Koala thought about that briefly and then raced to the bedroom, returning with the second slipper. She had created for herself a new evening chore that earned her two treats, one for each slipper.

Another day, while I was working at the computer in my home office, Koala put a crumpled piece of paper in my hand that she had picked up from the floor. I had meant to throw it away earlier, but my toss had been poor, and the paper had not made it into the trash basket. Then she stretched herself under my desk, retrieved a pen, and put that in my hand too. Then she raced out of the office and returned with a sock that must have been lying near, rather than in, the laundry basket. She exchanged each found item for a treat.

When I got up and walked into the kitchen for a glass of water, I found, to my surprise, that Koala's toys—which had been scattered around the house earlier that day—were now all in the toy basket. She had put them away on her own, with no prompting from me. As I made my discovery, Koala moved to the side of her toy basket, wagging her tail exuberantly. She knew that she had done something terrific. I was impressed enough that, in addition to giving her several treats, I also mixed a half can of sardines into her kibble for dinner that night.

As I got to know Koala better, I realized that Alberta had had more modest expectations of me than this new dog did. When I talked to Graham on the phone, he reinforced my thought that Alberta had decided early that there was only so much that she could expect from me. I asked him why he hadn't taught Alberta and me how to go through doors on harness the way Jim had shown me with Koala. Graham sighed. "Deni," he said, "I taught you and Alberta how to walk through left- and right-hinged doors correctly, but you were overwhelmed. You took in as much as you could in the ten days we worked together. I knew that you would forget things, but I wasn't worried because you were with Alberta. When you got home, she did what she does best. She improvised.

"From the time Alberta was a puppy, she looked for new and different ways to accomplish goals. When she realized you weren't doing doors right, she figured out a way to help you both go through safely. She was so proficient at manipulating you, you still don't consciously know the process she created. Koala won't let you get away with that, will she?"

"Definitely not," I said. "Koala obeys the rules that Guiding Eyes taught her and expects the same of me." When I hung up the phone, Koala appeared at my side, wagging her tail and pushing her nose into my thigh.

"Do you want to go outside?" I asked. I stood to open the door to the backyard. She backed up a few steps then stood still, wagging her tail. I hadn't guessed right. "You had dinner hours ago, so I know you're not hungry." She stood still and wagged. "Try again," she seemed to say.

"Show me," I said. Koala raced out of the office. I followed her to the laundry room. Her dog blanket was in the dryer. Koala was not allowed on the people bed without the dog blanket on top. She wanted to get on the bed now but needed her blanket first. She wagged enthusiastically when I pulled the warm blanket from the dryer and laid it across the bed. She jumped up on the bed, comfortable but waiting for me to join her once I finished my work and turned off the lights.

Alberta and Koala were each excellent guide dogs who pulled their unique partnership styles with me from different parts of my personality. I grew wiser thanks to Graham, Guiding Eyes for the Blind, and two exquisite dogs bred and trained there. A guide dog harness no longer represents disability to me. The harness lets me soar.

Thanks to Pam, I finally learned how to be truly independent by discovering how a professionally trained guide dog could make me a better person. Pam and I remain close friends. We visit one another, take trips together, and stay in touch with texts and phone calls. The dogs in our lives created a connection that we continue to share over years and miles.

I no longer wonder what it would be like to walk fully sighted. When my dog and I are in harness, our abilities augment one another. I let her know where we're heading. She keeps us safe along the way. As we combine our abilities, the sensory experience we share is superior to that of any sighted person. Together, we need no other, only each other.

RESOURCES

ANIMAL LEGAL AND HISTORICAL CENTER

https://www.animallaw.info/

The Animal Legal and Historical Center, based at the University of Michigan Law School, provides up-to-date information on domestic and international animal law on its website.

BERGIN COLLEGE OF CANINE STUDIES

https://www.berginu.edu/

The Bergin College of Canine Studies is the only US-based institution of higher education offering postsecondary degrees to students focused on understanding and improving human-canine partnerships.

BUCK'S BEST DOGS

https://bucksbestdogs.com/

Graham Buck, who helped develop and write **Catching Sight**, operates Buck's Best Dogs Inc., a private dog training business in Long Island, New York.

GUIDING EYES FOR THE BLIND

https://www.guidingeyes.org/

Guiding Eyes for the Blind is the third oldest of about a dozen guide dog schools in the US accredited by the International Guide Dog Federation—and the school where Deni, Graham, and Alberta met.

INTERNATIONAL GUIDE DOG FEDERATION

https://www.igdf.org.uk/

The International Guide Dog Federation (IGDF) sets standards and accredits guide dog schools around the world, which, at the time of this printing, includes one hundred member organizations in thirty-three countries.

INTERNATIONAL WORKING DOG ASSOCIATION

https://www.iwdba.org/

The International Working Dog Association (IWDA) supports genetics, breeding, and training of a variety of working dogs including service dogs, military dogs, and detection dogs by providing tools, educational materials, and training opportunities for members.

THINKING DOG BLOG

https://thinking.dog

Thinking Dog Blog is a weekly blog focused on canine cognitive abilities and demonstrations of how dogs think and problem-solve.

ACKNOWLEDGMENTS

We wish to first thank Jane Russenberger, the longtime breeder and geneticist for Guiding Eyes. Her work helped create the foundation for healthy purpose-bred guide dogs around the world. She also provided important background for the breeding and early canine development stories included in the content of this book.

We thank Miranda Beckmann, whose tireless dedication as a trainer and class supervisor has left a deep and lasting impact on generations of teams and who provided important background for the examples of canine and human education.

Thanks to Ted Zubrycki for always teaching Guiding Eyes instructors that the graduates and their dogs come first.

Thanks to Carol Andersen and Kris Anderson, who helped sort out science content in the early drafts. Thanks to Christina Phelps and Pam Balluck for excellent copyediting. Thanks to our agent, Barbara Hogenson, for her patience and tenacity. Thanks to friends in the storytelling world: Kathy Hourigan, Steve Weinberg, Michelle Brier, Lane DeGregory, Lillian Dunlap, and Jana Prewitt, who provided constant reassurance that this was a story worth telling. Thanks to editor Catherine Tung, who launched the manuscript at Beacon Press, and to associate editorial director Joanna Green, who saw it to publication. Thanks to Pam Hogle, who mentored me in creating my life story so that, so far, it has such a happy ending. Finally, thanks to my mom, Lottie Rhoads, who helped me believe in myself from the moment I was born until she died in February 2018. When she saw me with Alberta and read what I had written in my dog school journals, she urged me to write this book.

on Press
Davis
arnsworth Street
MA, 01773

s://www.beacon.org/gpsr
@beacon.org
486594

authorized representative in the EU for product safety and compliance is

Access System Europe
nu Konttnen
amäe tee 50
10621

s://www.easproject.com/gpsr/
requests@easproject.com
40 500 3575

. 9780807024850
ase ID: 157214236

www.ingramcontent.com/pod-product-compliance
Lightning Source LLC
LaVergne TN
LVHW080845170826
845678LV00006B/1708